WHERE EAST
MET WEST

POLAND

Oder

CZECH
REPUBLIC

Telč

MORAVIA

Slavonice

Mikulov

SLOVAKIA

Artstetten

MARCH-
FELD

Hainburg

VIENNA

BRATISLAVA

Neusiedlersee

Hegyeshalom

Andau

Sopron

BURGEN-
LAND

Esterháza

Köszeg

BUDAPEST

Ják

Sárvar

STYRIA

HUNGARY

Graz

Heiligenkreuz

Szentgotthárd

ŐRSÉG

Danube

SLOVENIA

CROATIA

SERBIA

Danube

BOSNIA

WHERE EAST
MET WEST

Something there is that doesn't love a wall ...

Before I built a wall I'd ask to know
What I was walling in or walling out,
And to whom I was like to give offence ...

He only says 'Good fences make good neighbours' ...

ROBERT FROST
'Mending Wall', 1914

And now, what will become of us without the barbarians?
Those people were a kind of solution.

CONSTANTINE CAVAFY
'Waiting for the Barbarians', 1904

Also by Peter Unwin

VOICE IN THE WILDERNESS: IMRE NAGY AND
THE HUNGARIAN REVOLUTION (1991)

BALTIC APPROACHES (1996)

HEARTS, MINDS & INTERESTS: BRITAIN'S PLACE IN THE WORLD (1998)

WHERE EAST MET WEST

A Central European Journey

PETER UNWIN

Peter Unwin (signature)

MICHAEL RUSSELL

FOR MY GRANDSON JOE
IN THE HOPE THAT ONE DAY
HE WILL EXPLORE CENTRAL EUROPE
FOR HIMSELF

First published in Great Britain 2000
by Michael Russell (Publishing) Ltd
Wilby Hall, Wilby, Norwich NR16 2JP

Typeset in Sabon by Waveney Typesetters,
Wymondham, Norfolk

Printed and bound in Great Britain
by Biddles Ltd, Guildford and King's Lynn

ISBN 0 85955 261 6

Contents

Preface

This is a book about the swathe of Central Europe that runs from Lübeck on the Baltic to Trieste on the Adriatic. As such, it follows what used to be the line of the Iron Curtain, across Germany and then between the Czech Republic and Austria, Austria and Hungary, Slovenia and Austria, and Slovenia and Italy. It is, in a sense, a book about the Iron Curtain in the Cold War and its legacy now that war is over. But it is, more broadly, about Central Europe: its history, its near-extinction for as long as the Cold War lasted, and its return to grace and prominence since the year of miracles, 1989.

You can look at Central Europe from many points of view. My approach is eclectic and discursive, touching on history here, politics there, the look of fields, woods, hill and cities, the people by the way, the prospects for the countries of the region and the region as a whole. So we dart from subject to subject, place to place, from one moment in history to another. But we stay close to the old dividing line, rarely straying east or west from it more than thirty miles; and our enduring concern is with Central Europe as an ancient and brilliant ingredient in the make-up of a brilliant and ancient continent.

Many people have helped me write this book; I take them in alphabetical order. Gordon Campbell of Croy told me about his near-fatal misadventures at the crossing of the Elbe in 1945. Keith Dobson, the former British Council representative in Germany, was encouraging, hospitable and wise. Martin Farndale gave me an absorbing account of how, if matters had ever come to East-West war, he would have led NATO's Northern Army Group to victory or defeat. Adrian and Jean Higham introduced me to Diocletian, Gibbon and Robert Frost. Alistair Hunter, who lived for many years in Germany, talked to me about things as diverse as East-West trade, the German soul and the Allied trains that plied between West Germany and Berlin; he also cast a critically helpful eye over the whole enterprise. My very old friend Martin Morton travelled with me over the hair-raising mountain passes of Slovenia. Nina Prentice described Hungary from a point of view very different from my own. Anthony Proctor provided the book with its

title. Hans-Joachim and Ingrid Seeler gave me German insights, information about the section of the Iron Curtain that separated Schleswig
Holstein from Mecklenburg, and an introduction to Egon Schwintowsky and his experiences as a West German customs officer on the
old border between the two Germanies. Frank Stewart told me how the
British Frontier Service worked. Kati and Tom Zombory recounted to
me the enthralling story of their escape from Hungary in 1956.

In my judgement this book does not need to be ballasted with foot-
notes, but I should acknowledge my debt to those few authors whom I
quote. Nicholas Bethell's *The Last Secret* remains a vivid account of the
handling of the Croat and Cossack tragedies in Carinthia in May 1945.
My account of Edward VII's Marienbad draws on Gordon Brook-
Shepherd's *Uncle of Europe*. In my nutshell description of the Austro-
Hungarian Empire I used *The Fall of the House of Habsburg* by
Edward Crankshaw; I so enjoyed his disobliging comments on Hungarian policy that I decided to run the risk of annoying my friends in
Hungary by including them. Martin Gilbert is indispensable on the
concentration camps and on World War Two generally. My account of
Bill Knowlton's adventures when he went looking for the Red Army in
May 1945 is mostly based on his article in *Armor,* the house magazine
of US armoured forces. The story of 'Dorf-Republik Rüterberg' comes
from Hans Rasenberger's lips and from his book on the same subject. In
her book *Fifty Years of Europe* Jan Morris almost persuaded me to like
Trieste as much as she does. The story of Pál Nagy's escape from Hungary in 1949 is recounted in his autobiography, *Sismánd*. Finally, the
quotations on the madness of Junot, Governor of Illyria, and on Italian
views of the Slovenes come from Rebecca West's great if prejudiced
book about Yugoslavia between the wars, *Black Lamb and Grey
Falcon*. For more general background reading, see the Bibliographical
Note on page 183.

From individuals and authors to two institutions. Martin Randall
Travel Ltd gave me post-retirement employment as a lecturer on their
tours of discovery. I have travelled with them in Poland, the Baltic
States and Kaliningrad as well as in Central Europe. They organised the
tours which I led along the line of the Iron Curtain in 1999, bringing
me the acquaintance and friendship of fifty of their wonderfully
engaged and indefatigable travellers. As for the Diplomatic Service, it
fed, watered and paid me for thirty-seven years; and wherever it sent
me the job nourished my love of history, geography and politics. I spent
six years in its service in Budapest and another six in Bonn, and there

and in London I worked on many of the issues which permeate this book. Living in Central Europe and studying its problems close up bred in me a curiosity about its history, politics and society; sharpened my eye for its cities, fields, hills and vineyards; and gave me an enduring concern for its people. I hope that something of all this is captured in this book.

I

Where the Iron Curtain Ran

In the spring of 1853 the European powers were lurching down the road that led to the Crimean War. The Ottoman Empire was sickly and Russia wanted free access to the Mediterranean and the guardianship of the Holy Places in Palestine. The Habsburgs feared the growth of Russian influence in the Balkans; and Britain and France were determined to check its advance into the Levant. The Chanceries of Europe conferred and calculated, and the world's newspapers fed sober comment and wild speculation to their readers.

At that time the *New York Tribune* enjoyed the biggest circulation in the world. On 12 April it offered its 200,000 readers an article on Russia's intentions. It was signed by Karl Marx, a regular contributor, but like many of his contributions it was probably ghost-written for him by Friedrich Engels. In magisterial terms it declared that if Britain failed to stop them in Turkey, the victorious Russians would go on to annex Hungary, Prussia and Galicia. The Russian Empire's western frontier lacked natural boundaries, a fact which a triumphant government in St Petersburg would want to rectify – 'and it would appear that the natural frontier of Russia lies from Danzig or perhaps Stettin to Trieste'.

Almost a hundred years later, in March 1946, it was Winston Churchill's turn to warn an American audience about Russian intentions. His fears were better founded than Marx's, but he fixed upon much the same geographical definition when he told an American college audience (and through it the world) that 'From Stettin in the Baltic to Trieste in the Adriatic an iron curtain has descended across the Continent'.

At the time the speech brought Churchill as much criticism and suspicion as applause; but the facts of Europe's division were there to see, and by the early 1950s it had hardened into an absolute separation of East from West. It ran not from Stettin, by now a Polish city, but from Lübeck, 150 miles further west. It drove a line of division through the heart of Germany, along Czechoslovakia's western frontier, through the middle of Austria, and down Italy's mountainous border with

Yugoslavia. Like Marx's dividing line and Churchill's, this continental divide ended at Trieste. But there were other, equally absolute East-West demarcations: in the Norwegian Arctic, along Finland's frontier with the Soviet Union, between Greece and its Balkan neighbours; and in Turkey's far east around Mount Ararat. Above all, the division between East and West ran through the heart of Berlin, at first no more than an administrative divide but in time, when the Wall was built, the most impervious section of the whole Iron Curtain.

This division of Europe persisted for more than forty years. To guard it and police it absorbed over the decades the energies of millions of human beings. It shaped the attitudes of West to East and of East to West, and it gave a long quietus to the concept of Central Europe – of *Mitteleuropa*. Hundreds died trying to cross it; in 1956 200,000 Hungarian refugees from the ruins of their defeated revolution went in search of new lives beyond it. Circumstances changed in places along its length when, for example, Austria won back its freedom from four-power occupation, when deals were struck about the disputed status of Trieste, and when East Germany and West Germany recognised each other's existence and began to do business together. Nevertheless, for four decades the Iron Curtain divided Europe as absolutely as the Roman *limes* separated the Empire's citizens from the barbarians or as the fluctuating line along which Hungarians and the Habsburgs struggled to keep the Turks at bay in western Hungary. It separated systems of belief, just like the old borders between Catholic, Orthodox and Protestant Europe. To the east of the line men and women gave their allegiance or paid their lip service to socialism, Marxism, planned production and the Soviet Union. To the west of it they looked instead to capitalism, democracy, competition and the United States. And along the line itself both sides prepared to tear each other apart if things ever came to war.

Eventually came the year of miracles, 1989. The Hungarians dug up their mines and tore down their barbed wire. East Germans in their thousands came to Hungary, to escape across the open border into Austria on their way to West Germany. The infection spread to Czechoslovakia and then back to East Germany itself, until the world saw on its television screens East and West Berliners gathered together, joyful if self-conscious in the glare of the floodlights, on the Wall itself. By the end of the year, even the Ceausescus were gone. 1990 was a year of elections, the first free elections in Central and Eastern Europe for more than 40 years. Communism vanished, and with it COMECON, the

Warsaw Pact and the Iron Curtain itself. Germany was reunited and the old Communist countries turned with expectant hope to NATO and the European Union.

Across Germany, most of the physical evidence of the Iron Curtain vanished, and what was left of it became the stuff of souvenirs, of commemoration. Elsewhere the line it had marked was now nothing more menacing than the borders between countries that wanted to be friends: Czechoslovakia and Germany, Austria and Hungary, and Italy and a newly-minted Slovenia. In the late 1990s I drove the length of the old divide, looking for what remained. There were only scraps of commemoration. Here was the machinery of the main crossing point on the Autobahn between Western Germany and Berlin, now become a desolate museum, there a boulder proclaiming reunion, there the remains of a watch-tower, here a reopened frontier crossing.

When I turned away from the old border itself and looked at the towns and villages it had divided, I found more differences. Western Germany was almost universally prosperous-looking, smug, complacent, unnaturally tidy. Eastern Germany was still very different, its recovery uneven, with a town restored here, a wilderness of abandoned Communist development there, its roads either new Autobahns that put western Germany to shame or cobbled roads unchanged since the time of Weimar. To enter the Czech Republic was to take a step back in time and progress, Slovakia even more so, yet both had changed for the better since I first knew Czechoslovakia in the early 1980s. Austria was as sleek as western Germany, and the Slovenian countryside nearly as sleek as Austria's. Hungary – the country which, with Germany, I knew best – had come far yet had far to go before it could rival Austrian or even Slovenian prosperity. And those bits of Italy which lay along the old Iron Curtain – the Julian Alps, Gorizia and Trieste – were something else again, Mediterranean hills and farms and towns butting up against the different ways of Central Europe.

But the essential changes had taken place and seemed safely nailed down for the future. The menace of Communist frontier guards and procedures had vanished; and if Europe still had threatening borders to show, they were to be found far away to the east, separating the countries of central and eastern Europe from the Balkans and the former Soviet Union. East Germany felt as safe and free as West, Hungary as Austria, Slovenia as Italy. Languages presented differing degrees of difficulty, cuisines of palatability. Hotels in the old east were mostly scruffier, their prices more affordable, their standards less predictable.

But in the 1990s Central Europe was re-emerging before one's eyes, a broad belt of Germany in the north, an even greater swathe of the Habsburg inheritance in the south. Lübeck was a proud Hanseatic city and Wismar was trying to re-establish its credentials. Quedlinburg told a story of the early Holy Roman Empire, just as Weimar, Coburg and Bayreuth spoke of the eighteenth-century Germany of the princes. Marianské Lazné retained some of the Edwardian grace it displayed as Marienbad, when half of Europe came there to set eyes on Edward VII, King-Emperor, and eye up the adventuresses his presence attracted. Vienna was the quintessential Central European city, just as Bratislava and Ljubljana were proud little capitals of proud little republics eager to wring every ounce of dignity and reputation out of their proud pasts. Finally, Trieste at the end of the line was a match for Lübeck at the beginning, like Lübeck a port and trading city, historically as important to the commerce of Central Europe and the Balkans as Lübeck was to trade up the Baltic to Poland, Russia and Scandinavia.

Along the line of the old Iron Curtain you can still see a few signs of the tragedy it represented: the wall that cut off Germans even from the view of other ordinary Germans, the deserted Communist-era prison camp which stands for the long oppression of the Czechs, the reconstruction of the broken bridge across which the Hungarian refugees fled in 1956. But there is a lot more modern history to uncover on the way from Lübeck to Trieste, much of it more tragic by far. If you fly to Hamburg to start your journey you land at Fuhlsbüttel, the spanking-clean airport of Europe's most prosperous city, built on the site of the concentration camp in which the Nazis re-educated and tormented their enemies. As you go south you pass not far from Belsen and Mittelbau-Dora, close to Buchenwald outside Weimar and Mauthausen on the Danube, and through the Loibl tunnel which links Austria and Slovenia, built by Nazi slave labour.

There are other reminders of horrors past to be seen where the Iron Curtain once ran. The Napoleonic battlefield of Aspern-Essling outside Vienna is one, the bridge in southern Austria across which the British despatched the Cossacks to their deaths at Soviet hands is another. So is the mountain battlefield of Caporetto, the scene of the Italian rout in 1917, now just inside Slovenia. But the reminders of the Nazi era tell a story which is specifically relevant to the Iron Curtain tragedies which came after them. They remind us that the division of Europe was not just a disaster for Europe and for Germany. It was also the natural, inevitable consequence of the aggressive war which Hitler provoked, at first to the fervent applause of so many Germans. The Iron Curtain is object-lesson as well as abomination.

Now even the oppression which took the place of Nazi tyranny has passed into history. A free Europe and a free Central Europe have taken the place of the old Europe divided. In 1999 I saw them through the eyes of two groups of British tourists whom I took exploring the line of the Iron Curtain. At the end, when at last we could put our feet up in Trieste, I asked them whether they thought that Europe had at last, in George Bush's phrase, been made whole. They were pretty well unanimous: it had not been, it would not be because it could not be.

I found their pessimism disappointing. The countries of Central Europe have far to go, but to my eyes the distance they have come since 1989 is cause for optimism. I told my companions what it was like even for a privileged diplomat to cross the Austrian-Hungarian border in the 1950s, about the bleak emptiness of Prague's exquisite streets and squares in 1985, about the mines and wire and automatic guns that guarded the Iron Curtain for so long. All this seemed like pre-history now; would not the differences and the shortcomings of today seem like pre-history tomorrow? What about the Central Europeans' passion to join NATO and the European Union? Did that not tell us that they thought themselves as much Europeans as Hungarians or Czechs?

I did not shake them; in their eyes national identity and historical difference were stamped too deep into the face of Central Europe for it to be sensible for anyone, American President or travel guide, to talk of making Europe whole. They may be right, or I may be. But whichever of us turns out to be right in the long run, the issue adds yet more zest, more spice to the flavour of Central Europe. You sense it everywhere you go along the line on which for so long East met West.

2

From the Baltic to the Elbe

The Continental Iron Curtain began and ended beside the seaside. In the north it reached the sea on the shores of Lübeck Bay, on the very edge of a suburb of Travemünde, Lübeck's port on the Baltic. A watchtower marked its northernmost extremity, and below the watchtower a line of obstacles blocked the beach and curled out into the waters of the bay itself. Like every yard of the Iron Curtain in Germany, this section was heavily fortified, with fences, barbed wire and mines. But these could not do the job alone. The divide required men and women, to watch, guard, patrol and intercept – if necessary to shoot to kill. These guards worked with obsessive thoroughness, watched over equally obsessively by their masters.

Let us take as an example one of these thousands of servants of the Iron Curtain, a man called Oskar Beck, who in the early 1970s did his duty by the German Democratic Republic as a border guard. For part of his time his duty station was precisely here, beside Lübeck Bay, at the place which an old-fashioned soldier might see as a post of honour, on the extreme right of the front which his country presented to its western enemies. Most of his duty hours were spent out on patrol along the border, checking the fences and the ploughed strip, scrutinising and photographing any over-curious sightseers who came right up to the dividing line on the West German side. And every third day he did a long stint in the watchtower beside the sea.

Beck's watchtower was built to give a commanding view right round the horizon. Behind him lay the empty fields of East German Mecklenburg. To his right he could see the frontier defences snaking out into Lübeck Bay, on his left the fences, minefields and mantraps which stretched away along the dividing line. At his feet were the walls and dogs and wire of totalitarian control. Before him were spread the good things with which western society taunted the society he served.

In the distance, across the water, Beck could see through his binoculars the beaches, casinos and hotels of Travemünde, Germany's Nordic summer playground. He could see the ferries going out on their journeys across the Baltic and the masts and yards of the grand old West

German sail-training ship *Passat* moored half a mile away. Around the *Passat*, Travemünde yacht harbour glistened with the finest playthings of West German plutocracy. Closer still was a colony of snugly tedious West German holiday homes, the nearest only a few metres away. And just below him, its blondes a provocation all summer long, lay Travemünde's nudist beach.

For forty years men like Oskar Beck stood guard here on the very edge of Travemünde. A few took seriously their mission of guarding East Germany against capitalist infection. Occasionally they had the excitement of tracking down an escaper, sometimes even an intruder from the west, more often drunk and disoriented than a true enemy of the Communist state. Every few years one of them made a run for it, tempted by the idea of freedom or the West's material allure. Most of them served out their conscript time without enthusiasm or conviction, and went home, duty done, to Gretchen or Renate in Leipzig or Magdeburg.

Now, with the division of Germany only a memory, you can meet men like Oskar Beck coming back to look at what it has left behind. Other men and women come with different memories. A very few remember an adventurous escape, many more arbitrary separation from loved ones beyond the wire. They come to re-celebrate the end of division, the old people among them still scarred by the indignity and tragedy of it all. Sightseers come in their thousands, and along the length of the German Iron Curtain alone there are thirty little museums of one kind and another which recall the divide. Schoolchildren come, looking for material for the essay about the separation of the German Democratic Republic and the Federal Republic of Germany which demanded their parents' fealty; and for them that division is already ancient history.

I met a group of people at the point where Beck's watchtower stood, where the Iron Curtain met the Baltic Sea. It was not a day to be out on a cold seashore and they were bundled up against the wind. But they lingered, looking for what there was to see. Between us, we found little. A notice still tells us that a footpath runs from here along the Federal German Baltic coast all the way to the Danish border, adding the pawky sentiment that this, its end, is also its beginning; and so far no one has taken the trouble to record that now long-distance walkers can go on walking all the way to the Polish border if the fancy takes them and that here, at Travemünde, they are not at a beginning or an end but, more tediously, merely half way between two of Germany's neighbours. At the foot of the notice someone has decorated a boulder with a more up-to-date sentiment: *'Nie wieder geteilt"* – 'Never divided again'. There is nothing else to remind you of the old days. The fence, mines and wire are gone, and so is Beck's watchtower.

All the same, a sudden transition remains. West of the divide stand those neat holiday houses in their ordered rows, shuttered at this time of the year against the Baltic winds. Sandy lanes run down to the beach, which is defended now with nothing more than notices about the limits of naked bathing. East of the old border stretch the still-desolate fields of Mecklenburg. On the border line itself, beside the boulder and the notice about the coastal path, there is a new notice, which is rapidly losing its fluorescent glory. It urges visitors on across the old death strip, to the cakes and cream that await them in a new coffee house a gentle walk away in Mecklenburg.

The Iron Curtain existed to keep not just people but whole worlds apart. In doing so, it separated cities that had interests in common that went back for centuries. We are going to look at two such places, Lübeck and Wismar, both of them Hanseatic cities on the German Baltic coast. The first lies just west of the dividing line, upstream from Travemünde, and its medieval spires were visible through Oskar Beck's binoculars. The second is thirty miles inside East Germany. To visit them both gives us a first fix on the differences between places that lay east and west of the divide, and on the changes that have taken place since it ceased to exist.

Lübeck is one of Germany's oldest cities. Here the Holy Roman Empire of the German Nation first established a footing on the Baltic. From Lübeck German merchants traded with Scandinavia, Russia and the peoples of the eastern Baltic. They started by shipping salt from the Lüneburg mines to the Baltic herring fisheries, and went on to despatch beer, cloth and weapons eastwards and to import furs, tar and timber in return. Lübeck merchants traded up the Baltic, and settled in places around it such as Danzig, Königsberg and Riga, Novgorod in Russia and Visby on the island of Gotland. Out of their business enterprises grew the Hanseatic League, that network of trading cities which extended right across northern Europe and for long monopolised east-west trade. For centuries Lübeck was the animating spirit of the Hanseatic League, its laws prevailing in most Hanseatic cities. The Emperor made it a Free City and recognised it as Germany's leading representative on the Baltic. When, a millennium later, I wanted to write a book about the Baltic, Lübeck was the obvious place to begin.

Out of the Hansa's monopoly of Baltic trade, Lübeck's leading merchants grew rich beyond all imagining, and even when the rise of the nation state trimmed the wings of the Hansa merchant cities, it remained a commercial force to reckon with. It stood sieges in the Napoleonic wars and went on to assert itself as a German city as the power of German nationalism and the Hohenzollern Empire increased. In *Buddenbrooks*, Thomas Mann captures the weariness of its decline, but also the pride which continued to sustain its Senators and men of affairs.

You can see relics of the city's medieval glories if you go to Lübeck today. Stand on the bank of the Trave and take in the vista of the old city's soaring spires. Cross the river and climb city streets lined with merchants' warehouses. Beyond are the medieval churches in Baltic brick, a masterful old Rathaus, successions of gabled houses. Go further and you enter quiet courtyards, an ancient hospice, a restaurant where once Lübeck merchants and Lübeck seamen contracted together for trading voyages.

There is still an air of civic confidence and self-importance in the streets of Lübeck today. It is one of the best places in Germany in which to wander, in short a delight. But it is a repackaged, reconstituted delight. On the night of 28–29 March 1942 Lübeck fell victim to Royal Air Force bombers. 234 aircraft took part in the raid on a city which, as the commander of Bomber Command recorded, was not 'a vital target.... but an industrial town of moderate importance', on which a second wave of attackers could practise the technique of aiming at a conflagration started by the first. Bomber Harris said he wanted his pilots 'blooded', 'to have a taste of success for a change'. This was area bombing; and depending on your point of view, it was either terror bombing or the righteous visitation on Germans of some of the horrors that they had already inflicted on most of Europe. Whatever the politics and the ethics of the affair, the attack destroyed 2,000 of Lübeck's buildings and eighty per cent of the city's medieval heart.

Lübeck continued to matter as the war ground to its conclusion. In its very last weeks Heinrich Himmler came here to meet Folke Bernadotte, asking him in vain to mediate a surrender of German forces to the Western powers, while they continued to resist the Russians. Four days earlier Winston Churchill had ordered Montgomery to concentrate his forces on a drive across the Elbe to Lübeck and the sea: 'Our arrival at Lübeck before our Russian friends from Stettin would save a lot of argument later on.' By 2 May, British forces had reached

Lübeck and, as Montgomery recorded, 'thus sealed off the Danish peninsula with about six hours to spare, before the Russians arrived'. Yet in the early hours of the following day German troops were still massacring Jewish prisoners who tried to get ashore from prison ships in Lübeck harbour. And with the end of the fighting came the refugees, fleeing on foot from the advancing Russians or coming by sea, shipped westward to make room for Polish settlers in East Prussia and Pomerania.

So Lübeck suffered even more than many other German cities. But on the day the war ended the British were in possession, and inter-allied agreements assigned it to the British zone of occupation. It underwent the same postwar privations as all Western Germany, and hunger, ruin, impoverishment and bereavement were intensified by the problems the refugees brought with them. But in the late 1940s and 1950s, German diligence went to work within the security which Western occupation provided. Lübeck arose out of the ruins, and you can see today what was achieved then. The Marienkirche, the proudest of all its churches, was restored, with only its shattered bells left as a reminder of wartime destruction. So, gradually, were all Lübeck's medieval treasures. Beside them you can see more brutal restoration, the crude boxy rebuilding of houses and shops in the hurried 1950s and 1960s; but none of this does much to detract from the old city's appeal. The heart of Lübeck today is a jewel, set on its hill between the river Trave and the Elbe-Baltic canal. Around it extends a major modern city. Within sight of it, on the other side of the canal, ran the Iron Curtain, a suburban presence throughout the Cold War years, closer here than to any other German city except West Berlin.

Wismar's story is a different one. Like Lübeck, it grew to glory in the Hanseatic centuries, and it too has its merchants' houses and its cathedral-like churches in Baltic brick. But in 1648 the Swedes conquered Wismar, made it into a stronghold, and held it for most of the following 150 years. In the course of them the city was first caught up in ferocious Swedish-Danish wars and then consigned to a protracted neglect. So Wismar was a big place but rarely a vital one. Its docks attracted Allied bombers in the Second World War, but they wreaked only moderate devastation. Western troops got there, as to Lübeck, ahead of the Russians. But the agreed demarcation line between British and Soviet zones ran along the border between Mecklenburg and Schleswig Holstein, well to the west of Wismar. Western troops withdrew and Soviet troops moved in.

So, as they intensified their grip on East Germany, did Communist functionaries, full of ideology, blowing up one of Wismar's medieval churches and abandoning the rest of them, and most of the centre of the city, as irrelevant to the people's needs. Wismar grew out of its wartime experiences into yet another East German city, its heart neglected, its commercial centre scarcely animate, the whole encircled by those terrible concrete boxes of Communist reconstruction which you can see all the way from the border with West Germany to the suburbs of St Petersburg. And in Wismar's case matters were made worse by its proximity to the border with West Germany, which required controls on visitors and on the movement of its citizens themselves.

So while Lübeck revived, Wismar stagnated. It was to become just another East German city, its Hanseatic connections denied, its citizens' energies compulsorily channelled into the search for peace, socialism and economic development on Communist terms. It lost its old love-hate relationship with Lübeck along the coast, and its exposure to the western seas and oceans. Instead its yards built ships for Soviet and East European customers and its people turned inwards upon themselves. Wismar's wakening Prince Charming came not in the 1940s and 1950s, nor in the 1970s when relations between East and West Germany became easier, not even in the revolutionary 1980s, but in the 1990s, with German reunification.

It was a slow awakening. I first went to Wismar in 1992 and found it stunned. Beneath the gloom and the casual squalor you could see that the place had wonders to revive. Its vast central square, its churches, the old houses on the waterfront, the dockyards extending out into Wismar Bay, all of these spoke of a substantial city. But Wismar lay under a patina of dirt, lethargy and disorganisation. When I went back, in 1997, things were stirring, and one or two places had been polished with the German zeal for improvement, but the city was still far removed from Lübeck's bustle and self-satisfaction.

By 1999 things were better again, and Wismar stands at level 2 on my descending scale from 1 to 5 of East German civic self-improvement. Around the square, the restaurants in the fine old houses now set out to please. A lugubrious man rushes to open one of the city's old brick churches for me, assuring me that its interior will delight me. They are cleaning up the old houses on the waterfront. Amid this progress is evidence of continuing failure to overcome the city's handicap of fifty years' neglect. The churches are being restored, but with the ineffable slowness that lack of resources imposes. Dirt and smoke and the stink of badly tuned diesel engines are everywhere. In ten years Wismar has just begun to resurrect itself, and it is far from overtaking Lübeck. But there is hope in the air and the beginnings of bustle. The city calls itself Hanseatic once again. It welcomes visitors and tries to separate them from their money in the best capitalist style. In another five years Wismar will have shed the rest of its inheritance from the Communist years, made itself more like Lübeck. In the process it will lose something of its sleazy charm and the visitor will mourn not the sloth of socialism but the arrogance of rampant capitalism. All the same, things are getting better in Wismar, as they are throughout eastern Germany.

A few years after my first solitary visit to the city I took my British travellers to look at the fine old churches of Wismar. For some this was a first exposure to what had been Communist Europe and I found myself answering questions about religion there in the bad old days. Were the clergy banned, or jailed, or seduced, or what? Were their churches closed, abandoned, made over into museums of atheism, or blown apart like the Georgenkirche in Wismar? Was it safe, indeed, for ordinary men and women to go to church at all?

The answers, I told them, depended on time and place. In Lithuania, for example, the churches had gone much the same way as in Russia proper, to near-extinction; whereas in Poland, one cardinal after another had wielded power on a scale to be compared with the Army's, or Solidarity's, or even the Communist Party's. But in both countries Catholicism had remained a passion, a central aspect of national identity. Other countries in the area had mixed the elements differently. On this as on so many things, Hungary had steered a middle course; and I found myself talking about conditions there, in the Communist country I had known best, in the hard days of the 1950s and the gentler ones of the early 1980s.

When I first lived in Hungary, Cardinal Mindszenty, the leader of the Roman Catholic Church, had been a refugee in the American Legation ever since the 1956 Revolution, cut off from the religious life outside its doors. To the handful of diplomats who went to mass there, he would fulminate in scarcely comprehensible English about atheism and materialism, and about the hardships visited on the faithful in Hungary. The bishops whom he had left behind had made their awkward compromises with the Communists, giving more than they gained. But their churches functioned, and the faithful, particularly the older faithful, still flocked to them. There were even a few religious schools, one of them in the monastery at Pannonhalma, half way between Budapest and Vienna, which had kept the faith for close on a thousand years. There was, in short, a sort of battle line drawn between Church and Party, a line along which the guns were silent, if only for a time.

Twenty-five years later, when we went back to Budapest, a kind of co-existence had taken the place of that old, wary hostility. I sometimes visited a cardinal whom Mindszenty, had he still lived, would have thought a Communist; but he used to tell me proudly, and with every appearance of conviction, that his policy, like that of the Church throughout Eastern Europe, was one of 'Little Steps' towards religious freedom. He still had his problems with the authorities, but by now both sides treated each other more gently, for the churches had seen their congregations shrink, and the Party's once-shrill ideology had softened.

The religious schools still survived, and at Pannonhalma the Abbot told me, having first turned up the volume of his radio, that one of his monks now knew how to locate the microphones which the secret police still planted around the place. As for the laity, if they cherished worldly ambitions they wore their religious faith discreetly, talked about it quietly, went across the city to have their children baptised in churches where they were strangers. But for ordinary people the old conflict was history. Religion was something they could take or leave, just as it was by now all over Europe, West as well as East.

The story was similar, give and take differences at the margins, in East Germany and Czechoslovakia. In these predominantly Protestant countries, congregations were smaller than in Hungary. But as in Hungary there were churchmen who argued for coming to terms with the Communist state, and others who, speaking more quietly, wanted nothing to do with it. The authorities were a shade more inflexible than the Hungarians, less willing to recognise that religion had a part to play in the nation's sense of self; but unlike the Hungarians they did not have to reckon with the wiles of the Vatican deployed directly against them.

Romania and Bulgaria were different again: regimes harsher, the mass of the population Orthodox rather than Western Christian, the scene complicated by a large, mostly Calvinist Hungarian minority in Romania and by large numbers of Turkish Moslems in Bulgaria. And Poland was different yet again, unique, self-aware, passionately Roman Catholic, the political power of its faith mightily reinforced when a Polish Pope came to the throne of St Peter. There are Poles who believe that it was their Pope more than any other single individual who spelt the end of Communism in Europe; and you do not have to agree with them entirely to see the power of their argument.

Most of my fellow-travellers seemed to have expected something harsher, a more absolute showdown between Church and State, God and Mammon. The story I told them was instead one of gradations, of grudging give-and-take, of a balance of power which was different in each country and which shifted over the decades. Both sides, I suppose, thought that time was on their side, that the convictions of the other would wither and die. In the end it was Communism which withered first; but as it died it took some of the Churches' convictions with it.

When I left Wismar, I went exploring other places in Mecklenburg. It formed the most remote corner of the old East Germany, as it is still the poorest part of the united country. But its capital, Schwerin, sees no reason to hide its head in shame. It lies at the centre of a belt of lakes which stretches right across northern Germany a few miles inland from the Baltic coast. Schwerin has ten lakes of its own, dividing the town into segments and bringing a holiday atmosphere to the whole place. It has its Castle on the water's edge, almost as fantastic as Bavaria's Neuschwanstein; a fine cathedral, opera house and art gallery to make a real city of it, and rows of dignified nineteenth-century terraces, as well as long views over the water and a spick-and-span air to it which is still hard to find in the old East Germany. It escaped wartime destruction, and its historic centre was big enough to keep its inevitable ring of Stalinist-era blocks of flats at a safe distance. The worst things you can see around Schwerin are the abandoned Soviet Army barracks, ramshackle and menacing, their training areas eating into Mecklenburg's woodlands. But if Wismar looks as if it will take decades to close the gap that separates it from Lübeck, Schwerin might almost have been a part of the prosperous Federal Republic all along. Add an amiable inebriate who came hiccoughing with me two miles out of his way when I lost myself among the lakes, and you have a town to gladden the heart.

Ludwigslust, a few miles further south from Schwerin, tells a different story. An eighteenth-century Duke of Mecklenburg built a palace here for his summer pleasure – hence its name – and it still dominates a town which is really not much more than a village. It is a grandiloquent but ramshackle place, open to the public but only half-restored, and that with a heavy hand that has wiped out the charm of whatever gave

Ludwig his pleasure. I found the town at the palace gates more pleasing: a north-German village of a place, low red brick houses and barns, but all laid out with a measured discipline that might have been brought here from Versailles.

I had promised that in my explorations of the old Iron Curtain I would resist divagations that took me too far from it. All the same, from Ludwigslust I took off to the east, in pursuit of a story half a century old. Someone had told me that years ago, at a NATO headquarters in Turkey, he had worked for an American general who told tall stories about a hairy adventure in this part of Germany at the very end of the Second World War. I tracked Bill Knowlton down, an old man now, living in retirement in Virginia just outside Washington, and this is the tale he told.

He was a young lieutenant in early May 1945, commanding a reconnaissance troop attached to the 82nd Airborne Division. The division had crossed the Elbe and taken Ludwigslust. Somewhere away to the east was the advancing Red Army, and between it and the Americans a shambles of what was left of the German Army. His commander told Knowlton to take a fighting patrol of sixty-five men to make contact with the Russians. He set off in his armoured car and was at once plunged into a sea of retreating Germans. They wanted above all to avoid surrender to the Russians, and many were happy to hand over their arms to Knowlton's little band of warriors. A corps commander with an SS escort, his face apoplectic with defeat, faced the Americans with stiffer challenges. But Knowlton maintained the pretence that American tanks were coming up close behind him. Somehow, he kept the hard men among the Germans at arm's length while their weaker brethren queued to surrender to him and accept his orders. For hours the Americans' fate was on a knife edge. For the moment they controlled a slice of rural Mecklenburg; an encounter with a fanatical SS unit could make of them the last American casualties of the war.

Finally, on 3 May, Knowlton found the Russians. His account of what happened then is hilarious. He met a rag-tag army. 'There seemed to be no system, and people just wandered in and out of the column at will, with apparently no order or particular jobs. Everyone grinned, saluted us, and yelled some unintelligible gibberish – while we grinned, saluted and grinned'. They catch up with the Russian colonel, 'a farmer-like individual, serenely driving a two-horse wagon as though it were Sunday in Central Park'. He gives them vodka and toasts victory. The divisional commander appears. More toasts, an orgy of toasts:

'Trrrooooman, Staaleen, Churchill'. The vodka takes its toll, on the general even more than on the Americans. He tries to give his officers orders. 'They looked at each other with that "the-old-man-is-drunk-again" look, folded up their books and yelled the Russian for "Hey gang, the bastards are over that way. Let's go".' This was the army that had fought Wehrmacht discipline, SS fanaticism and the German General Staff, all the way from Stalingrad to final surrender here on the road between Ludwigslust and Plau.

I found the bar in which Knowlton had set up a command post for a few anxious hours before he found the Russians and drank a beer to his achievement. Then I turned back towards Lübeck and stumbled across the village of Dassow. It is one of hundreds of Mecklenburg villages, with little to set it apart it from all the rest until the Iron Curtain brought it a distinction of a kind.

Dassow stands at the head of a lagoon which is linked by way of the Trave estuary with the sea. Throughout the years of German division, the waters of the lagoon were technically West German property, ballooning five miles into East Germany. So although Dassow was well inside East Germany by road, the threat of Western contagion by water came right to the end of its main street. The place was a frontier outpost, and here as everywhere else along the border, defences were erected. You can still see the base of a watchtower and odd traces of fence and wire among the reeds beside the lagoon.

A Communist-era bypass takes traffic from Lübeck to Wismar round Dassow, and beside the by-pass there have sprung up since reunification new detached houses that would be a credit to their builders even if they lay on the other side of the old border. But the heart of the village tells a different story, reminding you of Mecklenburg's poverty. It straggles along a main street which looks and feels as if it has not changed since the 1920s, before Hitler brought National Socialist exaltation to Mecklenburg. Shabby houses alternate with nondescript farm buildings, and two shops, a bar and an ancient garage add a sad sort of punctuation to the scene. The architectural medium throughout is north German brick, which in Lübeck, Wismar and cities all around the Baltic soars skywards in superb medieval churches and civic buildings. But Dassow's brick has a low-lying, uncherished look about it, which brings a kind of suburban weariness to the rustic scene. This run-down air adds to a sense of unchanged authenticity. In a Britain in love with the past, this street out of the 1890s, only lightly overlaid by the 1920s, would be preserved as a national treasure. But Germany is in love with the idea of making the eastern *Länder* gleam like the western ones, and they are starting work on the transition even here in Dassow. In a year or two it will have the same antiseptic polish as so much of western Germany..

Near Dassow I saw a sign summoning me to inspect 'a new development of executive homes in the heart of the health-giving Mecklenburg countryside'. I set off up a lane that rapidly became a track and then an obstacle course. I found the executive homes themselves being inserted between a duck pond and the buildings of an abandoned farm, with promise of a long view across the fields towards the Dassow lagoon. It was a Sunday, but a couple of men were at work, engaged when I was there in kicking plastic pipes. Never judge a housing development by the pile of stuff that is to become its wiring and plumbing; but I felt no conviction that when this lot was installed it would bring unalloyed satisfaction to the thrusting young businessmen at whom the houses were aimed. There was an air of fecklessness about the whole thing, the sort of hopeless resignation I remembered from factories I used to visit in Communist Hungary. It reminded me that this was still Mecklenburg, where the bleakest kind of Communism had reigned just a decade ago. It all seemed a far cry from Lübeck across the fields and the lagoon, even further from the richest city in Europe, Hamburg, only fifty miles away down the road.

I set off down that road and came to Selmsdorf. It lies within a couple of miles of the old border, and without the division of Germany it would have been absorbed into Lübeck's suburbs long ago. Indeed, it gave its name to the border crossing point at Lübeck's back gate. It was never a major crossing and it lent itself to the discreet transaction of East-West business. That, no doubt, is why a British government representative came here one September day in 1971, gave an East German government official a brown envelope containing 2,000 Deutschmarks and a receipt, and got from the East German a Cornish pasty manufacturer's light aircraft in exchange. The story of how officials, aircraft, Deutschmarks and receipt got to Selmsdorf tells you much about the realities and the inanities of the Cold War. I tell it as I remember it from my involvement, sitting in the Western European Department of the Foreign Office twenty-nine years ago.

The aircraft belonged to a Mr Robert Lewis, the owner of a firm called Oven Fresh Foods, which manufactured cakes and pastries in Cornwall. He set out to fly his Cessna on a business trip from Hamburg to Sweden. He lost his way, strayed over East German territory and was forced down close to the border by Soviet fighters. It was a serious mistake in those days, but a day later Mr Lewis and his companions were released and crossed the border back into West Germany. One might have expected the aircraft to follow as soon as a low-loader to bring it west could be arranged.

In fact it took more than a year before it was reunited with its owner. The two German states had by then been in existence for over twenty years. But West Germany and its Western allies still did not recognise the German Democratic Republic. Pending a peace treaty – on whose terms East and West would never have agreed – the four wartime allies were in Germany by right of conquest; their writ, at least in theory, ran throughout 'Germany as a whole'. Since the Western allies did not recognise East Germany, and since its rulers enjoyed no democratic legitimacy, we called them not 'the government' but 'the authorities'. The Hallstein Doctrine decreed that West Germany would not have dealings with any country which recognised its Eastern neighbour. Hard-liners called East Germany 'the Zone' – the Soviet zone of occupation. Ordinary West Germans talked about the other Germany as *'drüben'* – over there. It was one of those situations which look ludicrous in retrospect. It had its reasons, and we took it with deadly seriousness, but Mr Lewis's aeroplane was to test our doctrines to breaking-point.

Already, diplomacy was in hand which would, in the fullness of time, put an end to this doctrinal rigour. The time had come, all agreed, to try to ease tensions in Europe. The West was engaged in a series of complex negotiations with Moscow and its socialist partners. West Germany's *Ostpolitik* was part of the story. So were its attempts to negotiate humanitarian improvements for the people of East Germany. So also were the parallel negotiations between Britain, France, the Soviet Union and the United States about Berlin. Between us we were trying to put in place a series of agreements which would regulate relationships between East and West, draw a line under the consequences of Hitlerism, and make everyday life easier for East Germans and East Europeans.

In any negotiation, different parties want different things. We in the West held a trump card: the extension of diplomatic recognition to East Germany. But we wanted to secure a whole series of political benefits before we played that card. For their part, the East German regime wanted recognition, and this with the passion of a government which lived its life in the shadow of the superior attractions of the Federal

Republic and had built the Iron Curtain and the Berlin Wall to keep its people in. So the unofficial East German trade office in London, KFA Ltd, spent a lot of its time telling gullible British businessmen of the bonanza they could enjoy in the East German market if only the British government would be sensible and accept the reality that the German Democratic Republic was here to stay. Now it let it be known that it could easily arrange for the return of Mr Lewis's aircraft, if only the British government would talk to the competent East German authorities.

In the Foreign Office we detected no end of hidden dangers in this situation. We told ministers about 'slippery slopes', 'thin ends of wedges', 'Western solidarity' and even 'East German blackmail'. Mr Lewis's MP, David Mudd, got into the story and told us that we were behaving like obscurantist bureaucrats. Mr Lewis said that our attitude hindered his efforts to export Cornish pasties: leave the matter to businessmen and they could reach a businesslike solution.

Mr Lewis, Mr Mudd and the East Germans had got the Foreign Office over a small but moderately embarrassing barrel. We turned to the Soviet Commander-in-Chief in East Germany and told him that he was responsible for whatever happened in his zone of occupation. He referred us back to the East Germans. We turned to the West Germans, who seemed to have little difficulty in doing practical business with the East Germans when they needed to; but that line of inquiry led us nowhere. In a pompous submission we told ministers that for KFA Ltd to act as intermediaries would be 'an unacceptable enhancement of their status'. But we still had to find a way of getting Mr Lewis's aeroplane back for him.

Between us, we and the East Germans and the Russians turned the affair into a happy debate about angels standing on the points of needles. Finally, we scrambled together a deal between the Consulate in West Berlin and the East German Ministry of Transport. The low-loader rolled up to the crossing point in Selmsdorf. The Consul from Berlin signed a receipt, the fingers of his left hand crossed behind his back, while we in the Foreign Office swore black and blue that this was an isolated act and in no way a precedent for more substantial acts of recognition of the East German authorities. Mr Lewis got his plane back and Mr Mudd his picture in the Falmouth and Camborne newspapers. And as it turned out, East Germany had to wait another year before Britain (still in careful step with West Germany, America and France) recognised its diplomatic existence. But by then we had nailed down the advantages we wanted before we played our trump card.

I would have liked to spend longer in Lübeck, but the length of the Iron Curtain lay ahead. It was almost 900 miles to the end of the Inner-German divide, and as much again to the Adriatic. So I set off down the road to the south and soon I was back among lakes. The first of them, the Ratzeburger See, formed part of the old border with East Germany, and from Ratzeburg itself, a fine old town standing high above the water on its island, you could see the watchtowers beyond the trees. Here the Iron Curtain swerved briefly eastwards, to include in the Federal Republic the old petty Duchy of Lauenburg. The demarcation line cut erratically through woods and across lakes, and when, in the early days of settling inter-zonal borders, British army officers found that a friendly farmer would end up on the wrong side of the divide, they shipped all his animals and machinery down the Schaalsee to freedom under cover of darkness. But soon the dividing line was back beside the Elbe-Lübeck Canal and followed it the rest of the way to Lauenburg. It is a timid little waterway, edged by water meadows and shadowed by trees. Once it was the foundation of Lübeck's fortunes. Now you can take boat-trips along it on Sunday afternoons and watch the cattle chewing the cud as you drift past. In the old days they were Communist cows on one bank, capitalist cows on the other.

Lauenburg is an intriguing old town. On a hill overlooking the Elbe you can see what is left of the castle, but not much else except a rebuilt, restored, resplendent small West German town. At the foot of the hill, however, squeezed between the hill and the eternal current of the river, you find old Lauenburg. It is not much more than a church, houses clinging to the hillside and a single, riverside street of pubs and hotels and dead-beat shops, with a ship-repair yard just upstream beside the bridge. There is something down-at-heel and raffish about riverside Lauenburg, splendidly different from the ordered cleanliness on top of the hill.

Lauenburg owes its fame and its existence to the Elbe, which until the coming of the railways was the main link between eastern Germany and Bohemia and the North Sea. The river, which for fifty miles upstream from Lauenburg formed the border between East and West, properly entered the Federal Republic here. So Lauenburg acquired its border checkpoints, on the river itself and on the road which runs parallel to it. I asked a German friend to find me someone who could tell me about uniformed service on the western side of the Iron Curtain – as a frontier guard, perhaps, or a customs official. He came up with the name of Egon Schwintowsky, who had come to Schleswig Holstein as a

refugee from eastern Germany, worked for years for the customs department at the Lauenburg frontier control point and in retirement turned to
the town's civic affairs and to good works. Schwintowsky entered
wholeheartedly into the spirit of my enterprise, bombarding me with his
memories in brave letters of fractured Gerlish. In retrospect at least he
made the confrontation between East and West at this quiet point on the
Iron Curtain sound almost bucolic. He was obviously the best sort of
German official, and he would have found in me a captive audience for
his stories from the old days, but by the time I got to Lauenburg he was
dead. What follows comes from those gallant letters of his.

Schwintowsky's first story concerned two young boys who had
somehow escaped from East Germany and who, after six weeks in a
reception centre for refugees, presented themselves at his crossing
point. They wanted to go back to the East and take their punishment.
Schwintowsky asked them why. 'We are not happy in the West' they
told him. At the beginning the system had taken care of them but soon
it wanted them to stand on their own feet. Surely that was the freedom
they had come west to find? It was yet it wasn't. Western freedom
meant responsibility: 'We had to take decisions for ourselves and we
could not use to it' they told Schwintowsky. Decisions, decisions? Yes.
'In the DDR they tell us go straight on, go right, go left; they tell us
what we had to do. ... We like to live in the DDR.' And so they went
back, to face, if they were lucky, two years in gaol.

Another time, a busload of Russian students turned up at the Lauenburg border post. They were studying in West Germany and wanted to
go to Berlin. Schwintowsky told them that the East Germans did not
allow traffic for Berlin to use his little local crossing point. They would
have to go down to Helmstedt, where the Hanover-Berlin Autobahn
crossed the border. Soviet pride swept him aside: 'We are Russians.
They will allow us to use this road. They have to do it.' So Schwintowsky collected their exit cards but did not stamp them. Two hours
later they came back, subdued. Not even a busload of Russian students
in all their imperial pride could overrule East German regulations.

The same thing happened to Willy Brandt, one time Federal Chancellor. He lived in Hamburg and one day he came to the Lauenburg
border post on his way to Berlin. Schwintowsky, respectful, almost
awestruck, warned him that he would not get through. 'I'll try,' he said;
and an hour later he was back. Like the Russians, the man who had
done more than anyone else to open up more normal relations between
the two Germanies was defeated by the system.

Once an East German border guard got away across the fields. He came creeping, still armed, to the West Germans huddled in the fuggy warmth and cigarette smoke of their frontier post. They asked him why he had come. Politics? No. A better standard of living? No. Then why? 'To escape from my wife.' Your wife? 'She works for the customs back there. She is horrible.' 'We had heard for years', Schwintowsky explained in his letter, 'of the terrible customs official in Horst, over there. Now we knew' – and he meant from the horse's mouth – 'that she really was a horrible wife.'

One night Schwintowsky and his colleagues were preparing for a special event. Several West German prisoners were to be handed over to them after their release from the provincial East German gaol nearby. Special arrangements had been made to receive them. An hour early, a prison bus rolled up from the east, and three East German prison guards got out. They saw Schwintowsky in his West German uniform: 'You are in our state,' they told him, fingers itching for triggers. On the contrary, he replied: 'You are six hundred metres inside the Federal Republic.' I wish I could have seen Schwintowsky miming their consternation. 'What happens now? What happens to us now?' 'We sign for the prisoners and you go back where you came from.'

Behind the border post there was a brook which marked the border of East Germany. Beyond it was a meadow, a no-go area, patrolled only by East German frontier guards. But once a farmer was allowed in to mow the grass. He came with his tractor, and somehow he got away with bringing a trailer hitched behind it. In the trailer he had concealed his family. Suddenly he swung his tractor into the stream and into the Federal Republic, but the trailer stuck in the stream itself. Farmer and family stumbled out to freedom, but as far as their property was concerned, all remained to play for. The East Germans brought up a tractor to pull the contraption back to their side of the stream. The West Germans found a farmer with a bigger tractor which they coupled to their end of the contraption. A desperate tug-of-war ensued. Finally Western engineering triumphed. Infinitely slowly, tractor and trailer emerged from the stream to join their owner in freedom.

It was not all merry japes, even at the quiet crossing point between Horst and Lauenburg. One day Schwintowsky saw a group of soldiers gathered on the other side of the border. Suddenly one broke away and dashed across to the West German side of the line. He turned out to be an army doctor, a lieutenant. The East Germans demanded that the Western guards return him. Out of the question; Herr Doktor Oberleutnant Schmidt was a German citizen; he had won his freedom. But it was costly freedom, and short-lived. The East German security system got at the family he had left behind. The family sent him word of their punishment for his escape. So Schmidt went back, like the boys who could not hack it in the West. The price he paid was ten years in prison.

I talked to another man who paid a high price at Lauenburg. He is Gordon Campbell, now Lord Campbell of Croy, who in his time has been soldier, diplomat, member of parliament and cabinet minister. He first came to Lauenburg in late April 1945 with the 15th Scottish Division. We have seen that at the end of the war Churchill was set on getting to Lübeck ahead of the Russians. To do so, the British Army must force a crossing of the Elbe. The 15th Division, who had led the assault crossings of the Seine and of the Rhine, were the men to do it.

They came to the low western bank of the broad and fast-flowing river near Lauenburg. The far bank was higher, thickly wooded, and crowned by Lauenburg itself, giving the Germans a very strong defensive position. The tank superiority which had brought the British so far was useless here; they had to get across the river in assault boats, relying on accurate artillery fire to cover them, and then establish a position on the far bank. The battle began on 29 April, the day before Hitler's suicide. The Germans resisted fiercely, throwing everything they had got into the battle, even a few, last desperate Luftwaffe sorties. In the end the British consolidated their position and three days later they were in Lübeck.

But not Campbell. He had been with the 15th Division right through the campaign, winning a Military Cross along the way in Normandy and a bar to it in the Reichswald Forest. Lauenburg was to be his last battle. In the fighting in the woods he was shot through the body at short range, his legs paralysed. They brought him back across the river to a first aid post, unconscious, a bundle of mud and blood which the stretcher bearers took for the remains of a German and which the chaplain recognised only by the medal ribbons. He spent the next fourteen months in the hands of the doctors, while they patched him up and gave him back some movement in his legs.

In his entry in *Who's Who* Campbell says that he was 'wounded and disabled' at Lauenburg, and educated 'at Wellington and in hospital'. I asked him how, looking back, he felt about his wounds, suffered, in effect, not to defeat an already defeated enemy but to beat an ally to Lübeck and hence to control of the mouth of the Baltic. It was all a long time ago, he told me. In war you did what you were told; and forty years of Cold War had shown us that there was political wisdom in Churchill's military madness.

There is a sequel to Gordon Campbell's story. When his doctors released him he joined the Foreign Office, and there he became the desk-officer, the expert, on the affairs of Trieste. As West and East wrangled over who should hold what in and around Trieste it was he who prepared the British arguments. He went to the United Nations in New York and to the postwar meetings of Foreign Ministers to advise about the future of the city and its surroundings. He spent two weeks in the city itself, helping supervise municipal elections there. We shall look at the setting of all this activity when we come to Trieste at the end of this journey, but one feature of the story belongs here. West and East drew lines between the city and the country immediately around it. In the end the Yugoslavs got the country, Italy the city. In the early stages the line of division became known, in British circles at least, as 'the Campbell line'. So Gordon Campbell, who lost so much in the race to keep Lübeck on the western side of Europe's great divide, gave his name for a time to the line which did the same for Trieste at the Iron Curtain's other end.

Here at Lauenburg we have fifty miles of the old Iron Curtain behind us, and for another fifty we shall be following it up the Elbe. But thereafter the line takes off across the north German plain, through the Harz mountains, down to the Fulda Gap, and eastwards between Thuringia and Bavaria all the way to the Czech border. It follows that border, first with Germany and then with Austria until, east of Vienna, Hungary takes up the running. Finally the line swings back once again towards the west, along the southern border of Austria, before turning south through the mountains that separate Slovenia and Italy on its way to Trieste and the sea. Before we set out on that journey we need to see how the divide came about, and why it fell where it did.

At successive wartime meetings, Britain, the Soviet Union and the United States discussed how they would deal with Germany when victory was won. Disindustrialisation, dismemberment, reconciliation, crippling reparations, each was proposed and each contentiously pursued. But long before their troops entered Germany the Allies had reached agreement on the principle of a single Germany divided into three zones of occupation. Committees of officials went to work on the details. With Soviet troops in Poland, American forces pushing towards the Rhine and the British advancing into Belgium and the Netherlands, it was natural for the Russians to take the eastern, the British the north-western and the Americans the southern and south-western German provinces. And it was convenient to demarcate the exact borders by reference to existing German administrative boundaries. (When a French zone was added later it was carved out of the American zone of occupation.)

Gradually, land war was brought home to the Germans. In August 1944 Soviet troops entered East Prussia and in September the Americans crossed the Belgian-German border. In January 1945 the Russians forced a crossing of the Oder, and by March the Western allies were across the Rhine. Gradually the Germans were squeezed between the advancing armies until, in late April, United States and Soviet forces joined hands along the Elbe and cut what was left of German resistance in two. We have seen Bill Knowlton going in search of the Russians in northern Germany, and the British VIIIth Corps rushing to seize Lübeck ahead of them. At the other end of the line, other British troops occupied Trieste and advanced into Austria as Soviet troops entered it from Hungary and Yugoslav partisans from Slovenia. By 7 May it was all over, with Admiral Dönitz's unconditional surrender of what was left of the Third Reich.

The moment of German surrender found Soviet troops in most of eastern Germany, United States forces spread out across the south and centre of the country, and the British in northern Germany. Their positions corresponded only very roughly with the agreed zones of occupation. The Americans along the upper Elbe, in particular, were deep into what was to become the Soviet zone; and the Russians alone occupied Berlin. Gradually, however, the armies were shunted into their agreed positions. The Americans pulled back and British and American forces drove up the Autobahn to establish their presence beside the Russians in Berlin. Stalin reluctantly agreed to Western troops taking over their share of responsibility in Vienna. Gradually, West and East formed up along the line that was to become the Iron Curtain.

But at first the demarcation line, at least in Germany, was entirely porous. All Europe was on the move, as prisoners of war, forced labourers and demobilised soldiers set out, more often than not on foot, to find their way home. Other groups, like the Cossacks who had fought beside the Germans against the Russians, feared retribution and cast around for refuge. At the same time, a growing flood of refugees poured into the western zones of occupation. Their numbers were swollen by the Germans driven by the Poles from East Prussia, Pomerania and Silesia, and by the Czechs out of the Sudetenland. The armies were overwhelmed by this mass of wandering and suffering humanity. They did little more to police the zonal borders than to mark them with the blue and red-painted wooden posts you can still find in forgotten corners of Germany. Elsewhere, the Czechs, Hungarians and Yugoslavs staked out their national borders, but Austria, like Germany, was partitioned between the four allies: here the East-West divide ran at first not down Austria's eastern frontier but through the middle of the country; and Vienna, like Berlin, was occupied by all four powers.

While the soldiers sorted themselves out on the ground, at the political level tensions between the Soviet Union and the Western allies were growing. In Poland, the Russians were intent on installing a government dominated by Communists: their opponents were arrested and earlier Allied agreement on democratic institutions swept aside. The man on the New York and London omnibus still believed in 'Uncle Joe', but his political leaders knew what was happening in Eastern Europe, and feared Russian intentions further west. The summit conference at Potsdam in the summer of 1945 was intended to forge Allied agreement on the forthcoming assault upon Japan, but Truman, Churchill and Attlee were distracted by their concerns about Soviet activities in Europe, above all in Poland. The atomic bombs dropped on Japan brought a sudden end to the war in Asia but reinforced the fear which underlay Russia's determination to have its own way in the areas its troops occupied. Gradually suspicions of Soviet intentions spread. Ordinary soldiers and administrators began to see for themselves the human consequences of Soviet intransigence. Attitudes hardened, and the initial willingness to strike practical deals along the demarcation line evaporated. The East-West stand-off was beginning to take physical reality on the ground.

So matters rested in the late summer of 1945. Ordinary Europeans were preoccupied with the problems of survival. The occupying armies had their hands full with refugees, deportees and prisoners of war. As they tried to restart the machinery of peace they were handicapped by the universal destruction. East-West relations deteriorated. The winter was savage, and with it came further hardships. In February 1946 Stalin told a Soviet party conference that the ambitions of capitalism made a new war inevitable. George Kennan in the United States Embassy in Moscow composed his famous 'long telegram', bringing clarity, coherence and a new toughness to American thinking. And on 5

March Winston Churchill, out of office since the previous summer but still by a large margin the most famous of Western statesmen, delivered himself of the most important speech ever made by a British opposition leader when, at Fulton, Missouri, he gave public expression to the essence of Kennan's telegram.

In that speech Churchill famously warned the world that 'an iron curtain has descended across the Continent'. He was not the first man to use the phrase, but the fact that he used it made it famous. To the Soviet Union the speech was pure provocation. To many in the West it was too combative by half, a needless hindrance to better relations with Moscow. But to all those who had seen Soviet machinations in Central and Eastern Europe in the ten months since the end of the war it had the ring of truth.

In his speech Churchill placed his iron curtain between Stettin and Trieste. Stettin lies 150 miles to the east of Lübeck, where the Iron Curtain as we remember it reached the Baltic, and at Potsdam the wartime allies transferred it from Germany to Poland. Churchill was implying, therefore, that the Iron Curtain ran not through the middle of Germany but down its eastern border and that, divided into zones of occupation though Germany might be, the writ of the four allies as conquerors ran throughout its territories – a proposition that the Western allies maintained throughout the Cold War. The Soviet Union might dominate Poland, Rumania and Hungary by military occupation. It was not sole master of Germany and Austria, nor even at that date of Czechoslovakia.

But in the course of 1946 and 1947 Moscow tightened its grip in Central and Eastern Europe. The diplomats at the Paris Peace Conference could not draft their way round the facts of military occupation. Throughout Europe economic conditions, already desperate, deteriorated. In June 1947 George Marshall launched the economic recovery plan that later bore his name. When the Western Europeans gathered to plan their response to Marshall's offer, Stalin forbade the Easterners to attend. The Czechs resisted Soviet pressure longest, but succumbed when summoned to Moscow. 'I went to Moscow as the foreign minister of an independent state' Jan Masaryk told a friend. 'I returned as a Soviet slave.' Seven months later came the Communist coup in Prague; a month after that the murder of Masaryk.

By the spring of 1948, therefore, Poland, Czechoslovakia, Hungary and Yugoslavia were locked away behind an Iron Curtain that excluded all Western influence. Italy faced a general election that might make it Communist. In Germany and Austria the occupying powers squabbled. Then, on 20 March, the Soviet representative walked out of a meeting of the Allied Control Council in Berlin. His departure destroyed what was left of the four-power machinery established by the occupying powers to govern Germany as a whole. It doomed the two halves of Germany to develop separately (and, one German politician turned historian has argued, set the western half free over the decades that followed to help unite Europe through the European Union). Three months later the Western powers introduced a new currency into their zones of occupation. On the same day, 18 June 1948, the Russians sealed the border of their own zone. Then they shut off Western access to Berlin. The blockade of Berlin began and the Iron Curtain came down not just along the eastern frontier of Germany but through its very heart.

Yet on the ground the line of division was still porous, at least by comparison with what was to come later. Berlin, though besieged, remained a single city, to be divided by the Wall only thirteen years later. It was simple to move from the Soviet sector to the American or British: you walked or took a bus, and from the Western sectors you could fly to West Germany. Yugoslavia parted company with Moscow and accepted Marshall aid; it settled down to reasonably easygoing relations with its Western neighbours. After eleven months Moscow lifted the siege of Berlin: British and American aircraft had kept the people of the Western sectors fed and in doing so had beaten the blockade.

One crisis had been surmounted, but East-West relations became no easier. In October 1949 the Federal Republic of Germany and the German Democratic Republic were formed. Gradually the former made itself a major, universally accepted Western European state. But things were harder for the German Democratic Republic. To the West it was nothing more than the Soviet zone of occupation, its government a Soviet puppet. To its people it represented only a part of Germany, held in artificial isolation by Soviet occupation.

The East German regime became increasingly hysterical as it tried to assert its legitimacy. Throughout the 1950s it steadily tightened conditions along its western border. The Korean War provided one excuse, the brief 1953 rising in East Berlin another. Unreliable families were deported from border villages. Where a hamlet lay right on the border, it was levelled to the ground. Gradually, impassable barriers were set up, with a fence close to the line of the border, a belt of land immediately behind it, and another 2.5 metre fence behind that. These defences were guarded by armed patrols, attack dogs and watchtowers. Mine-fields and, later, automatic guns added to the hazards. They kept Western spies and saboteurs out and East Germans in.

The Czech and Hungarian governments were taking similar precautions along their own western borders, with even greater vigour when, in 1955, the Soviet Union signed up to Austrian independence and withdrew its occupation forces. Then, in October 1956, the Hungarian people rose in revolt. The Hungarian section of the Iron Curtain was briefly swept away. A few days later, when their revolution was crushed, 200,000 Hungarians fled to the west. As the Kádár regime asserted its authority, the Iron Curtain was re-established and re-equipped to keep Hungarians in and Western enemies out, a fully-equipped killing machine like the border across Germany.

Finally, in 1961, came the building of the Berlin Wall and the closure of the last loophole through which East German citizens could safely escape to the West. At the same time the Iron Curtain in Germany was again reinforced, first with wire mesh fences and later with new and massive concrete watchtowers. The Western papers still reported the occasional daring escape or brutal killing at the Wall or on the wire, but the East-West division was substantially complete. For twenty-eight years it divided Germany and Europe until, in 1989, all the assumptions that had gone into its creation were overturned and the Iron Curtain, an elemental fact of life, geography and politics for almost two generations, became instead an object of curiosity and even of nostalgia.

3
The North German Plain

The Elbe ranks with the Rhine and the Danube among Germany's great rivers. It flows from the Bohemian hills, north-westwards across central Germany, past Berlin and Lauenburg and through the heart of Hamburg. Before the railways it carried much of Germany's east-west trade, and even today the barges sweep past going down to the sea and thump their way back against the current towards the east. It provided a border too, first between the realms of the kings of Prussia and Saxony and, after the creation of the German Empire in 1871, between the provinces of Mecklenburg and Saxony. So it was natural that for fifty miles south-east from Lauenburg the Elbe should define the line of the Iron Curtain too. But at a little river-port called Schnackenburg, the demarcation line broke away from the river and swung back towards the west. The consequence was a West German peninsula jutting into Eastern Germany, encompassing an area known to history as the Wendland after its early inhabitants, the Slavonic Wends. An over-excitable East German geopolitician might have called it a dagger thrust between his country's ribs, but to Western strategists it was an excrescence, indefensible against attack from the east. To West Germans it was as much a part of their country, if an isolated part, as anywhere else. For the inhabitants – man-and-boy natives and a large influx of hippy artists alike – it was a place of rural peace marred by the presence of a threatening nuclear plant and by the absence of a major shopping-centre.

Upstream from Schnackenburg, the Elbe was a purely East German river. But historically it has always marked a European divide. In the dark ages Slav tribes such as the Wends lived well to the west of it, but by the time of the early Holy Roman Empire Teuton expansion had reached the river line. The Elbe then marked the division between Teutons and Slavs, Christian and heathen, West and East. Eventually the Slavs were driven back from it, and the tide of German conquest and settlement moved eastwards. In time it came to occupy all of what we think of as Germany today, as well as much of Poland and the whole Baltic coast to within a hundred miles of St Petersburg.

This German advance eastwards left the middle and lower Elbe flowing through an indisputably German landscape, yet the river continued to mark the difference between different Germanies. To the west and south were the easy-going Rhineland and Bavaria, to the east the Germany that grew up out of Brandenburg and Prussia. It was on the upper Elbe, at the Battle of Königgrätz in Bohemia, that in 1866 Prussia drove Austrian influence out of Germany. But even within the German Empire, Bavaria and the Rhineland remained as Catholic as the Habsburg lands and, in Prussian eyes, almost as slovenly, scruffy and imprecise.

Konrad Adenauer, the man who rebuilt Germany after the Second World War, was no Prussian. He came from the Rhineland; and apocrypha records that when he crossed the Elbe going east he used to murmur under his breath, yet in a voice well calculated to reach the ear of the recording angel, 'Asia, Asia'. He claimed that Sigmund Freud had once said of the Germany beyond the Elbe that it was 'baptised late, and very badly'. The West Germany that he built was a Roman Catholic sort of place as his Christian Democrats were a Catholic sort of party, and his government drew its strength from the Rhineland and from Bavaria. Atheistic East Germany, by contrast, remained Protestant in spirit, as do the new, free eastern Länder today. And only last year a garrulous old lady I met in the proudly Lutheran cathedral at Magdeburg confided to me that her Bavarian mother would be turning in her grave if she knew that her daughter had strayed 'up here, among the Protestant Prussians'.

We have seen that when they came to fix the borders between their zones of occupation the Allies based them on old German administrative divisions and that the Elbe by and large formed the border between Mecklenburg and Lower Saxony. But a few parishes of Saxony lay on the eastern bank of the Elbe, and in a fit of soldierly common sense the British surrendered them to the Russians. By doing so they doomed little places like Neuhaus and Kaarssen to develop for the next forty years in a quite different climate from that of their neighbours like Bleckede or Hitzacker on the western side of the river.

The river presented a pretty well impassable obstacle to clandestine movement between the two zones (though once an East German farmer got his family away to freedom in a cart converted into a boat) but for the Communist authorities it did not represent security enough. They set up their usual paraphernalia of control along it; and in one riverside village, Rüterberg, they built the first of their fences along the very river bank and the second a few hundred yards further back, so that for twenty-two years its inhabitants going home from market or the cinema in nearby Dömitz had to produce their documents to guards on duty at the only gate. When at last times changed, Rüterberg was quick to cash in on its experiences. One of the villagers petitioned the local authorities and the post office for a change of postal address, so Rüterberg became 'Village Republic Rüterberg'. Visitors came to get their postcards stamped with this distinction. The village pub started to serve meals and offer folders of documents about Rüterberg's past to go with them. The village flies its own flag, as vivid as a banana republic's. Passers-by rush to direct you to the home of Hans Rasenberger, the villager who got this cottage industry started; and when I went to see him it was clear that he had found his true entrepreneurial vocation in late middle age. He gave me five minutes of his valuable time, sold me his book, *Die Dorfrepublik*, presented me with a pile of free publicity material on Rüterberg, and as I was leaving told me that it would cost me a Deutschmark.

At the tip of the Western finger pointing into the old East Germany is Schnackenburg, a little riverside town and inland port, shut away by dikes from the occasional excesses of the Elbe. Here the West German frontier watchers were surrounded on three sides by East Germany. Rival patrol boats jockeyed against one another along the river, Western as aggressive as Eastern, particularly when they had American or British officers aboard to impress with the deadliness of division in the heart of Germany. Around Schnackenburg, the East Germans reared up even more than the usual quota of watchtowers, and on its landward side they rolled out first their barbed wire and then their death strip and attack dogs, their steel-mesh fences and their minefields. Just across the fields they destroyed a hamlet, Stresow. It had been there since the fourteenth century but it lay right on the border with West Germany. All their doings are neatly documented in an obsessive little museum in Schnackenburg.

There are other places to see around the Wendland beside Schnackenburg and Rüterberg. Dömitz makes less of its Cold War experiences than of its remoter history as an eighteenth-century Prussian stronghold on the Elbe. A little way back from the river, West German Lüchow does not feel all that different from East German Wittenberge, and on the river bank itself Gorleben's nuclear processing plant arouses equal concern on both sides of the old divide. Rural gentrification has gone further in the villages that used to lie west of the line, with the Wendland full of farmhouses converted into holiday homes for the middle classes of Hamburg; but change is coming in the east. In a quiet corner of East German Brandenburg, for example, I stumbled across the little spa town of Bad Wilsnack. Look in one direction and you see a decrepit main street distinguished only by a fine brick church which is big enough to be a cathedral. Turn a corner and you are faced by a spa hotel glittering with the plate glass and sophistication needed to woo the rich dyspeptics of the old western Länder of the Federal Republic.

As we watch the Elbe go by it is worth thinking a bit more about the Slav and Teutonic tides that have ebbed and flowed along it. Magdeburg is the principal city of the middle Elbe. This was where the great German push eastwards in the early Middle Ages crossed the river. But twenty-five miles away to the south west, nearer the Cold War border but still well inside the old East Germany, is the place where it began. Quedlinburg is a small medieval city almost untouched by the twentieth century. On a hill above the city Henry the Fowler built a cathedral and a palace in the early tenth century. He made the place a key centre of the Holy Roman Empire and the headquarters of its eastern expansion.

In his weird, mystical, frightful way, Heinrich Himmler worshipped Henry the Fowler as the father of the German nation. Pious guides who show you round the cathedral today will tell you that while the Communists respected the sanctity of the place, Himmler turned it into a ceremonial hall for the SS. He looked to Henry also as the man who started the German *Drang nach Osten* which, in our own time, took the Wehrmacht and the SS's death squads into Poland, Russia and the Ukraine. But before that last mad dénouement, German expansion across the Elbe shaped eastern Europe for a thousand years. The Teutonic Knights conquered East Prussia and Livonia. They waged war on Europe's last heathens in Lithuania, until the Lithuanians turned Christian and got together with the Poles to defeat them at Tannenberg. German peasants settled in Brandenburg, Pomerania and Silesia. German merchants of the Hanseatic League created East-West trade, and with it the Hansa cities of the Baltic. German artisans were invited by ambitious princes to settle in places as far away as Transylvania and Lithuania. German barons ruled what are today Latvia and Estonia and served the Russian Empire as loyally as others served Brandenburg and Prussia. Throughout eastern Europe and in Russia itself, German settlements provided as much of a social and economic leaven as did the settlements of the Jews.

Woodrow Wilson's reshaping of Europe, creating Czechoslovakia and giving Poland its access to the Baltic, blunted this German presence in eastern Europe, but it left a solid German province beyond the Vistula in East Prussia, as well as German settlers throughout the region. Hitler's Eastern Policy sought to convert this German presence into German domination. When his armies reached the Volga at Stalingrad in 1942, they had advanced further into Russia than western troops had ever gone before. Their entrenchments among the ruins of the city marked the high water mark of the *Drang nach Osten,* just as their extinction was its most spectacular defeat. Three years later the Red Army swept into Germany and put the divide of power between Teutons and Slavs back where it had stood ten centuries earlier, along the Elbe.

Now in their turn Russian troops are gone from the north German plain. Their barracks and their training areas straggle abandoned across the German landscape. Poland is part of NATO, and the British troops still based in Germany despatch a brigade to the east every year to practise war with their Polish allies. The Russians are back behind the Pripet marshes. In the last ten years the unending struggle between Slav and Teuton has moved far from the line of the Elbe on which it began. Those who believe that we have seen the end of history are convinced that it will never be resumed.

After this Wendland diversion, the Iron Curtain resumed its march southwards across the empty spaces of northern Germany. Now you can see little of the old divide. Lower Saxony is on your right, Saxony Anhalt on your left, village succeeding forgotten village, with little to choose between those which once housed Ossis and others for Wessis. The landscape is one of marshes and empty fields which seem to extend into infinity, with empty skies speaking of eternity. Gradually, however, what seems to be the skyline of a great city rises up before you on the southern horizon. You cross a big canal and enter the empire of the Volkswagen.

You are in a world of superlatives, expressed in square metres and Deutschmarks and guest workers and cars rolling by the hundreds of thousand off the production lines. But well into the 1930s Wolfsburg was a village as nondescript as any other in Lower Saxony, distinguished only by one of the province's moated manor houses. Then came the decision to produce the People's Car here, right in the middle of Germany and precisely here in a quiet corner of Lower Saxony. Nazi drive and subscriptions by ordinary Germans got production started just in time for it to serve the needs of war. The Wolfsburg factory was given over to producing military vehicles. Then, as the war turned against Germany, production of Hitler's secret weapon, the V1 cruise missile, was moved here from Peenemünde. But Wolfsburg attracted the Allied bombers and V1 production went underground, at the concentration camp Mittelbau-Dora which we shall visit later in this journey. When Allied troops arrived in April 1945, what was left of Volkswagen at Wolfsburg was in ruins.

British occupation officials famously came to see whether the People's Car was worth taking away by way of reparations. They decided that the Volkswagen had no future, and left the Germans to get production going in Wolfsburg. The Beetle's very defects – its cheap construction and crude simplicity – made it the perfect car for a Europe digging itself out of the ruins of war. It sold in its millions, sucking in workers, first from East Germany and then from Italy and Turkey, to build up production. It powered the postwar German economic miracle, and Wolfsburg became a place of pilgrimage. In the 1970s Volkswagen nearly went under, as more affluent Europeans looked for something more sophisticated than its only product, the Beetle. The company saw the writing on the wall, transferred the Beetle production lines to Latin America and set about building middle-class cars in Wolfsburg for a middle-class continent. In the years since that crisis it has gradually acquired other companies: Audi, whose cars are Volkswagens with an added touch of class which sell at a premium, and foreign producers of lesser breeds of Volkswagen, SEAT in Spain and Skoda in the Czech Republic. Soon it will be building Bentleys.

Now Volkswagen employs half of the people of Wolfsburg. The cars on its streets are mostly Golfs and Passats and Polos, and here in 1999 I saw my first retro-Beetle, built by Volkswagen in Mexico to give the nostalgic an alternative to the Golf. Wolfsburg's rare individualists drive BMWs, its impoverished clapped-out Japanese cars; and one brave Renault dealer has his showroom right in the middle of town.

Volkswagen has made Wolfsburg a substantial modern city of 130,000 people. Nature does nothing to rein it in and it sprawls across the plain, a place of a weak centre and scattered suburbs. The Volkswagen plants sprawl also, dominating the place; but Wolfsburg is no industrial hell-hole, rather an exemplar of all the civic strengths and all the architectural blandness of a dynamically successful new town. Volkswagen has the resources to subsidise distinction, whether in a football stadium or in a scattering of painfully elegant civic buildings.

Of course, Wolfsburg is more than Volkswagen City. Here, right on what used to be the edge of the Western world, it stood as a symbol of the success of Western industrial society. And – to push the argument one step further – it provided an example of the qualities that brought the West victory in the Cold War. Here, Western capitalism (with a strong dash also of subsidy from a provincial government desperate for the jobs that Volkswagen could provide) produced good cars that ordinary people could afford. Here it integrated 'guest workers' into the German work force. Here it gave ordinary people good lives in freedom. And by outproducing the East, Wolfsburg and so many places like it all over the Western world made Soviet defeat in the long term inevitable.

The East Germans too had a car plant close to the line of the Iron Curtain. In Eisenach in Thuringia they produced the Wartburg, big brother of the Trabant, with half its charm and all its inadequacy. We shall go there later, not to study the Wartburg factory which, rebuilt with Western money, now produces Opels for General Motors, but to visit the medieval Wartburg castle after which the car was named. Now we set off to compare East with West in Oebisfelde across the fields from Wolfsburg and just inside East Germany.

When I was learning German, much too late in life, I was taught a sentence that was supposed to encapsulate the rhythm of simple German: 'Der Zug von Berlin nach Hamburg fährt über Hannover'. That *Zug*, that train, travelled also through Oebisfelde, lying as it does on a main line between Western Germany and Berlin. Oebisfelde became as important a railway town as Crewe or Swindon. Today Oebisfelde station looks dead-beat, and the town itself has as decrepit an air as so many East German towns in the back of beyond, with only an exquisite little manor house behind a pond to lift the visitor's spirits.

I asked three men drinking in a pub in Oebisfelde to talk to me about life there in the bad old days, so close to Wolfsburg and so far away. Could they see Volkswagen's chimneys? Not from the town, but easily from their allotments. What did they think about Volkswagen then? Envy, they told me; and not just of West Germans but of the Turks and the Italians. And when reunification came? Did men from Oebisfelde now work for Volkswagen? Surprisingly few, seemed to be the answer: the Turks had the jobs, and there was an edge to the resentment with which they said it. But the worst thing was what had happened to the Reichsbahn railway works here in Oebisfelde. Employment in them had collapsed, whether because the local works were obsolete or because West German shysters had stolen the work away noone seemed to be sure. As for the prosperous Germans of Wolfsburg, 'Wir sind Ossis und sie sind Wessis', and as far as they were concerned the twain never seemed likely to meet.

In my time in Germany twenty-five years ago, I used to think in a whimsical kind of way that if the West Germans built enough Wolfsburgs along their eastern border they would provide an unbroken obstacle to the Soviet Blitzkrieg we were all supposed to expect. To capture the factories of Wolfsburg, courageously defended, would certainly have required the sort of yard by yard clearance by infantry which first the Germans and then the Russians tried in Stalingrad. I tried my theory once on an officer of the Royal Engineers, who dismissed it for the impracticality it was. But NATO could, he believed, have made things easier for itself by judicious field works, to canalise Soviet attacks and lead them into dead-end killing grounds. It could even have built a few fortresses like Maginot's.

Nothing on these lines was ever attempted on any scale, and the Allies prepared to fight a tank war of movement if they were attacked. Perhaps the West Germans saw insuperable objections to anything that added to the division of their country: certainly they spent a lot of money on building schools right on the border, their windows looking east. Schoolchildren were brought to them from all over the Federal Republic to learn about the other Germany – Germany *'drüben'* – and about the iniquities of division. Or perhaps the explanation is simply that the Allied commanders were tank generals with no time for the theories of the engineers and that they were learning yesterday's lessons as generals have always done, preparing to fight the Third World War on the same lines as the Second. Whatever the reason, Germany never got its Maginot Line.

Even at the height of the Cold War, there were many openings in the Iron Curtain. But in Germany vehicles travelling to and from Berlin used only three of them, as did long-distance East-West traffic. Each served an Autobahn that lead to the city from Hamburg, from Hanover and the Ruhr, and from Munich. Of the three routes, the most important was the middle one, which entered East German territory at Marienborn, just south of Wolfsburg. And at Marienborn you can still see today what is left of an extraordinary road traffic marshalling yard.

Marienborn today is a sketch of a museum with ambitions. The enthusiasts who have dedicated themselves to its preservation provide all the vital statistics about the machinery of control. The complex sprawled over thirty-five hectares of concrete. At night 100-foot-high flood lights loomed over the scene. There were sixteen lanes for checking private cars, and ramps on which goods vehicles could be examined and, if suspicious, taken apart. One thousand people were employed at Marienborn by the East German customs, by passport control and by the frontier guards. The different parts of the complex were linked by tunnels and watched over by cameras and hidden microphones. A bridge concealed gamma-ray testing equipment, and officials ran the operation from an airport-sized control tower. They were linked with observation points and with a control system that ran all the way along the Autobahn to Berlin. If they found themselves faced with a mad attempt to break through their defences by force they could deploy across the exit roads electrically-operated rams capable of stopping a heavy truck travelling at thirty miles an hour. And at the edge of the site were the quite separate facilities for handling military and civilian traffic of the three Western allies, each insisting that with the Russians they had rights and responsibilities in Germany as a whole, transcending whatever the East Germans chose to do to West German traffic.

The people who show you Marienborn today are eager to remind you of the evil which it represented: the division into two of a nation which wanted to be one. In their enthusiasm they sometimes suggest that there was something uniquely terrible both about that division, and about Marienborn. The place itself looks the part, as grey, watchful and inhuman as a concentration camp, with its watchtowers and floodlights, its wire fences and mean barrack buildings. You need to remind yourself of the fundamental differences between the two very different qualities of horror which you can see commemorated across the heart of Germany. For even at the worst of times, the division of Germany served a rational and even positive purpose – the preservation of a German Democratic Republic in which some few of its citizens believed. You would have to try hard to find any similar rationale for the concentration camps.

A moment's thought at Marienborn reminds you of something which we will examine in more detail when we reach the end of the German Iron Curtain and come to reflect upon the Germans. The division of their country which the Iron Curtain represented was a tragedy for ordinary Germans. But it was a direct consequence of crimes committed in Germany's name in the course of an aggressive and brutal war which, for no want of trying, the Germans eventually lost. In this sense

Marienborn, grim as it is and tragic as are the facts for which it stood, was a direct consequence of places like Buchenwald and Mauthausen which we shall visit on this journey.

There is a second ironical thing about Marienborn. It came to its full grey concrete flowering not in the worst years of the Cold War but in 1974, when détente between Communist East and capitalist West was at its peak and after a whole series of agreements to ease relationships between the two Germanies had been painfully negotiated. The 1971 four-power agreement on Berlin provided for many improvements. The agreement between the two Germanies which followed permitted freer movement between the two. The Marienborn processing facilities came into existence to handle the consequences of these improvements, yet they look like the product of the worst years of East-West confrontation.

At Marienborn today you can still see many testimonies to the obsessive perfectionism of the Teutonic totalitarian mind. The Hanover-Berlin Autobahn is being widened to accommodate the traffic which swishes by uninterrupted and unchecked on its way to Berlin, but inside the frontier station the old buildings bear witness to the old days. Guides show you where your travel documents went when you put them into the outstretched hand of the functionary behind the window. They made their way up conveyor belts that look as if they were lashed up by thick-thumbed handymen in their spare time, but which were watched over by supervisors ever alert for carelessness or worse on the part of their juniors. Helmut Schneider's documents were pigeon-holed, if necessary for hours, while East German intelligence went to work to establish whether this was or was not the Helmut Schneider who, four years ago, had been caught smuggling *Playboy* into their country. And if Helmut Schneider panicked at the delay, it was evidence of a guilty conscience, perhaps over some contraband like *Playboy,* perhaps over something even worse he had concealed in his luggage, perhaps for the evil thoughts he entertained towards the people's republic.

Outside the marshalling yard itself, along the actual border, there remains a short section of the old concrete panel walls erected to foil anyone who made a dash for freedom on foot from Marienborn. You can see such walls at various points along the line of the old Iron Curtain, concrete here, steel mesh there, as well as the watchtowers and the death strip. In some places, such as Hötensleben, just south of Marienborn, they give you a vivid impression of the impact of the Iron Curtain on ordinary people in ordinary villages and, if you climb up into one of the watchtowers, of the wearisome life of the border guards as well. But to see and understand separation and control practised on an industrial scale, go to Marienborn.

Trains as well as cars, trucks and buses crossed the Iron Curtain. They too were controlled, inspected, minutely examined, their upholstery if necessary torn apart in the search for forbidden goods. As with road traffic, the East Germans had two motives. First to ensure that noone and nothing left the German Democratic Republic illegally (and, they would have argued, that no Western spy or saboteur entered it undetected). Second, to assert the sovereignty of a regime which, even after it was internationally recognised in 1973, still wore upon its shoulder an ill-concealed chip of inferiority.

As at Marienborn, the Western allies had rail facilities of their own, notably the British and American military trains. These ran to and from Berlin daily, as much to assert a right-of-way as to carry passengers to useful destinations. The British train left Hanover every morning, the American Frankfurt every evening. Each bore its share of military pomp, personified by a train commander. At Helmstedt, just on the Western side of the border opposite Marienborn, the train commander disembarked. On the platform he met a Soviet officer in his broad-brimmed cap and ankle-length overcoat. Stiff salutes were exchanged, careful scripts recited. The train proceeded on its way into East Germany, its doors locked, armed British or American soldiers patrolling its corridors. Its way lay through empty Saxon forests, but beside the track ran a high mesh fence topped with barbed wire. Here, deep inside East Germany, watchtowers still reigned, and attack dogs prowled along a track of their own, shut in by a second fence, this one electrified. East German authority was thus protected, Allied rights in Germany thus asserted, at whatever cost to common sense.

But anyone could fly to West Berlin, along three corridors from the West prescribed by four-power agreement. It was flights along these corridors which saved Berlin from starvation in the blockade of 1948–49, and for forty years thereafter, in civil aircraft of British Airways, Pan Am and Air France, an ever-increasing number of businessmen and family travellers winged their way to Berlin over the German Democratic Republic as if they were on a simple German domestic flight. But Allied use of the air corridors was never an entirely simple matter.

In 1970 I was dealing with Germany in the Western European Department of the Foreign Office. The best part of our days was taken up with the *Ostpolitik*, with plotting that complex of agreements which eventually eased relations between East and West in Europe and made life better for ordinary East Germans and East Europeans. But there were going to be no cost-free agreements, as the endless difficulties we faced over Mr Lewis's aeroplane a year later showed. And if necessary the bear could bite. One September morning the Russian controller in the Berlin Air Safety Centre informed his Allied counterparts that an area of East Germany fifty miles across would be closed to air traffic for two hours in the early hours of the following morning. The effect of this would be to shut the north and central air corridors to Berlin. It was the first attempt to interfere with Allied use of the corridors for a quarter of a century.

At the time the Warsaw Pact was conducting military exercises in Germany. They might, military intelligence told us, involve surface-to-surface missiles and parachute drops. The closure may have been intended as no more than a safety measure, at a time in the small hours when Allied flights were unlikely to be incommoded. The Russians may have seen it as a bit of routine that went wrong. But throughout the Cold War the Western Allies brought to Berlin business a suspicion of any Soviet move that might appear to erode their rights in Germany as conquerors. Successive generations of officials were brought up to remember the Berlin Blockade, the Berlin Wall, and ludicrous but potentially catastrophic disputes about whether or not the Allies should lower the tailgates of their military vehicles to allow the Russians to count the number of passengers. Anything might be the thin end of a wedge, not least a Russian claim to close an Allied air corridor.

In London we went into spasms of enjoyable if nervous excitement. We were clear that Allied aircraft must be put through the corridors to demonstrate that only the agreement of all four allies could close them. We so recommended to the Foreign Secretary, Alec Douglas-Home. He telephoned the Prime Minister: 'We've got a spot of trouble in the Berlin corridors, Ted. We recommend a probe.' 'Harrumph' said Edward Heath at the other end of the line, and agreed that the Royal Air Force should join our allies in a probing flight through the corridor and face the Russians down.

Not for the first time, American policy-making was in a mess. Nixon and Kissinger were on a United States aircraft carrier in the Mediterranean, preoccupied with other issues. The State Department, having said one thing to London and Paris, said something else to the President and recommended against a probe. The President and Kissinger went along with it: no United States flight would be available. We determined to go ahead with the French alone; but by the evening hours the Quai d'Orsay, earlier gung-ho, had had second thoughts and the French pilots had gone out to a party or home to bed. Finally, very early on 30 September, a Royal Air Force aircraft went through the corridor alone, while in London, Washington, Berlin and Bonn officials sat anxiously by their telephones and crossed their fingers and toes. As it approached Berlin a missile was fired, some said five miles from the aircraft, some twelve. The probe landed safely in Berlin.

We still did not know whether the Soviet controller's statement that the corridors would be closed was a try-on authorised at high level or a junior officer's mistake. The day after the probe the Allied ambassadors registered a protest with their Soviet colleague – low key because there seemed no point in shoving the Russians into a corner in which they might turn defiant. A few days later he replied, saying that the statement about the closure of the corridor had been made without reference to higher authority. The air traffic controller would be 'severely punished'. So far so good. But the ambassador added that the Soviet side reserved the right to control flight in the corridors. So far so very objectionable. We told him, still low key, that we trusted there would be no further incidents which might infringe the rights of the Allies in the corridors. The incident passed into history, with only a grace note a few weeks later. Henry Kissinger, not a man given to apology, then told a British official that he and the President had been weary, unfocused that evening. The credit for identifying the right course and sticking to it belonged entirely to the British Foreign Secretary. His clear-headedness had saved President Nixon from making 'a very serious and damaging miscalculation'.

Now that the division of Germany is a memory you would have thought that walls separating Germans from Germans would be no more than a bad dream. Almost everywhere now, the concrete walls or steel mesh fences that made their political statement across the face of Germany have gone. The panels were shattered, the pillars which supported them extracted like teeth at a giant dentist's. You can see only souvenir-scraps of the Wall in Berlin, and only museum mementoes at places along the old Iron Curtain. But it is as if the wall builders cannot rest. For years now, walls serving a different purpose have been going up all over western Germany. Along roads throughout the old Federal Republic you can see walls erected to shelter towns and villages from the roar of traffic. When I lived there, in the early 1980s, they were occasional eyesores, mostly beside the Autobahns, and only defending considerable conurbations. Now they are everywhere, and even quiet little back roads have their fifty yards of wall or embankment to protect a single house, half a mile of defences to protect a village – and sometimes, it seems, a stretch of wall to protect the ruminations of a solitary cow.

Of course, says the voice of reason, the Germans are not alone. We too have our walls to baffle traffic noise, to protect the peace of suburban streets and quiet villages. But nowhere else in Europe has taken wall-building to the lengths you see in Germany. And now the disease is spreading into what used to be the German Democratic Republic, as if walls were necessary signs of bourgeois respectability. They are going up not just along the Autobahn east of Marienborn, shutting it in even more effectively than the East Germans' precautions against spies in transit to Berlin ever did, but along back roads in Mecklenburg and Saxony Anhalt, in Brandenburg and Thuringia. In places they bring necessary relief to the ears of the man-in-the street assailed by passing traffic. But at the same time they bring offence to his eyes, where grim blank walls overshadow villages or single houses. The process has gone beyond all reason. Germany, having lost its Communist Wall, is becoming a land of walls, decent, democratic, environmentally friendly walls no doubt, but far more walls than a sense of proportion would suggest was reasonable.

At the end of the Autobahn which crossed the old divide at Marienborn lies Berlin, now the capital of a united Germany. Throughout the Cold War it was, like Germany, famously divided between East and West. Here the two alliance systems, the two world orders met most directly, intensively and dangerously. Here the diplomats watched one another, the spies spied on one another and the statesmen threw down their challenges to one another. This was where the Third World War might have started. The Berlin Wall marked the East-West divide at its starkest; this was the Iron Curtain in spades.

It is instructive to recall how this situation came about. In the wartime negotiations about zonal arrangements in a conquered Germany, the Western allies insisted on having a presence in Berlin. They saw it as the essential capital of a Germany which the four powers would administer as a single unit. So insisting, they put their necks into a noose which Moscow could tighten at any time it dared. For years the temperature of relations between East and West was regulated in Berlin.

We have seen the occupying powers' manoeuvres in the early post-war years. In 1948 Britain and the United States, desperate to bring Germany back to life, merged the economies of their zones. To the Soviet Union it was the ultimate provocation or the perfect excuse to divide Germany into two. The Soviet representative walked out of the four powers' Control Council. Moscow closed road, rail and canal access to Berlin from the West. Britain and the United States began to fly in supplies through those air routes which we have seen the Soviet Union claiming to close one summer's night twenty-two years later. Several times in the next few months the world seemed near to war, but in the end the East blinked before the West and the Berlin Air Lift beat the Berlin Blockade.

Four years later, Stalin died. There were hopes of better times, but in East Berlin they led to the rising of 17 June 1953. Soviet tanks fired on East German demonstrators. A man tore down the Soviet flag from the Brandenburg Gate. East Germany's leader declared that the rising was the work of 'provocateurs and Fascist agents', and East Berlin was temporarily shut off from the Western sectors. Yet still Berlin was a single city, and still the four occupying powers claimed rights over the city as a whole.

For eight more years, Berlin remained one. You could walk between the sectors, take a train, take a bus, take a taxi. Over the years, three million East Germans passed from East to West Berlin and on into the Federal Republic and the Western world. East Germany was bleeding to death as its citizens fled and at last, in 1961, the Soviet Union allowed its East German satraps to build the Berlin Wall. Again war was close, but this time it was the West which backed away from the challenge.

The Wall insulted the people of Berlin, East and West, but it saved the German Democratic Republic. It ruined the lives of many thousands of Berliners, but it made possible a rough and ready political *modus vivendi* in the city. For a decade, divided Berlin was an insistent source of neuralgia in East-West relations, with the nagging pain of shootings on the Wall and the sudden fierce pain that blazed up in occasional, potentially dangerous disputes over Western access to the city.

The Berlin and Two Germanies agreements of 1971–72 were palliatives, not cures; but they improved the circumstances of the ordinary lives of Berliners. They made things as ordinary as they could be in a city with a wall and a killing zone driven right through its heart. But in Berlin as everywhere in human affairs, improvement gradually brought demands for more. They came to a head in 1989. Moscow did most to bring about change in that miraculous year and Budapest opened the gap in the Iron Curtain which spelt its end. But it was the crowds dancing on the Berlin Wall who most vividly demonstrated that the Iron Curtain was finished. Crowds of East Berliners streamed westwards, men took pickaxes and sledgehammers to the very fabric of the divide, the border guards looked on in sheepish impotence.

For more than twenty-five years the Wall had been by far the most important element in the story of Berlin. When it came down, its physical manifestations vanished quickly, broken up into souvenirs, taken away to museums. Berlin is Germany's capital again, as important as the Hohenzollerns willed that it should be. New buildings are changing the face of the city, blotting out the killing zones and the blighted wastelands along the Wall. But the distinctions which its existence imposed on the two halves of the city have a more enduring reality, and it will be another century before the last of them is forgotten.

Whatever their reasoning, the Western allies never built their Maginot Line across Germany, but they took the Soviet threat with deadly seriousness. For more than forty years their armies in Germany prepared to fight the father and mother of armoured battles to stop and destroy a massed Soviet tank attack. Two generations of British military families lived much of their lives in the garrison towns of northern Germany, convinced that it was the British Army of the Rhine that held the most vulnerable sector of the entire front along the line of the Iron Curtain. Further south, where the Fulda Gap seemed to offer the Russians an easy road to Frankfurt, American forces believed that they rather than the British stood at the point of maximum danger. In the 1950s a rearmed Germany began to add its military strength to theirs, until in the end it provided some of Nato's most formidable divisions. There were plans for Dutch and Belgian corps to move up into the line in the north German plain, and for a Danish division to come down from Jutland and help block a Soviet thrust towards Hamburg and the Danish frontier. The French Army was a less certain quantity, but there were hopes, never quite solidified into conviction, that if war came the French too would come forward and play their part in defeating a Soviet offensive.

Martin Farndale was one of the many British officers who spent the best part of their lives in Germany, preparing for the war that never came. Over the decades he held appointments at every level, from troop commander to the command of Northern Army Group, responsible for the front all the way from the Elbe to the Harz mountains. I asked him how he would have fought his Armageddon.

Like all Allied commanders, he told me, he assumed that if the day had ever come the West would have been hit by a tidal wave of Soviet armoured divisions, moving forward in two great strategic echelons. The Russians had learned their tank warfare from the Wehrmacht and their use of overwhelming numbers from their own military history. The British Corps, holding a 50-kilometre front just south of Braunschweig, would have faced the Third Shock Army. The country there is gentle, open fields regularly punctuated by insignificant villages and broken by low hills and scattered woods. It is country which favours an armoured attacker, and the Russians would have punched their way easily through the covering force of scouts and armoured reconnaissance regiments. They would have run up against the British fighting divisions somewhere on the line of the little River Oker, which flows out of the Harz mountains and northwards across the plain to join the Aller and the Weser on their way to the North Sea. After I had talked with Farndale I went looking for the Oker and found something that is not much more than a sweetly flowing stream, as physically insignificant as the Somme. On the day of Armageddon, I reflected, the Oker would have become as significant as the Somme in British folk memory, if any of us had survived for its memories to haunt us.

The commander of a British armoured division, Farndale told me, had at his disposal nine armoured regiments – say 300 tanks; 3,000 infantry; 70 guns; minelaying and bridge-blowing engineers; about 15,000 men when fully reinforced for war. First British Corps contained three such divisions as well as the covering force and Corps reserves – say 50,000 men. On its left it had a German and a Dutch corps, on its right a Belgian corps and the Harz mountains. Between them their task was to slow and then stop the first echelon of a Soviet thrust across the north German plain towards the Ruhr and the Rhine.

At every level, Farndale told me, an Allied commander would face similar problems. The Russians would outnumber his forces by a factor of at least three to one. They would come forward in waves, preceded by air attack and supported by low-flying attack helicopters. A Western brigade commander who was wise would not stand and fight these hammer blows head on. He would let the Russians advance where the lie of the land took them, then strike back in large-scale ambushes with tanks and guns from behind woods and hills and minefields. To fight effectively he would have to commit his forces, but he must constantly

be rebuilding his reserves, pulling units out of the fighting and reposi-
tioning them to fight again. He would make maximum use of artillery
fire power and of air support.

I asked Farndale if he thought that he could have held such a Soviet
attack. That, he said, was what Margaret Thatcher had asked him
every time she visited Rhine Army. In retrospect, knowing what we
know now of Soviet weakness, he thought that he probably could have
stopped the first echelon of the Russian attack somewhere in Lower
Saxony. At the time he had been less confident. 'On balance, and taking
everything into account', British officers used to tell each other, 'military history does tend to suggest that, everything else being equal, big
armies will usually defeat little armies'. It was black humour which
masked the reality that in the first forty-eight hours of onslaught, First
British Corps expected to lose fifty per cent of its men. And behind the
Soviet first echelon would come the second strategic echelon: Russian
hordes in very deed.

A key factor in the days of the Cold War was a simple matter of
housekeeping: ammunition stocks. Modern war has a frightening
appetite for supplies. To pre-position ammunition in Germany in quantity cost budget-breaking sums of money. So Allied commanders prepared for war with the haunting fear that if the real thing came they
might run short of ordnance and spares. It was that factor rather than
fighting capacity, Farndale had told Margaret Thatcher, which might
bring defeat – unless, that is, the Russians outran their supplies before
the Allies exhausted theirs.

But the Allies would be fighting not just to stop the Russians, but to
postpone the deadly moment of decision to go nuclear. In the time the
soldiers won for them, the politicians and diplomats could go about the
desperate business of trying to find a peaceful end to the fighting. But if
they failed (and they would probably have had no more than twenty-
four hours to do their job) the Allies would have faced the choice
between accepting defeat and turning to nuclear weapons. Intermedi-
ate-range weapons would have been used first, striking at Soviet
reserves, supplies and communications in East Germany and Poland.
Next, to destroy Soviet forward concentrations, it might have been necessary to use the short-range weapons – this in thickly populated
friendly country. The last resort would have been the strategic weapons
targeted on Moscow and other Soviet cities – true Armageddon

Into this deadly brew Farndale mixed two other ingredients. There
were plans for the American Third Corps to fly from its base at Fort

Hood in Texas into position behind Northern Army Group. Its equipment was pre-positioned in Germany, but the aircraft carrying its men would have to fly the gauntlet of attack by Soviet fighters. If the Third Corps made it, it would bring to Northern Army Group the capacity for a major counter-stroke against Soviet lodgements in North West Germany. And there were plans, too, if the main Soviet blow fell in Northern Germany, for the American troops concentrated further south at the Fulda Gap to strike north eastwards into the Russian lines of communication. Each of these might have saved the world from the consequences of a fateful resort to nuclear weapons.

All this, Farndale and I thought, sounded fanciful in 1999, ten years after the Berlin Wall came down. It was not fanciful in the Cold War years in which he commanded first his troop and then his regiment, his brigade, his division, his corps and his army group in Germany. The exercises in which the British Army and its allies endlessly practised for these events were, he told me, deadly realistic affairs. You might spend days cooped up in armoured command vehicles, fed with information by radio, telephone and computer, immersed in an imagined sea of war, cut off from the reality of the world outside. You might spend hours, for that matter, in anti-gas suits, breathing filtered air, fighting the demands of nature in clothing you could not get out of. You ended up believing that outside the protection of your armoured vehicles the scenes you were exercising were real. When you finally emerged into the sunshine it was the everyday German field or farmyard which seemed the fairy tale.

I got another perspective on all this from a more junior officer, who in his time had served on nuclear targeting staffs. He shared Farndale's memories of exercises, and added one more sinister touch. He remembered obsessive men with lists prowling these practice battlefields. The lists recorded the size of German villages. If in the course of exercises events reached the stage where a tactical nuclear strike was being considered, these lists had their relevance. For policy dictated that villages with over 500 inhabitants should if at all possible be spared. Like Farndale, he remembered the awful realism of these exercises, as if the next little village across the fields might go up in nuclear smoke. And, added Farndale, 'My German Chief of Staff grew up here; this was his part of Germany.'

The big exercises, Farndale told me, were planned many months in advance. But First British Corps, like all the Allied armies, lived under the shadow of a sudden Blitzkrieg attack. Of course there were likely to be warning signs of increasing tension: political developments, diplomatic contacts, unusual patterns of communication, intelligence signals. But the fighting units had to be ready to move to battle positions at short notice. For forty years, one million men in NATO's front line from northern Norway to Italy lived at four to eight hours' notice of a move to their battle positions. Officers at many levels were authorised to call Exercise Quicktrain into life. If one of them did, officers and men had four hours in which to get back to barracks. They might then be ordered to 'bomb up', to break open ammunition packs ready for war. (This too, Farndale told me, was an appallingly expensive thing to do – the housekeeping again – but it could be and had been ordered.) Thereafter the units had another four hours to get into their battle positions – and some British units had sixty miles of congested north German roads to cover to get there. The worst time for Quicktrain, Farndale told me, was early evening. You were on your way out to dinner when all hell broke loose. You had to turn away from the prospect of cocktails, get out of your black tie (those black ties so beloved of British military dinner parties), get into combat gear and move into position to fight a war to the death.

There was one exercise in particular which Farndale remembered: Reforger 1987. The life of the Cold War seemed to be moving peacefully towards its close, but still the Allies practised the tactics of real war. Reforger 1987 was no Quicktrain, but a long-planned and enormously ambitious exercise. It involved deploying all four European corps of Northern Army Group against the clock to meet the first wave of Soviet attacks. Into this maelstrom would arrive the men of the Third United States Corps from Fort Hood, equipped with the guns, vehicles and gear which awaited them in depots along the German-Dutch border. To become integrated into the Allied order of battle the Americans would have to pass through positions occupied by Dutch and German corps, covered not by their own guns but by First British Corps artillery. It was, said Farndale, one of the most difficult of military manoeuvres, demanding the complete integration of Allied forces. He was glad, he said, that as Commander of Northern Army Group he commanded not just the allied corps but the attacking 'enemy' as well. Whichever side came out on top in Reforger 1987, he could claim to have won it. In the event, in this clash of 400 tanks, 600 other armoured vehicles as well as guns and missiles on the Hanover plain, with 2nd Allied Tactical Air Force joining in from the sky, the Allies 'won'. Men, machines, systems and controls were tested to breaking point. It was, said Farndale, the most realistic of all the exercises to which he had devoted so much of his life.

By this stage of the Cold War, he had to reckon not just with his Soviet opposite number away behind his shock armies on the other side of the Iron Curtain but also with a Soviet shadow, a Russian general attached to Northern Army Group headquarters. The Russian's attachment, like that of Allied officers to the Soviet commander-in-chief in Germany, was a confidence-building measure. Watchful and suspicious at first, the Russian followed Farndale everywhere, or nearly everywhere, as he went about his business of running this supremely testing exercise. Gradually he became friendly and talkative. In the end, as the exercise ended and the exhausted troops crawled back to barracks, the Russian turned to Farndale in a rare gesture of openness. 'It was a great exercise, General,' he said. 'We could not have done what you did.'

That was the moment, Farndale told me, when he felt that the West had won the Cold War and, in Reforger 1987, had fought its last battle. He quoted the words of Sun Tzu, the Chinese military sage: 'To fight and win a hundred battles is not proof of superior excellence; the supreme achievement is to bend the resistance of the enemy without fighting him.' For forty years of peace the members of the Atlantic Alliance had kept a million men ready for battle at eight hours' notice. Victory without bloodshed was their reward.

Every army gathers specialists and auxiliaries around it. As I dug deeper into the affairs of the armies on watch in Germany, two stories particularly intrigued me.

The British Frontier Service developed out of an organisation scratched together in the first days of the peace in 1945 to deal with the problems of displaced persons and refugees. As the Allied armies crushed the last life out of the Nazi regime they were confronted with vast floods of people on the move. Soldiers returning home or fleeing from vengeance were one source, the hundreds of thousands released from Nazi concentration camps and prisoner-of-war camps another. German civilian refugees moved westwards, at first on their own initiative, to escape the advancing Russians, and then at the point of a gun, as Poland and Czechoslovakia took over areas acquired from the Reich. In the British zone of occupation Lübeck in particular was swamped, with refugees coming overland from Mecklenburg and northern Germany and with tens of thousands more shipped down the Baltic from the old German provinces of East Prussia and Pomerania.

The Army looked around for help in settling this flood of humanity and the Royal Navy came to its assistance. With the sinking or surrender of what was left of the German submarine fleet, the Navy had lost its main wartime purpose. It offered whole units to serve ashore beside the Army. The blue uniform became as familiar as the khaki at the checkpoints and reception areas for people on the move.

Nothing endures like the provisional; and out of this naval deployment ashore grew the British Frontier Service. As the problems of the great migrations were gradually resolved, the problems of controlling the zonal borders increased. The British Frontier Service in its naval caps went out on patrol. As, in the 1950s, West Germany began to build up its own capacity to guard its frontiers, the role of the Frontier Service diminished. But on the border with the Soviet zone it still provided a reminder that the occupying power was as interested as the Germans in safeguarding West German territory; and there as on Germany's other borders the Frontier Service processed the British Army's own needs for immigration and customs control.

So throughout the Cold War the British Frontier Service provided a presence and a reassurance along the line of the Iron Curtain in northern Germany. Its patrols, like those of the West German frontier troops, went right up to the demarcation line. Like the men on the other side they were under strict orders about their conduct there. Studying the other side too intently through binoculars could easily be seen as provocation, trespass across the demarcation line as invasion. But men pursuing parallel avocations find their own ways to talk to one another, even to drink with one another when higher authority's back is turned. So it was with the solution of the mystery of the boundary markers.

Some time in the course of the Cold War, the East Germans set out new markers along the line of the border. They were concrete, squat, and roughly tapered. Laboriously the East Germans painted each in tricolour bands of their national colours. But the concrete and the painted bands were not the object of the West's concern. Instead, Western intelligence focused on little wires that protruded from the top of each concrete marker. Were the East Germans installing a line of listening devices or of electronic triggers along the border? The mystery remained unsolved for a decade. But gradually relationships along the Iron Curtain thawed a little. The day came when Western frontier guards went drinking with the East Germans, then gossiping with them. Finally they admitted to their suspicions about the wires. The hard men of the East German frontier guards broke for once into smiles, even into laughter. The wires were there to stop birds alighting on the concrete markers and shitting on the national colours.

The work of the Frontier Service was mainly about security, together with a little snooping when occasion offered. The work of the Missions to the Soviet Forces in Germany was about both: in one incarnation a kind of insurance policy and in another licensed spying. BRIXMIS (like SOXMIS and every other SUCHMIS) grew out of the realisation that if British, United States and Soviet forces were to occupy Germany jointly, they needed mechanisms of communication between them. Initially, these were assured at top level by the Allied Control Council in Berlin. But in March 1948 the Soviet representative walked out. He went in protest at being denied information about the Western allies' plans to develop in their zones the mechanisms that were to lead to the establishment of the Federal Republic, but his departure was almost immediately followed by the blockade of Berlin. The Russians never returned to the Allied Control Council, and its functions at the political level were gradually taken over by diplomats, meeting in Berlin but answerable to their embassies in Bonn and, ultimately, to their foreign ministries. At the military level, the role of the individual missions to the headquarters of the other occupying powers increased.

Throughout the Cold War the officers and men of BRIXMIS lived and worked close to the headquarters of the Soviet commander-in-chief in Potsdam. Its head served a quasi-diplomatic function, as a channel of communication between the two commanders-in-chief. But his men were always out on the road, snooping on Soviet military activity right across Germany. They were there when the Russians manoeuvred their Shock Armies, pounded their training sites with rocket fire or laid assault bridges across the Elbe. And they were there when we flew our probe through the Berlin corridor.

BRIXMIS, like SOXMIS and USMIS, snatched photographs of new equipment whenever they got the opportunity: they were licensed narks, after all, and military intelligence was as much their game as liaison. BRIXMIS sent back a steady stream of photographs of Soviet tanks and guns for the technical intelligence staffs to work on; and when, after the Suez war, the Israelis gave us the vital statistics of a new Soviet tank they had captured from the Egyptians, the photogrammetry team I worked with as a National Service dogsbody found that their drawings based on BRIXMIS photographs were 97% accurate.

BRIXMIS, someone told me who never served with them and had therefore no *parti pris*, had 'a particular flair' for this kind of work along the shadowy border between liaison and spying. The Americans never got the same results and neither, we trusted, did the Soviet mission to our own forces in Germany. But BRIXMIS, like the Americans and Russians, took risks. In the 1970s an American officer who pushed too hard was shot dead by a Soviet sentry; and every so often an incident in the field led to sharp exchanges between the diplomats who otherwise turned half a blind eye to the activities that led to it. One story in particular illustrates both the danger and the flair.

Some time in the 1970s, Soviet forces in Germany acquired a new artillery piece. The West wanted to know more about it and the missions went to work. A BRIXMIS patrol got itself alongside a slowly-moving Soviet military train loaded with the new guns. There were armed guards at front and rear, but a sergeant from the patrol got aboard undetected with his camera. He started to unlace the muzzle cover on one of the guns. A guard saw him and fired. This was no time for more photography, but our sergeant still had not established the calibre of the gun. But he had his picnic in his pocket and dessert that day was an apple. He jammed it into the gun, pulled it out with the size of the muzzle clearly bitten into the peel, and dived with his evidence into the safety of a ditch. The guns went on their way to join their units and the sergeant's apple found its way back to British technical intelligence. Devilish cunning, BRIXMIS.

4

The Heart of Germany

We leave behind us the north German plain, with its memories of apples stuck in gun barrels and plans for Armageddon, and start the long climb into the Harz mountains. There is nothing here to challenge the Alps, but this is the most significant area of high ground in central Germany; and the summit of the Harz, the Brocken, rises getting on for 4,000 feet above the plain. The road creeps up heavily wooded ravines, carved by rivers like the Oker, which we have seen ambling across the front on which the First British Corps would have fought in war. Here and there the darkness of the valley is broken by the silver sparkle of the water in mountain reservoirs; and higher up still you break out into open hill-top country. The Harz form a solid block of country, twenty-five miles from north to south and rather more than that from east to west. There have always been ways through it, but it presents a serious obstacle to movement, particularly by armies; and their allies, with the loyalty of all good allies, will tell you that one of the reasons why the troops of the Belgian corps in Northern Army Group were assigned this section of the front was that noone could imagine the Russians being mad enough to attack here.

The Iron Curtain ran right through the middle of the Harz, passing just west of the summit of the Brocken. And even if noone envisaged fighting battles among these hills and woods, the dividing line between east and west remained a serious reality here. In little museums at Sorge and Bad Sachsa you can see pathetic relics of the machinery of control, and throughout the region you come across traces of the different societies which grew up on each side of the line. So Bad Harzburg, on the western side of the line where it enters the Harz, is a wildly prosperous spa, and Braunlage, ten miles to the south and still just in the old Federal Republic, is an equally prosperous winter sport resort. Places in the eastern Harz, like Wernigerode, Schierke and Elend, are antique, unspoiled, rather scruffy by contrast. But, west or east, Germans come to the Harz to walk and wander, to breathe fresh air and take healing waters, and above all to wonder at the splendours of nature in the wild.

For the Harz is to German sensibilities what the Lake District was to Wordsworth and his disciples. It has a particular appeal to the old and

serious, untempted by Caribbean beaches. There is something solemn
about the bus excursionists and the lines of walkers you encounter here;
and if they have a book in their hands it is as likely to be a volume of
Heine's poetry as a twentieth-century guide to the place. Goethe lost his
head and heart to the Harz; the romanticism which it represented fired
his imagination. He was beguiled by wild places in general and by
ghosts and demons, celebrated annually in the Harz on *Walpurgis-
nacht,* in particular. So in November 1777 he absconded from his
duties at the court of Weimar and made off on horseback, incognito,
into the Harz. For him it was as much a journey of self-identification as
of exploration, and as he rode he composed his poem *Harzreise im
Winter.* He got to Torfhaus at the western foot of the Brocken, determined to find a way to the top. The locals assured him that it was
impossible, the approach paths were already blocked by snow. Goethe
insisted, and eventually a woodsman took him, struggling through the
snow, to the summit. He came down, in a mood of exaltation, suffused
with the splendour of nature and a new assurance about his own des-
tiny. Goethe's love of the Harz and his admirers' worship of Goethe
have fed German affection for the Harz ever since.

But Goslar, the centre of the western Harz, tells a different story
about this mountain region. It was for centuries a silver-mining town,
and in consequence one of the richest cities of Germany. The Emperor
needed the wealth they produced, and he made Goslar a Free City of
the Holy Roman Empire. So Goslar is heavy with history, with historical memories stamped on every street-corner, but in a way different
from most small German cities. No prince ruled here, though the
Emperors themselves came frequently to hold court and take their share
of the silver that came out of the mountain behind the town. The citizens of Goslar were assertive and independent-minded, like those of
Hamburg or Lübeck, not subservient like the subjects of the German
principalities. The Emperor needed them, their skills and hard work,
their silver production, and so they struck with him a relationship
almost of equals.

You see something of this if you wander the streets of Goslar. There
is an imperial palace on the edge of the town, reconstructed with a
heavy hand in the nineteenth century, but the heart of the matter in
Goslar is burghers' territory, gabled house succeeding wildly decorated
house, the city's dignity massively celebrated in the Rathaus and the
houses of the guilds. Across the market square from the Rathaus a
modern city benefactor has provided a *Glockenspiel,* a performing

clock which acts out the discovery of the city's silver and its tireless exploitation. The mines are finished now, but Goslar still shines with prosperity. Nothing much here was destroyed in war, nothing much here needed restoration afterwards. You find in Goslar as nowhere else in the western Harz the essence of an older Germany, carried forward effortlessly into the present.

To compare and contrast East and West once again, go to Quedlinburg on the very edge of the eastern Harz. We have seen that here Henry the Fowler laid the foundations for German expansion eastwards across the Elbe in the early Middle Ages, and Heinrich Himmler held his weird SS ceremonies. But there is much more to the place than the imprint of these two individuals. We have left the last of north German brick behind us and Quedlinburg's streets and squares are lined with half-timbered houses, proudly medieval still, or medieval with a Renaissance facade tacked on. Quedlinburg is more expansive, less cramped than Goslar, and it lacks its polished sheen. For Quedlinburg slept untouched through the Communist years, and only now are the improvers taking it in hand. In the back streets you can see them shoring up a collapsing house. In the squares the work of spit and polish has begun. But Quedlinburg remains shabbier by far than Goslar, an uneven sort of place, with far to go before the improvers have given it Goslar's gloss and, therefore, still shabby, real, and as yet almost unharmed. It will be another ten years before we shall see whether the improvers can carry Quedlinburg's past as successfully into the present as they have done in Goslar.

Wernigerode, between Goslar and Quedlinburg and, like the latter, a star in the old East German crown, is something else again. It lacks Goslar's wealth, ancient and modern, and Quedlinburg's imperial connections. But its old houses are as extravagant as theirs, its steep streets as charming. It too has a castle, rebuilt at the same time as the Emperor's palace in Goslar but with twice the verve and conviction. Above all it has a steam train that looks as if it had puffed off the set of *Anna Karenina*. It crawls out of the town at walking pace on its way up into the mountains. An out-and-out moderniser might see its antiquity as a pimple on the face of the Federal Republic, an almost shameful hangover from Communist days. Other kinds of Germans celebrate it – and because of it Wernigerode attracts steam train buffs from all over Germany.

Wernigerode is fifteen miles from Goslar, about the same from Quedlinburg. All three places are products of Germany's decentralised history, each self-sufficient in a way typical of so many German towns and cities which you will find very rarely in Britain. At the same time, their histories preach an identity in common, a product of the Holy Roman Empire, of the German language, and of a sense of German nationhood which existed long before there was thought of a German state. Then, in 1870, the citizens of Goslar, Quedlinburg and Wernigerode got their German statehood. They enjoyed it and abused it for seventy years. Then came the price, the isolation of Goslar from its eastern neighbours for half a century. For most people throughout the Cold War they might have been on different planets. Now the citizens of the three towns go back and forth as they please. Once again they enjoy their common statehood; some regret it, hankering for the years of division; a few abuse it. Germany's future, like that of any of its neighbours, is a closed book to us. It will be written as much in little places like these as in big cities such as Munich, Hamburg and Berlin.

The Harz mountains told me one side of German history. Leaving them, I decided to go looking for a different story that was played out all over Europe and along the line which divided the continent for so long. I was in search of the concentration camp Mittelbau-Dora, and I found it outside Nordhausen, a ramshackle industrial town just inside the old East Germany. On a back road that leads from town to camp I noticed a plaque built into a wall. I stopped, expecting some commemoration of the men and women brought this way to forced labour and, too often, extinction. I found something very different. Here a nineteenth-century worthy had committed to bronze a statement that Goethe had passed this way on his winter journey into the Harz. For me it pointed to something you cannot escape if you travel far along the old German divide: the way in which the best and the worst of this most diverse of countries stand together cheek by jowl, bringing together here Goethe's poetry, the Nazis and the Iron Curtain.

Much of Dora still survives: parade ground, huts, guards' quarters neatly laid out on a gentle, sunlit slope from which you can just about see the roofs of Nordhausen. So, out of sight and underground, does its *raison d'être*. For unlike most concentration camps, Dora served a recognisable war-fighting purpose. In 1943 slave workers were brought here by the thousand to develop an existing tunnel system into an underground factory. The work was pushed forward with appalling

brutality, but so effectively that Albert Speer, the Nazi industrial production overlord, put in writing his astonished thanks for the achievement. And in the underground factory the Nazis pressed ahead with the
production of the V1 cruise missiles and V2 rockets which were used
against London and Antwerp in the last year of the war. 20,000 prisoners died in creating the underground factory and in building in it
Hitler's last 'victory' weapons, perhaps four times the number of their
British and Belgian victims.

A guide led me through the vast echoing spaces of the tunnels and
workshops. His torch picked out bits and pieces that were left behind
when the underground factory was abandoned: a Volkswagen jeep, a
row of lavatory bowls specially installed, he told me, when free workers
were brought in to join the slaves. In a corner lay a V2 motor that was
still incomplete when, in April 1945, the Americans arrived. My guide
had spent too long in those terrible places, and he was haunted by the
horror of his subject, the statistics of death, and the hell that was created there half a century ago.

Dora is but one of the concentration camps in the belt of country on
either side of the old Cold War divide. Buchenwald, perhaps the most
famous of them, lies only fifty miles further along our Iron Curtain way,
and supplied Dora with its first slave workers. This was the concentration camp, on a hilltop just outside Weimar, which the Nazis set up soon
after they came to power, and it grew with Hitler's ambitions and successes. At first it was used to house the Nazis' domestic enemies, and in
the early days the place seems to have maintained a tenuous kind of order,
with the prisoners occasionally arguing back and making representa-
tions to the authorities about conditions. But later, deportees and resistance fighters and prisoners of war from all over Europe were brought
here also. They were reduced to the usual half-life of concentration camp
prisoners, and in the twelve years of its existence as a Nazi camp, nearly
60,000 died in Buchenwald, three times as many as at Dora; and after the
Nazis were gone first the Russians and then the East German authorities
put their own political enemies away behind its gates.

Buchenwald shows you the essence of a concentration camp. The
prisoners' barracks were destroyed but their foundations are still there,
laid out in perfect regularity on the windswept hillside. So is the vast
parade ground as well as the SS control buildings and the punishment
cells. A flogging post has been preserved, and near it a clumsy wagon
piled with boulders, which prisoners, weakened by starvation and disease, were forced to haul up the long slope. Nearby is the stump of the

tree which the prisoners called Goethe's Oak, the oak among the beeches of Buchenwald, German genius in terrible company. Built into the metal of the main gate, facing inwards towards the prisoners, is a mocking slogan, *'Jedem das Seine'* – 'To each his own' or 'You brought this on yourself'. Sicklier still is the little zoo, just outside the wire and under their starving prisoners' noses, in which the SS kept well-fed animals. Like Dora, Buchenwald is a monstrous place. Like Dora, too, it looks out over long rural vistas; and it offers a kind of physical tranquillity to the visitor, to put beside its anxious and evil memories. Above all, standing on the hill above Weimar, which Germans see as the epitome of their country's virtues, it illustrates the terrifying juxtaposition of the best and the worst faces of mankind.

The camp at Mauthausen in Austria sends the same kind of signals. The town itself is a pretty little place beside the Danube, in which promises of Big Macs and leggy advertisements for tights and stockings distract the eye from the discreet signpost which points you to the concentration camp. You find it two kilometres out of town up a quiet little glen, once again laid out on a hilltop: like Dora and Buchenwald, Mauthausen offered any of its inmates with the strength to lift their heads views over glorious countryside. But first impressions of Mauthausen itself are more imposing by far than Dora's or Buchenwald's, for its barracks stand behind granite ramparts that look as if they could have stood an eighteenth-century siege.

Like Buchenwald, Mauthausen was an early concentration camp, established immediately after Hitler's march into Austria. In it a small minority of distinguished prisoners of one kind or another led to the moment of the camp's liberation magically protected lives. But for the vast majority it was as much a hell as any other camp, and the death toll here was more than twice that of Buchenwald: 127,000 people from every country in Europe. They are commemorated on plaques set into the walls: by nation, by category, by method of their extermination. They are remembered too on the steps in the camp's granite quarry (the town by the river still boasts that it is the granite capital of Europe) up which prisoners were driven under crushing loads of stone.

These are some of the evil machines from the Nazi era to be found along the line of the Iron Curtain. But around them and between them were hundreds more internment camps, concentration camps, labour camps and prisoner of war camps. The French historian Fernand Braudel, for example, spent four years as a prisoner of war near Lübeck. Somehow he mobilised the resources of intellect, memory and willpower to compose up there beside the Baltic his magisterial work about the Mediterranean in the reign of Philip II. At the other end of the line, in the Holy Saturday district on the outskirts of Trieste, you can find a rice factory which was turned into a concentration camp for Italian Jews before their deportation. In the prison at Sopron Köhida in the extreme western tip of Hungary, the retreating Nazis and their Hungarian sympathisers executed their prisoners as a last act before they withdrew into Austria. On the very line of what became the Iron Curtain, on the Yugoslav-Austrian border, forced labourers from camps at either end dug the tunnel through the Loibl Pass which we use today. In Hamburg the Nazis built two concentration camps, at Neuengamme and at Fuhlsbüttel, now Hamburg's civic airport: between them they accounted for 50,000 victims; and in the very last days of the war, at Bullenhuser Damm just across the Elbe from Hamburg, they hanged twenty Jewish children when advancing British troops had reached the next town, only five miles away. And in 1997, in the woods between Marianské Lazné and the German-Czech border, I came across a substantial prison camp that looked as if it had only very recently been abandoned.

But of all these places of horror the most haunting is Bergen-Belsen. It lies among the British Army's old training areas in the heathland of Lower Saxony and just down the road from the site of the concentration camp a barracks, shut away behind grim green metal fences, still proclaims itself 'The Home of the 7th Armoured Brigade'. It is haunting in part because of its emptiness: little is left of Bergen-Belsen itself except a desolation among the woods. Discreet markers record that here are buried 10,000 victims, and here 5,000, and here 8,000. The museum presents the usual vicious litany of grainy black and white photographs, from the first notices proclaiming 'Jews not wanted here' to old ladies scrubbing pavements and then to Kristallnacht, to shootings in Poland and the ramp at Auschwitz and the shoes, false teeth and teddy bears the victims left behind.

These factories of death bear witness to a frightening obsessiveness. At every level obsession was at work, from the clerks who registered new prisoners to the guards who counted and recounted them and the men at the top who insisted, to the very moment of their own defeat, that one way or another their prisoners should die. But Bergen-Belsen demonstrates an equally terrible characteristic, an irresponsible and incompetent fecklessness which somehow coexists beside the thoroughness. For when British troops reached Bergen-Belsen and found

40,000 people dying of famine and disease they were discovering a camp that had been intended to preserve the lives of prisoners, not destroy them. In the last months of the war, the SS saw Bergen-Belsen as a holding camp, in which prisoners of value to them should be concentrated. Here they brought prisoners from neutral countries, and prisoners who might be bartered for some political or military concession from the advancing Allies. But Himmler, who conceived this high political game, found himself distracted, or perhaps the functionaries who were to bring it about were killed in an air raid on Berlin. The prisoners stayed, unexchanged, at Bergen-Belsen.

In the camp typhoid broke out, and the administration panicked. German thoroughness collapsed, as it so easily does when faced with the unexpected. While their prisoners died by the thousand, the guards did nothing beyond episodic attempts to impose brutal discipline upon the dying. The German army area commander got wind of the disaster and proposed a truce in which relief could be rushed to the camp. But even as British troops entered Belsen, some of the guards – Hungarians as much as Germans – were still shooting their prisoners. Water supplies were sabotaged. The British found an untouched food depot just down the road from the starving camp. As they took charge of Bergen-Belsen they found themselves dealing not just with the consequences of obsessive thoroughness but also of an almost frivolous ineffectuality.

The progress of some East German cities since reunification is easy to assess. When I visited it Wismar seemed a potentially glorious place, on the way to recovery from fifty years' deliberate abuse and casual neglect. Schwerin, just down the road, looked by contrast as if it had come through the war and the Communist years almost untouched. In Halberstadt they are building new shops and apartment blocks around its three bleak medieval churches, to replace the boxes that were run up quickly in the wake of wartime bombing. In Quedlinburg, by contrast, the only concession to modern life which I could find among its medieval and Renaissance buildings was one way streets leading to dead ends.

But Eisenach escapes generalisation. It is a huddled, muddled place right on the old border, crowded together at the foot of the Thuringian hills. It has walls and gates that date from the early Middle Ages and two fine medieval churches. But it also has all the pros and cons of an industrial city, focused on the motor car. The factory that built the infamous Wartburg was one of Germany's oldest, and between the wars it produced far more distinguished vehicles. Now, rebuilt and re-equipped with Western capital, it is back in shiny production again. But industry attracted bombers in the Second World War and the damage they did lingered long after the war was over. Now bomb damage, the detritus of hurried industrialisation and the legacies of Communism are all being swept away. In time Eisenach will become a splendid place but when I explored it several years ago I found a gridlocked building site which to my bilious eye seemed the next best thing to hell.

Noone in Eisenach would accept so partisan a judgement, and the city fathers make much of its links with schoolboy Martin Luther and court musician Johann Sebastian Bach, with classic cars and with Fritz Reuter, a beloved nineteenth-century author. But it owes its historic importance to its Landgraves, who in their early days ruled Thuringia from the Wartburg castle which rears up above the city. And it is the castle which brings tourists in their thousands to compound the chaos of Eisenach before making their way up the hill to the castle gates.

The Wartburg is Germany's most famous medieval-shading-into-Renaissance castle. It offers the visitor the same mixture of joys and disappointment as any other castle. They are a taste that I have never acquired and I went to the Wartburg only because I wanted to understand better the hold it exercises over the German imagination. I found myself among a crowd of tourists uttering cries of enthusiastic appreciation. The splendours and the significance of the castle escaped me. But I discovered two things about it which made up for the steep climb up through the woods from the city below.

The first was its views. The Wartburg stands in a commanding position high among the hills under which Eisenach nestles. From its walls and terraces you can look deep into the woods of Thuringia, north towards the Harz forty miles away, or westwards into Hessen. From the walls of the Wartburg you could almost lob a cannon ball into a finger of the old West Germany which prods to within three miles of Eisenach. Heart of Thuringia as the Wartburg once was, it is nevertheless a border castle.

My second discovery concerned Martin Luther. In 1521, on the run from his condemnation at the Diet of Worms, he took refuge in the Wartburg from his Catholic enemies. There the Protestant lord of the Wartburg tucked him away while religious tempers cooled. He lived under his protection for nearly a year, half-heartedly disguised as a visiting farmer but spending his time in writing. Above all he produced, writing at his usual frenetic speed, a translation of the New Testament into German.

This was not the first New Testament in the vernacular, but it stood apart from the others in its literary excellence. Scholars will tell you that it is in its way as masterly as the King James version, and it had a similar seminal importance. It reinforced the Protestant argument that ordinary men and women should have direct access to God's word, without priestly mediation. And it laid the foundation for modern German, that language which held Germany together as a nation through the centuries, long after Luther's time, in which it remained divided by dynasties and politics into a hotchpotch of princely states. So at a stroke Luther divided Germany into Protestant and Catholic camps, while uniting it linguistically, and so socially and culturally. As I tramped round the Wartburg in the company of legions of Germans celebrating its contribution to their national identity, I was struck by the irony that he made this contribution to German paradox in this castle in the very heart of Germany, on the borders between one princely state and another, and within cannon shot of the divide which the Iron Curtain represented for so long.

As I was trying to find the way out of Eisenach past its car factories, I found myself thinking about the automotive cleavage that used to run through Europe along the line of the political divide.

West of the Iron Curtain was the world of BMW and Mercedes, Volkswagen, Fiat and Renault. On our side of the line cars were state-of-the-art products, which functioned with a glorious, sometimes almost boring predictability. On the other side was the world of the Trabant and the Skoda, of Wartburgs, Ladas and the out-of-date replicas of old cars from the West that trundled off the production lines in Poland and Romania. Over there, cars usually worked after their cardboard and sticking plaster fashion, slow, uncomfortable, unreliable, leaving a trail of pollution behind them; though when, once in the mid 1980s, my Rover broke down on a back road in northern Hungary, I was glad enough to thumb a lift from a Hungarian in a clapped-out Lada.

A decent car was the material asset ordinary Easterners most coveted. Mercedes stood at the pinnacle of desire, but almost anything Western attracted attention. Occasionally, an Eastern European government would import a job lot of a few hundred Western cars, with which to buy a little popularity, quieten unrest, suggest that good times were just around the corner. But most of the time ordinary Eastern

Europeans put their names down for a Lada or a Trabi to be delivered
years hence if they were lucky, and thought it was Christmas when the
vehicle finally arrived.

Each of the Eastern marques had its devotees, almost its fan club;
and the very quirkiness of the Trabi, for example, gladdened some Eastern hearts. But there were few who did not lust after something Western. So when I left Hungary there were friends who longed to buy my
Rover, unreliable and past-it as it was; but rules and regulations got in
their way. Hence the run on the second-hand showrooms of western
Germany as soon as the Wall came down. The most decrepit Opels or
Renaults then became the pride of someone in the East who had hitherto known only Ladas and Trabants.

Once in 1985 a Budapest dissenter was put on trial. His real offence
was political; but by then the Communist regime was on its best behav-
iour and charged him with a collection of less controversial offences.
One of them was speeding in a back street in Buda. His lawyer's turn
came to cross-examine a police witness.

'Where did the alleged offence take place?'

'Fillér utca' – a street which climbs one of Buda's many hills.

'Was my client driving northward or southward?'

'Northward.'

'Uphill, therefore?'

'Yes.'

'What car was he driving?'

'His Trabant.'

The court fell about laughing. A Trabant exceeding the speed limit
going up Fillér utca was too ludicrous to contemplate.

Case dismissed.

Leaving Eisenach I decided to go looking for the Fulda Gap through
which, we were told throughout the Cold War, Soviet troops would
come pouring if ever they went to war. To the geographer the gap is a
stretch of relatively open country between the hills that form the border
between Bavaria and Thuringia to the east, and the uplands of the Harz
to the north. The schoolboy's map shows that this is the place where
the line of the old Iron Curtain, which has so far run roughly from
north to south, turns away eastwards towards Czechoslovakia, enclos-
ing Bavaria in the capitalist world. To the tactician this was good country for a tank attack, as good as the open fields of the north German
plain. For the strategist it offered the Russians an even better road to

the Rhine. The Iron Curtain here ran within sixty-five miles of Frankfurt, eighty-five of the Rhine. Even in the 1980s it did not seem too fanciful that a massed attack by Soviet armour could drive a spearhead through the heart of NATO, reach the Rhine in forty-eight hours and leave it to Russian diplomats to dictate the terms of peace in Europe.

But as I drove south westward from Eisenach towards Fulda on the back roads of western Thuringia I found it difficult to detect any signs of the famous gap. I remembered that a more expert and interested observer had had the same difficulty. Once, at a NATO seminar in Copenhagen, I found myself sitting beside the American commander of the Central Army Group. I tried him out with the old Anglo-American chestnut, whether Rhine Army or the Americans in the south held the more vulnerable sector of NATO's front line. My general was one of those sharp Americans who affect a goo' ol' southern boy charm. 'Ah went lookin' in the north once,' he said, 'an' the ol' north German plain seemed pretty up an' down to me.' But then, fearing he had been too hard on British sensibilities, he added: 'The Fulda gap's the same. I'm darned if I can see anythin' you'd call a gap in my part of Germany.'

There is a relatively low-lying gap in front of Fulda, however, significantly more open country than the Harz or the Thuringian hills. Behind it the plain opens out steadily on its way to the Main and the Rhine. Frankfurt, Wiesbaden, Aschaffenburg and Mainz lie at the end of this funnel. The Roman *limes* ran this way, defending the Roman settlements on the Rhine and Mosel from the Teutonic tribes in the woods of central Germany. American troops assigned to hold the Fulda Gap had a similar job. Geography gave them little room for manoeuvre or withdrawal; if they were to save Frankfurt they would have had to stop the Russians within forty miles of their start line. Near a little place called Rasdorf, just to the west of the old dividing line, you can find an exhibition that brings back something of the particular tensions at this point on the Iron Curtain. Here you can see in close proximity the usual paraphernalia of the East German border controls; a Soviet observation post; and the United States Army's 'Observation Post Alpha'. Here were based the reconnaissance troops of the 11th Armored Cavalry, the first men and women who would have died if the Russians had poured across the border. Further back down the road that leads to Frankfurt the Russians would have run up against the heavy allied forces, the American and German armoured divisions which practised here in Hessen as assiduously as the men of Northern Army Group for the day of Armageddon.

With the threat of the Iron Curtain removed, this is sweet and unspoiled country, dotted with small versions of national parks and, along its southern edges, one hill after the other from which to view the famous gap. Along the old border line itself here runs one of Germany's beloved long-distance footpaths. It forms part of a Europe-spanning footpath I came across in Lauenburg which professed to run from the Baltic to the Adriatic, which you can find documented – on maps, way-markers and exhortations to get out of your car and walk – at many points along our route.

Then I went to look at Fulda itself and found one of those glorious German provincial cities which go so grievously unsung. That evening I was summoned by bells to accompany the faithful to Vespers. For Fulda is a city of churches. The Anglo-Saxon monk Boniface came here in the eighth century. He founded a monastery, and after his martyrdom his tomb became a goal of pilgrimage. Over the centuries abbots became bishops, and bishops became princes, and along the way they built churches, monasteries, episcopal palaces and a fine cathedral.

Today Roman Catholicism predominates in Fulda, but the Protestant churches of Germany hold their annual convention here. Priests, nuns and clergymen flutter through the streets. Only in Italy and Spain have I seen so resolutely ecclesiastical a city. If the Russians had ever smashed through the American forces to the east of the city, I reflected, they would still have had to deal with the Church Militant when they got within its walls.

The line of the Iron Curtain makes a decisive change of direction near Fulda. It has run from north to south for 250 miles from the Baltic to the middle of Germany, more or less on longitude 11 degrees east, only once deviating more than thirty miles from the fold down the middle of my road map of Germany. But here it turns away to run eastwards till it reaches the Czech frontier. At the actual turning it embraces the little village of Birx, in the extreme bottom left-hand corner of Thuringia, with Hessen just across the fields to the west and Bavaria as near to the south and east. So for nearly fifty years the villagers lived their lives in the German Democratic Republic, their only link with it a third-class road to Frankenheim and Ellenbogen, a road as closely guarded by the frontier troops as the approach to Dorfrepublik Rüterberg beside the Elbe.

Birx is therefore a good place to pause and look at the journey that still lies ahead of us. Ask an American or Briton about the Iron Curtain and he will talk about the part of it we have explored already. Most Germans will think either of the north-south divide through their country or of the division of Berlin itself. Yet we are still 120 miles short of the Czech frontier, and a 1,000-mile journey from Trieste. What lies ahead?

First comes the stretch where the divide between the two Germanies continues, but running not from north to south but from east to west. There was always something relatively relaxed about this southern-facing part of the German Iron Curtain. For one thing, noone expected that the main thrust of a Soviet attack would be aimed at Munich rather than at Frankfurt and the Ruhr, so the military presence on both sides was lighter than in the north and centre. For another, the line of the border runs mostly through the hills of the Thuringian and Bavarian woods, the least populated areas of Germany: there was no pressure of people here to grieve over the division of their country. Nevertheless, the fact of division was as real as in the north. The watchtowers brooded on their hilltops and the patrols still combed the woods; and the men and women who ran unsuccessfully from the patrols ended up just as dead as those gunned down at the Berlin Wall.

Paradoxically, down here the border followed a divide historically more deeply rooted than in the north. To its south lies Bavaria, to whose inhabitants it is a proudly distinct part of Germany, with its own royal house of Wittelsbach incomparably older than the Prussian Hohenzollerns. Bavaria's Catholicism was untouched by the Reformation, its conservatism scarcely influenced by more modulated attitudes in the rest of Germany. In a strangely savage, almost racist phrase, Bavaria is to ill-disposed northern Germans the 'transition between Austrians and human beings'. But Bavarians and north Germans are agreed on one thing, that Bavaria is different.

Thuringia, on the other side of the Bavarian and Thuringian woods, lies at the geographical heart of Germany, and even Germans from far afield will concede that in it is distilled, in castles like the Wartburg and in a city like Weimar, some of the essence of Germany. Thuringia was *par excellence* the Germany of the smaller princely houses, of the family of Saxe-Coburg-Gotha, for example, from which Queen Victoria's Albert came. It is mostly Protestant, if without the asceticism of northern Germany. It breathes a very different air from the southern, almost Mediterranean air of Munich and the Danube valley. The division here between Federal and Democratic Republics reflected, therefore, a more real, more organic division between parts of Germany than did the fiercer Iron Curtain further north.

An ancient cross-country path runs through the Thuringian forest, more or less parallel with the line of the Iron Curtain, all the way from the Wartburg to the Czech border. It feeds the German appetite to drive out, park beneath the trees and wander in the countryside, to seek the deep peace of nature; and the path from the Baltic to the Adriatic which we came across at Lauenburg on the Elbe and again in the Fulda Gap joins it and brings it more committed walkers. But its origins go back to a more political purpose, as a line marking the division between Teutons and Franks in the Dark Ages, and between Bavaria and Thuringia for 1,000 years thereafter.

The story of that path is a quiet reminder that the Iron Curtain was not the first great European divide, as it will not be the last, and that some of those earlier divisions ran close to the Iron Curtain. We saw that the Romans fortified a line just to the west of it in Hessen, and we will find another stretch of the *limes* when we reach the Danube. Between Vienna and Bratislava, just north of the Danube and, therefore, just outside the Roman Empire, is the killing-field of the Marchfeld, where so many of Europe's battles, from the Romans' to Napoleon's, have been fought. The Elbe was a reminder of the divide between Slavs and Teutons, and we shall find that divide repeated further south.

We find it first on the Czech frontier. Where Czechs met Germans and Austrians, the Slav world met the Teutonic. Subjects and masters within the Habsburg Empire met along part of the same line. As recently as 1938 and 1945 those rivalries were acted out along what is now the western edges of Bohemia, when first the Germans seized the Sudetenland and when, seven years later, the Czechs came back for their righteous, wrathful revenge.

You can tell something of the same story along Austria's southern border, where it faces Slovenia. It is once again a story of collision between Teuton and Slav, between Habsburg master and Slovenian servant, between two different views of who should be master of Carinthia. And the play continues, with a change of actor, when the Iron Curtain turns another corner and runs from north to south once again, separating Slovene from Italian right through the Julian Alps to the Adriatic. There, in the last stretch of our journey, the Latin world meets the Slav. Trieste, our destination, has seen Habsburg and Slav and Italian come and go, dominated first by one and then by another; with the Iron Curtain merely representing for a time a division that goes back all the way to Venice's struggles with Constantinople in the early Middle Ages for power, influence and trade.

But the most vivid example of these European divisions that pre-ceded the Iron Curtain is to be found where Austrians face their lin-guistically and ethnically unique Hungarian neighbours. We shall spend a lot of time exploring that Austrian-Hungarian border, for it twice played a dramatic part in the history of the Iron Curtain. In 1956 it showed us Hungarian refugees scrambling to safety in neutral Austria, and in 1989, after the barbed wire had been torn down and the frontier opened, it was the scene of the exodus of East German holidaymakers which doomed the whole East European political system. But its his-tory as a divide goes back much further. There, in the eastern outskirts of Vienna, Metternich asserted that Europe ended and the Balkans (or, in another version, Asia) began. Long before his time, this same border region saw for 150 years the ebb and flow of one of Europe's most sig-nificant divides, that between Christendom and Islam. So in Hungary today we shall see, not twenty miles from the border, fortresses held by Christian defenders against Turkish assault. In Vienna you can stand where the Turks stood in their last siege of the city, in 1683, at the high water mark of their assault on Christendom. Upstream you can see where Jan Sobieski crossed the Danube as he rode to raise the siege, and in the Vienna woods you can trace the route his warriors took as they fell upon the Turkish camp just outside the city's walls. In a Vienna café, drinking Turkish coffee and eating the roll that the Turks brought to Austria, you can ponder what might have become of Europe if he had failed.

A friend of mine did business for many years in Germany on both sides of the divide. I asked him what he made of the East Germans when there was an East Germany, and how they changed when the Wall came down.

They were recognisably Germans, he said, like the ones we knew in the West. A few of them were Communists, a few more committed socialists, the vast majority, he imagined, people who kept their mouths shut and did what they were told. Like all their fellow-victims of Com-munism, they lived a lie, to which some accommodated more easily than others.

Observers in the West, he reminded me, had overestimated the strength of the old East Germany for years. Its people were educated, self-disciplined, hard-working, respectful of authority, the heirs of a long industrial tradition. Their leaders told us of a rate of economic growth which, projected not too far into the future, would put East

Germany ahead of Britain in terms of GDP per head. We were half-prepared to believe that these were people who could make a success of Communism.

In fact, of course, the success of the East German economy was a fiction imposed on us – and perhaps on the East Berlin Politburo itself – by the painstaking thoroughness of the German character. Every factory manager had his target to meet, set for him from on high. Decade after decade, factory managers carefully falsified their figures to demonstrate that they were meeting their quotas. The figures went up the hierarchy to a Politburo cocooned by security measures from everyday reality. So the leaders never asked themselves why, in chaotic Poland or backward Czechoslovakia, you could buy a Polski Fiat or a Skoda off the shelf, whereas in progressive East Germany you waited twelve years to take delivery of a two-stroke Trabi or a cardboard Wartburg.

Ordinary East Germans lived with other pretences too; and my friend, who is as much committed to the arts as to business, offered me a theatrical example. An East Berlin business partner took him to see *Fiddler on the Roof*. The production was frightful, the cast visibly uneasy in their roles – 'and slowly it dawned on me why'.

This was a piece about the persecution of the Jews of a Russian village. For East Germans, the Holocaust was an unexplored subject. They had been taught that it was an atrocity committed by the Nazis, of whom East Germany's good Communists also had been victims and whom the Soviet Union had destroyed. Unlike the Federal Republic, they were told, East Germany bore no historical responsibility for the destruction of the Jews. Yet it was a subject which continued to haunt ordinary East Germans; and here an audience of East Germans was confronted by a musical in which the persecutors were Russians, the people whom they had been trained to believe were their closest friends. The result was a tangle of emotions, half-examined, unexpressed, on stage and among the audience. They created their own confused dynamic; the point of the piece was lost; the consequence was theatrical catastrophe.

There was confusion too when change in Eastern Europe came. Poland and Hungary knew where they were going: back to their proud historical sovereignty. So did Czechoslovakia: back to its democracy. East Germany, by contrast, was not a nation, merely the smaller, less successful part of a larger Germany. So the prospect of change put the leadership in a panic and left the people uncertain where they were heading. By the autumn of 1989 matters were coming to a head. Soviet protection was withdrawn, leaving the regime at the mercy of events. It dithered, between repression, concession and surrender. The crowds asserted their power, without any certainty about how to use it. The outcome might have been the restoration of order by terror, a course which the Politburo considered, or a truly democratic German Democratic Republic, which the emerging opposition around the writer Stefan Zweig favoured, or the urge to unification which came so suddenly out of nowhere and quickly swept all before it with the battle cry 'We are one people'.

Afterwards, the Germans in the East experienced all the joys and sorrows of the other, suddenly liberated peoples of Eastern Europe. But again, their experiences were more convoluted than the Hungarians' or the Poles'. They had many advantages, not least their rapid absorption into the Federal Republic and the lavish financial assistance which flowed from West to East. But the East German economy was shown up for the sham it had always been. Standards of living collapsed, unemployment spread. West Germans appeared from nowhere to reclaim property lost in the 1940s. Administrators came from the West to help rescue the Eastern *Länder*: usually well-meaning, often helpful, sometimes overbearing and arrogant. 'We are one people' remained the doctrine, but for the present at least, '*Wir sind Ossis, sie sind Wessis*' was too often the reality.

We finish our Bockbier in Birx, defer ideas of drinking coffee in Vienna and set off eastwards on the second leg of this journey. Here in Thuringia we are in the heart of Germany, and Erfurt is at its geographical centre. It is a city which can show us, also, one of Germany's finest examples of historical continuity, little marred by wartime destruction. We can see here the Augustinians' cloister in which Martin Luther served his religious apprenticeship and the churches which, when the Reformation came, a wise Cardinal Archbishop of Erfurt shared out equally between the rival parties. The city is rich in houses and palaces, medieval, Renaissance, baroque; its cathedral broods over it on its hill; and there is even a bridge of shops like the Ponte Vecchio in Florence. All these are pretty well untouched by time, looking as they looked when Napoleon came here in 1808 and Goethe rode over from neighbouring Weimar to meet him. The whole place reeks of German history, like Berlin but without its viciousness.

For us, however, the interest of Erfurt lies more in modern politics than in the architectural and artistic evidence of its remoter past. For here the two Germanies started the process of talking and doing business together which led in time to a wary acceptance of one another's existence and legitimacy. The process was a key part of West Germany's *Ostpolitik*, the regularisation of its relationships with Moscow and with eastern Europe as well as East Germany, which consumed so much of its political and diplomatic energies in the early 1970s. It led also to East Germany's emergence as a member of the United Nations and as a country which, for a time, seemed to be working the trick of running a collectivised economy efficiently.

On 19 March 1970 Willy Brandt travelled to Erfurt to meet the East German leader, Willi Stoph. Five months earlier he had become post-war Germany's first Social Democratic Federal Chancellor, with a programme of restructuring his country's 'eastern' policies, its relationships with the Soviet Union, Eastern Europe and East Germany. No Federal Chancellor had set foot in East Germany before him, and West German hard-liners maintained that the very fact of going 'over there', to 'the zone', the pariah state, was a concession too far. Others welcomed the contact: at last each of the two Germanies was recognising realities, and the fact that the other was there. The press called it the meeting of the two Willies. But the applause of the Erfurt crowds made it clear that it was West Germany's Willy, not their own, Communist Willi, whom they were welcoming.

Two months later Stoph made a return visit to the West German city of Kassel, seventy miles away to the west, a place which can boast few of Erfurt's splendours. Battered by Allied bombers, it enjoys none of Erfurt's splendid continuity. It has its glories, but the bleak marks of reconstruction and the modern world predominate. Its citizens rejoice in the city's ownership of the Brothers Grimm, who gave modern Germany edited, regulated and improved versions of its fairy tales and folk stories. They enjoy the largest and wildest city park in Germany and one of its finest civic art galleries. But Kassel cannot claim a place beside Erfurt among Germany's fine provincial cities.

Few of its citizens wanted to welcome Willi Stoph, a man publicly reviled in West Germany, and his talks with Brandt made far less public impact than the meeting in Erfurt. But Brandt put his own *desiderata* on the table – his 'twenty points'. The concept of Germans talking officially to Germans was launched, and before the end of the year the negotiations themselves had started. At the same time, the Federal Republic came to terms with Moscow. Willy Brandt, paying his famous visit to Warsaw, shattered two nations' preconceptions when he went down on his knees at the site of the Warsaw Ghetto. The Western Allies started talking to the Russians about Berlin, a process which culminated in September 1971 in a quadripartite agreement on the status of the city. That autumn, and in the first half of 1972, one agreement between the two Germanies followed another: on postal and telephone services, on transit to Berlin and on traffic more generally. By the end of 1972, West Germany's relations with all its Eastern neighbours had been regularised, a line drawn under the consequences of the war.

The way was clear to start in Helsinki the Conference on Security and Co-operation in Europe. For year after weary year the process continued, talks shifting from one European capital to another and another, subject matter always shifting between one topic – grouped in what the jargon called 'baskets' – and another. At the end of it all the Soviet Union and its Communist allies had secured copper-bottomed assurances that the West accepted their position in Central and Eastern Europe. The West had secured an opening up of the socialist camp to contact, information and international involvement. It was another fifteen years before the year of miracles – 1989 – demonstrated that the West had got the better part of the bargain, and a year after that the Germanies were reunited.

But long before that happy day, the process started in Erfurt and Kassel had improved practical relationships between the two Germanies and ameliorated the lives of ordinary Germans, particularly in the East. In doing so, it altered circumstances along the Iron Curtain. Before the German-German agreements were signed, it was difficult for West Germans to travel to see family and friends on the other side of the divide. Even contact by telephone was difficult. The few East Germans who were permitted to go west could take no money with them. West Germans going east paid dearly for the privilege, buying Ostmarks at a rigged rate of exchange. Land transit to Berlin was zealously controlled. In the German Democratic Republic itself West Germans found themselves in an intrusively suspicious environment. It felt almost foreign; and the fact that in the eyes of the East German authorities it was indeed a different country, whose inhabitants were policed quite as severely as visitors, brought no comfort to West Germans used to their own state's more easygoing ways.

All these circumstances were improved by the inner-German agreements. In West German terminology, the object was to improve conditions for Germans who happened to live in East Germany. The East German government wanted something different, the normalisation of relations between two sovereign states whose peoples happened to speak the same language and were, regrettably from its point of view, inextricably interrelated.

Along the border, the effect of the agreements was to increase human contacts of every kind. More crossing-points were opened, more use made of them in both directions. Trade between the two Germanies developed, more traffic crossed East Germany on its way to and from Berlin, and from Eastern Europe. But all these increasing contacts might threaten the East German government's ability to control its own people and to frustrate the attacks of its Western enemies. It was determined to control and contain them. The apparatus of control we saw at Marienborn dates not from the time the Iron Curtain was established, in the late 1940s and early 1950s, but from the 1970s, precisely the period in which German-German contacts were so dramatically increasing. When they signed their agreements with West Germany the East German authorities did not abdicate one jot of their pretensions to control and defend their state. More East-West movement merely increased the need for resources to regulate it. A dual passion for order and regulation was brought to the process: the passion of good, efficient German officialdom; and the passion of authoritarian regimes everywhere.

The circumstances created by West Germany's *Ostpolitik*, and by the German-German agreements in particular, might have persisted indefinitely. They would have normalised ordinary human contacts between the people of two sovereign states at the heart of Europe. There would still have been the occasional tragic shooting on the Berlin Wall, periodic scandals of East German spies seducing West German secretaries, alarms from time to time over Allied access to Berlin. But by and large the inescapable difficulties of running two such different countries, interrelated, speaking the same language, would have been contained. Instead, changes came to make that order unsustainable and finally brought it to so dramatic an ending. All of them originated outside Germany.

In Moscow, Gorbachev had the courage to recognise the fact of Soviet failure and to abandon the Soviet Union's pretensions to control its Eastern European empire. The Poles, restless ever since the 1970s, asserted their will to sovereign nationhood in freedom. The Hungarians, who had been pushing at the limits on their freedom of action ever since their reforms of 1969, opened their western border. In the summer of 1989 all those hundreds of thousands of Germans who still could not travel to the West saw that Hungary offered them a way out. When they were denied travel to Hungary they went to Czechoslovakia instead. Finally they demanded the right to visit their German neighbours not via Hungary, Austria or Czechoslovakia but directly, through the folds of the German Iron Curtain.

Even then, with Eastern Europe crumbling, the East German leaders thought that with Soviet support they could defy their people. That Soviet support was denied them. 'We are the people' chanted the crowds, first in Erfurt and then in all East Germany's cities. Their leaders' nerve cracked, and the Berlin Wall came down. The Iron Curtain's checkpoints were opened. For all practical purposes East and West Germans found themselves one people. They demanded political recognition of that reality: 'We are one people'. Russia, France and Britain all had their reservations, but they were swept aside by the Germans' will to unity. Now, eleven years after the Wall came down and almost thirty after the meetings in Erfurt and Kassel, 'Ossis' and 'Wessis' still cherish their mutual resentments, their sense of difference, their occasional contempt and dislike for one another. But politically today, they can without fear of contradiction call themselves 'one people'.

There are still good things to be seen before we reach the Czech border and the end of the old German divide. Weimar, Coburg and Bayreuth are three of them, straddling the old inner-German border. Weimar in Thuringia was a cherished East German city, Bayreuth and Coburg are both Bavarian, the latter only by adoption. Taken together they tell us relatively little about the contrasts between what was East and what West, but much about Germany's past, nature and prospects.

Coburg lies right up against Bavaria's border with Thuringia. Indeed, through most of its history it was a Thuringian principality, tied to its neighbours there by princely connections. But when the last Duke of Saxe-Coburg-Gotha abdicated after the First World War, the citizens of Coburg voted to join Bavaria instead. In doing so they unwittingly elected themselves citizens of the free world when Germany's division came twenty-five years later. Throughout the Cold War, therefore, NATO protected the citizens of Coburg, just as the Warsaw Pact protected their neighbours up the road in Gotha, Jena and Weimar.

So in 1920 history smiled upon Coburg. Geography was less kind to it since. The Iron Curtain, curling round three sides of the place, cut it off from those northern neighbours. It is far from the prosperous heartland of Bavaria. The black woods of the Franconian forest press in upon it. It lies in one of the most backward corners of Germany. The town was always a navel-gazing sort of place in an out-of-the-way area, and a flood of refugees from Silesia and the Sudetenland, driven westward by the Poles and Czechs in 1945, added to the embittered introversion of the whole region.

There is therefore a sense of pettiness about the streets of Coburg. The Ehrenburg Palace, the residence of the Saxe-Coburgs in the town itself, looks like a cramped Houses of Parliament, dominating its neighbours. Fine town houses line the streets and squares but they are squeezed together, overshadowed. To my mind at least Coburg summons a good German word, '*spiessbürgerlich*', which the dictionary renders as 'narrow-minded, commonplace, humdrum'.

Yet there was nothing *spiessbürgerlich* about Coburg's rulers, the house of Saxe-Coburg-Gotha. Like other princely families they invested their subjects' wealth in the glorification of their pint-sized principality. Unlike them, they also sought glory outside its boundaries, engaging themselves vigorously in international affairs. Aided perhaps by the unusual physical beauty of their males, the Saxe-Coburg-Gothas succeeded in forging dynastic links with the royal houses of Portugal, Bulgaria and Belgium. It was a Saxe-Coburg uncle, himself safely established in the new Kingdom of the Belgians, who first brought Prince Albert of Saxe-Coburg-Gotha to the attention of the English statesmen who were looking for a suitable bridegroom for young Vickie.

The minds of all of us outside the magic circle of royalty may boggle at the thought of Prince Albert's transmogrification from little Coburg to the grandeurs of Windsor and St James's. If it troubled him, he did not show it. He had enjoyed a rustic, almost bucolic childhood, spent in Coburg itself and at the little palace of Rosenau nearby. He had been quietly educated in Brussels and Bonn. But the *Almanach de Gotha* was the *Who's Who* of royal and aristocratic Europe. The Saxe-Coburgs-Gothas, like his mother's family of Saxe-Gotha-Altenburg, had given their names to it, and had their assured place in its pages. Cousin Albert went to London with the absolute confidence of the insider.

He had also the didactic assurance typical of the educated German, a quality as impressive as it is irritating to less organised human beings. Without hesitation he set about designing better principles and institutions for his wife's dominions. In doing so he brought to England things that England needed, like deductive reasoning, intellectual seriousness about politics, and a concern for matters of the mind and of the spirit.

Unabashed by comparisons of scale, he took Victoria to see the place whence he had sprung. Coburg installed its first water-closet for her, and rewarded him with a fine statue which still dominates the main square. The last four decades of the nineteenth century carried Victoria, Britain and the Empire to their heights, their supreme glories. God knows what more they might not have achieved if Albert, their mentor, had not died in 1861, weakened by his own unremitting zeal and finished off by typhoid fever at the age of forty-two.

Bayreuth was the home, property and principality of a lesser family of German nobility, its Margraves. On today's maps it looks a lesser place than Coburg and it shares some of its geographical disadvantages, tucked away in the woods of the north-eastern corner of Bavaria, close to the Czech frontier. But an eighteenth-century Margravine, a sister of Frederick the Great, made it a pole of attraction for artistic and cultural life. She adorned it with stately public buildings, laid out on a scale which makes Bayreuth as openly welcoming as Coburg is oppressive. And a century later enlightened patronage of Richard Wagner brought a new and enduring if often shadowed genius to the town. You do not have to love *Parsifal* or worship *The Ring* to enjoy a visit to Bayreuth.

Yet Bayreuth's significance is a chequered one, like that of so many German towns and cities. The Palace, the Opera House and the Palace Church are delights of much restored eighteenth-century architectural delicacy. The whole town provides a setting and a shrine for the music of a German genius, which conjures up profundities out of the German soul. Like all profundities, they had their share of bad as well as good, and Wagner's genius unleashed some German daemons. An appeal to the spirit of the Germans became entangled with resentment of things less German. It is almost as if Shakespeare's evocation of 'this happy breed of men ... this England' were taken up by an intellectual wing of the British National Party. The overt anti-Semitism of Wagner's heirs added to the dangers of the brew. So did Nazi patronage. For another century at least, Bayreuth, like Salzburg, will trigger political concerns beside its musical sublimities.

In Bayreuth I came across a very down-to-earth example of the things that still sometimes bother those who venture into these Teutonic backwoods. It was a Sunday afternoon out of season and I was wandering aimlessly, looking for straws in the wind to supplement what I was learning from the guide books and works of history. A taxi-driver might have provided *vox populi* insights, but business was quiet that Sunday and the taxis had retired from the streets. Something in a telephone kiosk notice caught my passing eye.

Printed in Gothic script, it told the Germans of a town in Silesia to assemble with one piece of hand baggage for deportation to the West. It was dated 1945 and signed by the Polish town commandant. Fifty years later an organisation of German expellees had reprinted it, topped it and tailed it in an appeal to sympathy and support for its demand that what once was German should be German again. 'That was our "Liberation"' it said, dripping with irony and self-pity. It left me reflecting on the enduring nature of resentment; on that preoccupation with one's own group's sufferings to the exclusion of the sufferings it has inflicted on others – a preoccupation I used to think of as peculiarly German but now see cultivated also by the Serbs; and on the paucity of a historical imagination which tries, with the benefit of fifty years' hindsight, to suggest that Germans in Silesia could have expected 'Liberation' rather than brutal expulsion in 1945.

But if you are looking for things to praise and blame and ponder in the German experience, it is Weimar, in all its compact complexity, which takes the prize. It is as if the whole essence of Britain's historical experience – the good and the bad, the proud and the shameful – were distilled in a place like Winchester.

Weimar is the biggest of our three mid-German towns, but even today it is only a middling-sized place and throughout its heyday as the cultural capital of Germany the population of the whole principality never much exceeded 100,000. It grew up as a village to serve a court, and a fairly petty court at that. Outside the circles of court officials it never generated a middle class, or middle class amenities. Yet decade after decade it attracted Germany's best minds and spirits.

It is customary to start with Goethe and his princely patron, Karl August, in the 1770s. But Weimar's extraordinary story really starts two centuries earlier, when the defeated Elector of Saxony tried to create a new kingdom for himself in Thuringia. It fragmented: into Saxe-Coburg-Gotha and Saxe-Gotha-Altenburg, as we have seen, and into Saxe-Weimar. The new rulers of Weimar attracted artists to their court, and Lucas Cranach and Johann Sebastian Bach were among its earlier ornaments. Goethe, a universal genius in the making, came here from Frankfurt in 1775.

The story of Goethe's long years in Weimar is often told. Karl August's mother, Anna Amalia, adopted a conscious policy of attracting the stars of German cultural life to the Weimar court. In 1775 Karl

August came of age. Between them he and his mother decided that Goethe, himself only twenty-six, should become the prince's companion and mentor. He stayed, with few interruptions, until his death in 1832. In that half-century he delivered himself of his literary and philosophical masterpieces. Having brought Karl August to maturity he became his most trusted minister. He made of Weimar both the 'German Athens' and a quiet model of sound administration. He gave all Germany a model of rounded intellectual and political development which prevailed for the best part of a century, until Bismarck and the Hohenzollerns opted for a more centralised, dynamic, power-obsessed and ultimately unstable alternative.

Goethe's story is not a chronicle of calm and measured wisdom alone. We have seen him abandoning his duties more or less on a whim, to go climbing central Germany's highest mountain in mid-winter. He led Karl August astray, with irresponsibly romantic, and occasionally vicious, forays into the countryside. He quarrelled with the ruler's young wife. He conducted a protracted and in the end fruitless courtship of the wife of a senior court official, endlessly disputing with her the rights and wrongs of addressing her as 'Du' rather than 'Sie'. He took a younger woman for his mistress, keeping her waiting for marriage for eighteen years in an unsanctified relationship which scandalised all Weimar.

In these years Goethe added his own gigantic contribution to German literature and sensibility and the whole world has remembered him ever since a writer of genius. But in some ways his political contribution was as important. He chose, consciously, to base himself not in Frankfurt, where he grew up, or in Berlin, where the German centralisers around the Hohenzollerns believed that he belonged, but in a provincial court of no political importance in the backwoods of middle Germany. He lent the weight of his literary and moral reputation to the Germany of the principalities, not the Germany of the kingdoms or the big battalions. He did this at a time when divided Germany found itself at the mercy of revolutionary France and of Napoleon; and then in a period when Germany began to shape itself around Prussia against France. He stood aside from the clash of Titans, and depending on your point of view you can argue either that in the process he preserved Germany's soul and reputation or that he betrayed Germany in the hour of its national need. Between them Goethe and the men who gathered around him in Weimar – Schiller, Herder and Weiland most prominent among them – made the city's reputation and at the same time endowed all Germany with an enduring intellectual and artistic legacy.

In consequence Weimar remained something precious to Germany's sense of self. Later generations of German artists and thinkers brought it their own tributes. Liszt, Strauss and Nietzsche all spent time there. Walter Gropius established the Bauhaus in Weimar, and attracted Klee and Kandinsky to work with him there. After the First World War Germany's democratic constitution was drawn up in Weimar, and the Weimar Republic deserves better than its reputation for moral depravity on the one hand and as the supine predecessor of Nazi Germany on the other. In four centuries the little city added far more of the good than the bad to Germany's record.

But the Nazis came to patronise Weimar. On the one hand they wanted to bask in its reputation as the well-spring of German culture. On the other they wanted to assert there a different aspect of Germany. They found waiting for them in Weimar something of the *spiessbürgerlich* attitudes of provincial Germany which they wanted to enlist in their service. Long before the Nazis, the city fathers of Weimar had driven the Bauhaus out of the city. Now they responded to Nazi favour. Weimar became a Nazi stronghold.

Weimar presented East Germany's Communist rulers with conceptual difficulties. They wanted to claim it as the expression of a historical purity of which they were the heirs and at the same time to distance themselves from Weimar's Nazi connections. So Weimar became a place of high ideological and propaganda significance. But it came more or less undamaged through the strains of those years. Today it bundles together the elegant simplicity of one of Germany's old princely cities, the attentions of trippers sentimental about its history, an enduring worship of Germany's cultural glories, the ever more pressing demands of tourism, and the continuing need to serve this part of rural Thuringia as its market town. So in 1999 Weimar won the accolade of 'Europe's City of Culture', which brought culturally-minded tourists in their thousands; and on the day in October on which the city's annual Onion Festival is held, even more thousands came from the countryside around, to swamp what by then remained of the tourists.

It does not do to overload history with symbolism, but Weimar tempts one to excess. You can walk across the centre of the little city in half an hour, passing Schiller's house, Goethe's house, the theatre, a church with a Cranach altar-piece and the princely palace along the way. On Weimar's eastern side lies the palace park, in which stands Goethe's country cottage, where he lived the simple life, slept under the stars, entertained his friends and his friends' children and created some of the marvels of German literature. On the other side of the city, high on a hill, the Nazis created Buchenwald – a place of horror throughout their twelve years in power and continuing after their fall. For in Buchenwald first the Russians and then the East German Communist regime continued what the Nazis had begun, the incarceration and liquidation of political enemies. More than Coburg and Bayreuth, more than anywhere else in Germany, Weimar sums up the best and the worst of Germany.

Throughout our journey we have been visiting German places, examining German attitudes, with only passing excursions into the doings of their enemies, victims, allies and friends. Now we are approaching the Czech border. Ahead lies the inheritance of the Habsburgs in all its multi-coloured variety. This is our last chance to turn back to the Germans and get to understand them better.

I have spent most of my working life among foreigners. Everywhere, even in Denmark, I found unexpected paradoxes: when closely examined, human beings as individuals or in groups always turn out to be full of contradictions. And the Germans, among whom I lived or with whom I worked for almost a decade, were quite as paradoxical as any of the others. Contradiction runs through the individual personality and society alike. You can find it at every turn in German history.

It means, for one thing, that Germans are unusually capable of extremes both of good and evil. They bring to both more than their fair share of idealism, determination, moral sense and sentimentality. It seems to me that in the last fifty years, ever since their defeat in 1945, the Germans have shown an enormous capacity for good. They have worked themselves, and their country, back to prosperity. They have learned the ways of democracy and produced, in their federal system and in the individual *Länder*, flourishing and effective democratic structures. At the same time, as individuals and as a nation they have done pretty well as much as a society can do to come to terms with and make amends for the spectres of their shameful past. In doing so they have accepted personal and social responsibility for the crimes committed by Germans and in Germany's name, in a way unique among the nations. Compare their honesty about the horrors of the Second World War, for example, with the attitudes of the Japanese and the Austrians to the crimes then committed by their own fellow-citizens; with our own myopia and America's double standards; or, for that matter, with Russian detachment from any sense of personal responsibility for the evils of the Soviet years.

From all this flows the Germans' record as good neighbours. They have committed themselves wholeheartedly to NATO and the European Union, bearing much of the heat of the day in both. They have taken in guest workers and refugees by the million, and their record with both is better than that of their neighbours. West Germans have undertaken with reasonably good grace the huge task of integrating the eastern *Länder* into the Federal Republic. Germans also carry much of the financial burden of caring for eastern Europe. Yet their record in the Third World is equally admirable. They have even made their peace with Israel.

This, in short, is a society which for fifty years has reflected the goodness and moral seriousness which, throughout the centuries, has been the mark of a very numerous category of Germans.

But for almost the whole century leading up to 1945, German society showed a very different face to the world. The contrast between that face and the good German face adds to the sense of paradox which confronts those who study Germany. And memories, personal or collective, of that infamous period of German history feed a continuing suspicion of Germans, even prejudice against Germans, even among people, such as myself, who consider themselves friends of Germany.

For the German record in the century to 1945 was appalling; and in it large numbers of individual Germans committed themselves actively to the horrors committed in Germany's name. Bismarck built the German Empire by chicanery and force, and most politically-conscious Germans supported him. German society in the years before the First World War achieved much, but its tone was set by hysteria and bluster which doomed it to friction and worse with its neighbours. After all the revisions of history have been digested, Germany remains marginally more responsible than the other European powers for the horrors of the First World War. German irresponsibility and self-pity undermined the postwar settlement, and millions of individual Germans welcomed the rise of Hitler and supported him enthusiastically almost to the end. Finally, many elements in German society, extending far beyond the Nazi Party and the SS, share some of the responsibility for the Nazis' crimes against the Jews, the Russians, the gypsies and the Poles.

The consequences which followed the collapse of this bandit state were also terrible. It was at the feet of its conquerors, who had little reason to show it mercy. The German inhabitants who did not flee before the Russians arrived were driven out of East Prussia and Pomerania, the Sudetenland and Silesia. Within what was left of Germany, reconstruction started at Point Zero. Partition, when it came, was brutal. It was also well-nigh inevitable. And while the Germans thought it the harshest and most unjust of afflictions, to their friends and their enemies it was an inevitable and in a way appropriate consequence of the history that Germany had made. Few of those friends and enemies expected that the division of Germany would come to an end; none of them saw reason to pay any serious price to bring it about.

But end it did, for reasons mostly extraneous to Germany; and the biggest of them was Gorbachev. Germany was the prime beneficiary of the fall of the Warsaw Pact, of the Soviet Union and of Communism. Its history ever since has been the story of the attempt to unite Germany in fact as well as in name; and to reposition a united Germany in the heart of a Europe which needs it, admires it and fears it in more or less equal proportions.

Such, in brief, is the story of modern Germany, showing us such paradoxical contradictions about the Germans. The way to make sense of them is to dig deeper into the German psyche. To do so takes us much further back into German history.

Germans, many of their friends observe, are unusually anxious people. They crave security, predictability, certainty. Their anxiety feeds in them a thoroughness, a concern for the facts and the evidence, a desire above all for legal certainty, which buttresses German moral seriousness. A German does not speak off the cuff or act instinctively; he is not frivolous; he suspects the promptings of inspiration. He finds such traits in others suspect, even despicable. His moral seriousness can become first pompous, then didactic, then domineering, and finally dangerous. But its motivation is virtuous.

The anxiety stems in part from the Germans' historical experience. While nation states formed around Renaissance kings in France, England and Spain, Germany remained fragmented into little societies under princes, dukes, bishops, margraves and city fathers. The only political expression of anything wider was provided by the Holy Roman Empire, which could offer the Germans no real national focus, led as it was by Habsburgs whose lands and concerns extended far beyond the boundaries of the German nation. The Reformation, splitting the Germans religiously, only underlined their fragmentation, and the experiences of the Thirty Years War brought home to them their vulnerability. So did Napoleon, shattering the armies of Austria and Prussia and dictating his own reforms to Germany.

When reaction came, therefore, it was natural for Germans to seek security above all. They found it by rallying around the one centre,

Prussia, able and willing to bring unity to most of those who thought themselves Germans. So at last, 300 years after its Western neighbours, Germany was able to bring together blood, language, political power and national identity under the German Emperor. But in less than half a century, he led them to defeat. Hitler offered them the same unity – '*Ein Reich, ein Volk, ein Führer*' – and in twelve years he led them to a far more terrible destruction.

Out of that came a renewed fragmentation of Germany. There were individuals among the Allies who saw the solution to the German problem in a forced reversion to the little units of the principalities and city states. Together with the deindustrialisation which the same men advocated, this would have reduced millions of Germans to penury and impotence. But even though they rejected such measures, in practice the Allies in 1945 broke Germany into fragments. We have traced the line of division drawn between East and West Germany. But to the Germans there were also other Germanies, all transferred to Germany's former victims, in Pomerania, Silesia, East Prussia and the Sudetenland. There was the revival of Austria as a republic and the separation, enforced by treaty, of Austrian Germans from other Germans. And there was the loss of the Germans of the Baltic States and Transylvania, of the German settlements scattered across Russia, all of them expelled or persecuted and subdued.

For all the years I lived and worked with Germans, this fragmentation was a factor in their everyday calculations and their profounder psyche. Whatever they said, it was something they could not bring themselves to accept in its totality. All sensible Germans knew that the fragmentation was Hitler's doing, the consequence of the defeat of his lust for conquest. Most Germans knew that the other Germanies beyond the Oder-Neisse line were lost for good, fit only for the nostalgia of ageing expellees. But no West Germans and few in the German Democratic Republic accepted that the essential Germany between France on the one side and the new Polish frontier on the other should forever remain divided between Communist and free.

The facts of power, expressed so vividly along the Berlin Wall and the Iron Curtain, suggested otherwise. In their efforts to draw a line under the consequences of the Second World War, to build better relations with Moscow and their Eastern neighbours and to bring better conditions of life to ordinary East Germans, the West Germans made many agreements which, at least by implication, seemed to accept the division. But at the same time they clung to the letter of the legal position.

They held themselves apart from the pragmatism of their allies, who assumed that common sense and the facts of power would keep the two Germanies separate for decades and perhaps for ever. On this subject, and on this subject alone, Germans went on believing in something for which almost all the evidence was lacking. And in the end, in 1989, they found their faith justified. The Soviet Union started a process which brought down Communism in Eastern Europe. Poland and Hungary carried it forward. Others joined in, and the Germans benefited. The Berlin Wall came down and the Iron Curtain was dismantled. Germans danced on the Wall, and all along the line of the divide they went visiting the neighbours from whom they had so long been isolated. 'We are one people' became a reality, and within a year Germany was politically united, as it has been so rarely in it history.

So in the end Germany won one of the twentieth century's most glittering prizes. Today, eleven years later, Germans can see the costs as well as the joys of reunification. They grumble, and some of them say that things were better in the time of partition. But for most of them the game of making Germany truly one is still well worth the candle. West German wealth has been poured into Eastern Germany, and in some places reconstruction has brought a glossiness which outshines even polished West German cities. For the individual, the gap between East and West – a gap in terms of wealth, self-confidence and sophistication – is beginning to close. But a gap remains, and will remain for decades yet. So will resentments: Eastern resentment of Western arrogance, Western resentment of Eastern dependence.

But outweighing all this is the fact of German unity, and what it does to Germany and the Germans. It has created a single, Central European state of 80 million people in place of a Western European and an Eastern European country. It has shifted the Germans' focus of attention eastwards, with the very capital migrating from the Rhine to the Spree. It has increased still further Germany's salience in Europe and its importance to the European Union, while complicating the relationship between that body and its weightiest member. Germans see themselves today as Germans, as Wessis or Ossis, as Rhinelanders or Brandenburgers or Bavarians. They are also, most of them, modestly committed Europeans, reluctantly content to share their Deutschmark and their well-being with other Europeans. They see themselves as the Americans' equals: not in military terms, self-evidently, or scientific, but in economics and banking and business; and the Americans' superiors in terms of culture, civilisation and maturity. They look to the rest of the world with the self-confidence of a powerful country which has lived down its past and now deserves the respect of its neighbours. With good reason, Germans today think of their country as a place of righteousness; and in doing so they run the risk, not always avoided, of self-righteousness as well.

5
Czechs and Teutons

My journey along what used to be the Inner German border brought me at last to Hof, a nondescript little town in the extreme top right-hand corner of Bavaria. I had been to Bayreuth the previous day and been tempted to go on from there in search once again of the best and the worst of Germany. For just a hundred miles away to the south was Regensburg, a glorious city astride the Danube whose origins go back beyond the Romans; and as it lay not all that far from the Czech border I could surely find some relevance to my Iron Curtain story. On my way there I could go looking for yet another of the Nazis' concentration camps, at Flossenbürg, where at the very end of the war the SS hanged a last trio of Hitler's enemies, Admiral Canaris, General Oster and Dietrich Bonhoeffer, and where the among the inmates the American army found Léon Blum, Kurt Schuschnigg and Martin Niemöller. But to stay in Germany while I drove further south would mean bypassing north-western Bohemia and its three major towns: Karlovy Vary, which to the Germans who used to live there was Karlsbad; Cheb, which they called Eger; and Marianské Lazné, which Edwardian Europe knew as Marienbad.

So from Hof I went to the small Bavarian frontier town of Selb, and from Selb drove up the back road leading to its Bohemian neighbour, Aš. I was entering the extreme western tip of the Czech Republic, leaving behind me a minor, impeccably groomed German road and a quiet German frontier post and committing myself to what for a moment looked like Balkan chaos. The Czech frontier post was being repositioned, remodelled and rebuilt. Traffic in and out of the country competed for a single lane of broken tarmac. Diesel smoke belched from unattended trucks. I had driven far that day and did not know where I would lay my head. I was leaving a language I knew for one which promised to mystify me in every particular. For a moment my heart failed me. My morale was restored by common humanity, as it so often is if you wander open-minded in those parts of Central Europe which used to lie beyond the Iron Curtain. A brisk customs girl melted into friendliness. She came to collect my passport before I had disentangled myself from my safety belt. She stamped it on the spot, wished me a good journey, told me where I could get petrol round the next corner, and sent me on my way restored. The girl at the petrol pump gave me a promotional yellow lollipop. They were light years removed from the Czech functionaries I remembered from the bad old days.

The main square of Cheb, too, lifts the heart if you come to it as an outsider eager to be pleased by old houses, quiet charm and lots of history. For Germans, even the reconstructed Germans who, by my observation, outnumber the others by a factor of fifty to one, it is another matter. Until 1938, Cheb, as Eger, was essentially a German city, lying just within the extreme western end of Czechoslovakia, with German territory around it on three sides out of four. At Munich, Britain and France forced the Czechs to cede it with the rest of the Sudetenland to Hitler, and the people of Eger cheered as his troops marched in. For seven years the Teutons of Eger lorded it over the Czechs, while everywhere terrible crimes were committed in Germany's name. So when the Czechs' turn came, in 1945, their deeds too were terrible. In Martin Gilbert's words, 'what had begun as a great adventure for German-speaking people all over Europe, during the euphoria of Hitler's early victories, was one more tragic ending in a war which had seen every variety of tragedy and disaster'. Out went the Sudeten Germans with only what they could carry, 'literally beaten across the border', to fester for years as refugees, mostly in northern Bavaria – and we have seen that the old people among them who still survive are disproportionately prominent among unreconstructed Germans in the Federal Republic. Today there are no heel-taps about the fact that Cheb is purely Czech; though the first thing I encountered there was a second-hand clothes market run entirely by Vietnamese.

The consequence of these expulsions for Cheb and all of western Bohemia is a sense of under-population, even now more than fifty years afterwards. To me Cheb felt like a half-empty city and the woods and fields around seemed unnaturally empty; and when you get to Marianské Lazné it feels like a gracious but decrepit passenger liner beached on a gently sloping shore. The only enterprises that seem to flourish along the roads that take you there are 'night clubs' housed in abandoned farm buildings, their customers mostly Germans coming across the border for cheap sex, just as, later in this journey, we shall see Austrians looking for cut-price cream cakes in Moravia and cheap dentistry in Hungary.

Leaving these profoundly uninviting night clubs behind you, you drive into Marianské Lazné across a rackety level crossing and up a long avenue of buildings in which peasant cottages gradually give way to white stucco palaces. The stucco is crumbling here and stained with damp there, but the spa city still wears an aura of magnificence, if scruffy magnificence. The hotels are majestic in principle if dead beat and fraying in detail. The spa is elegant, the casino positively grandiloquent. Restoration is going its methodical way. The day will come when Marianské Lazné recovers most of the glories of Marienbad.

Those glories were at their peak in the first years of this century. For seven years in a row Edward VII spent six weeks in the early autumn in Marienbad. In a lively account of the king's impact on the place, Gordon Brook-Shepherd remarks that it 'was established as the unofficial midsummer capital not merely of Bohemia, or of Austria-Hungary, but of the entire Continent ... from mid-August onwards the spa guests came to include almost everyone of rank and importance whom the King wished to see there.' They included also Hungarian horse-breeders with promising racehorses to sell to the king, Berlin tailors there to copy the fashion he set, and at least one adventuress who took the train from Vienna hoping to sleep with the king and who, frustrated on that point, suggested she might as well sleep with his private secretary to cover the cost of her ticket.

Henry Campbell-Bannerman, prime minister from 1905 until his death in 1908, had been an habitué of Marienbad since the 1870s. He took a dim view of what his king's patronage was doing to his favourite spa and wrote Cassandra-like to a friend: '... wherever the eagle is, there will the carcasses be gathered together ... extraordinary number of tainted ladies ... we thought of wearing our marriage certificate as a sort of order on our coats.' The king's private secretary wrote equally censorious but more vivid accounts of Marienbad: of an Englishwoman in her thirties with snow-white hair who was known only as 'Mrs X'; of another lady 'with an eye-glass, short skirts and a murky past'; and of yet another, an entertainer who got herself expelled from Marienbad when she danced before her enraptured Edwardian audience in 'two oyster shells and a five-franc piece'.

But two policemen whom the Austrian authorities charged with King Edward's safety make the most fascinating characters in Brook-Shepherd's story. One, posted to Marienbad from Prague, hired an assassin to make an attempt on the king's life, confident that by foiling it he would establish his reputation as a bodyguard. Another, posted there from Vienna, was more conventional, contenting himself with keeping onlookers at a respectful distance while the king took the waters. But the chancer from Prague went down into obscurity, whereas the solid citizen from Vienna lived on to engage himself in politics after the fall of the Habsburgs and finally to emerge as Hans Schober, President of the Austrian Republic.

Marianské Lazné today is a less vivid place, but it brings together an engaging mix of visitors. In Communism's good old days most of its clientele were workers, sent for a cure by their factories and trade unions; some of them linger on, in uneasy juxtaposition with sober middle-class Germans and the less-than-sober Czech new rich. And when I went to dinner in a small, private casino I ran into yet more exotic specimens. In the gaming room, looking bored out of their minds and chatting in a corner behind their cigarette smoke, sat three Czech whores, in skirts that would have given Campbell-Bannerman apoplexy; and at the roulette tables sat three men to whom they had attached themselves: bulky, greasy, very Russian, Mafia-like figures winning and losing vast sums at the turn of the wheel. I went downstairs and asked the head waiter in the deserted dining room what they were doing in this quiet corner of Marianské Lazné. He was one of those decent, ordinary Czechs who will never get rich but who try so hard to understand the avalanche of money and money-makers that has descended on their country. He was not about to indulge in gossip about his customers. 'They are welcome visitors in our house,' he told me, 'they bring dollars from St Petersburg.'

My route next day took me from Marianské Lazné to southern Bohemia. I wanted to keep as close to the Bavarian frontier as I could, but a map will show you that the Czechs have only a fraction of the road density of the Germans over the border. So I picked my way, lost more often than not, along minor roads through places like Domazlice and Klatovy, Prachatice and Volary, and their details are lost in a grey soup in my overloaded memory.

Gradually the darkness closed in around me, until it seemed almost palpable. The back roads of Bohemia are not the most reassuring of places for a stranger on a dark night. As usual I did not know where I would sleep, and I sensed, at 7.30 and 8 and 8.30 in the evening, that already doors were being locked and bolted. But my headlights picked up a finger inscribed Cesky Krumlov and I followed it into even inkier darkness. Krumlov, when I got there, seemed bleakly deserted, and a single light was a beacon of hope in a threatening world. It marked a round tower, stone built under a steep peak, a veritable medieval forti-fication. Below the light was a notice in shakily hand-written English: 'Bed and breakfast'.

A woman behind a desk beneath the stairs told me the tower was part of the medieval civil wall, but she had privatised it five years ago. She took me up the spiral staircase to a wedge-shaped room under the eaves, showed me where I could get breakfast in the morning, handed me a front-door key the size of a hand-grenade, and told me to take care of it because she was going home and I would be alone in my tower that night. 'Where can I eat?' I moaned. She gave me a map of the town and bade me a firm goodnight.

The map and what I could sense in the darkness suggested impass-able streets, so I set off on foot. The night smelt of that heavy east Euro-pean blend of coal smoke and wood smoke and diesel fumes and doubtful drains. Faint lights on street corners guided me as I stumbled and slithered on icy cobbles. A medieval muddle of twisting streets con-vinced me that I would never find my way back to my tower. I was hungry; I needed a drink; I was frightened in an uncertain kind of way; and I turned a corner into a film set.

Far below me was a noisy little river. Around me was the stygian darkness of an ancient town. In front, forming a great floodlit amphitheatre, rose a sheer castle wall, curling round the bend of the river, capped with roofs and towers floodlit against the blackness of the sky. No townscape I have seen – the innumerable vistas of Venice, St Petersburg across the Neva, Buda across the Danube – has filled me with such awed surprise.

Man does not live by film sets alone. I was getting seriously hun-gry, and again I followed a light. It marked a restaurant of sorts, bereft of customers, staffed by an emaciated young waiter. I told him in German what I wanted and he told me in German what I could have. Then I asked him if he could manage a cucumber salad as well; and used the Hungarian word '*uborka*' rather than '*Gurke*' by mis-take. He answered in a stream of Hungarian, far faster than I could understand. Was he Hungarian, I asked. 'No, Slovak.' But he spoke a bewildering range of central European languages. 'They are my love, my passion, my concern.' What was he doing here, waiting? 'I have tried many spheres. Now I must make my fortune.' Here, in this abandoned restaurant? 'In summer the Germans come. I shall greet them in their own language.' Perhaps he has made his fortune, but I doubt it.

I ate what he brought me and left him, still effervescent with his linguistic abilities, and made my way down a steep and empty street towards the river. At the bottom, staring at the massive floodlit wall above them, were three young people. 'Awesome,' said the girl. 'Awesome,' said the boys. 'What brings you here on an October night?' I asked them, more for the sake of Anglo-Saxon rapport than because I cared. 'My father was raised here,' said the girl, 'we're touring Bohemia. But where are you from?' 'London,' I said, concerned at the turn the conversation was taking. 'London, England?' they asked, and then told me they were from Missouri. There was no more to be said and I evaporated into the darkness. 'Awesome,' they were saying as I moved out of earshot.

I found my way through the darkness back to my bed-and-breakfast tower. Thuds and thumps emerged from the open door. Inside four young men were humping their luggage up the winding stair. 'Good evening,' I said; and one of them swore, not at me but at his impedimenta, in unmistakable Australian: 'Goddam drum. Goddam stair.' 'Can't leave them in the van,' said another to me by way of explanation as they struggled up the stairs with drums and guitars. Next morning, at breakfast, I asked the drummer where they were playing. 'Prague,' he said, 'and Pilzen, and Ceske bloody somewhere.' 'Ceske bloody Budweiser,' said the guitarist, 'like the bloody beer.'

I walked back into town after breakfast; but first I put my bag in the car. A man of my age loomed out of the morning smog. He came from Salzburg, he said, but now he lived here in Krumlov. '*Meine Kameradin*' had brought him here, he explained, his fingers digging into his wallet for her photograph. She was a crudely glamorous creature, at a guess one-third his age. 'Pretty,' I said politely. 'Beautiful,' he corrected. 'Is she Czech?' I asked. 'Czech,' he confirmed, 'but beautiful.' He dug something else out of his wallet. 'Me, with my brother,' he said, pressing upon me a dog-eared photograph of the two of them posed in front of my tower. 'Thank you,' I said, returning it. 'It is for you,' he explained, 'a souvenir of your hotel.'

Ceske Krumlov was marginally less awesome in what passed for daylight on an October morning. But the castle was as imposing, the crooked streets as intriguing as they had been in the floodlights and the darkness. I had done my homework in my wedge-shaped room, and now I knew something about Krumlov's story. They had filmed much of *Amadeus* here. The artist Egon Schiele had come here in 1911, with his disreputable friends and his seventeen-year-old model mistress: they had scandalised the solid Austrian citizens of Krumau. For in 1911 the population of Krumau was solidly German; and the German-speakers had gone only in 1945, when Czechoslovakia wreaked its revenge on Germans and Austrians alike.

I went up to the castle, home of one of the historic families of Austria and Bohemia, the Schwarzenbergs. In Hungary they remember a Prince Schwarzenberg as the man who put down the Hungarians after their war with the Habsburgs in 1849, remarking that reconciliation was all very well, but first he would prefer to have some hangings. The family's name is more glorious elsewhere in the Habsburg lands, and here in Krumlov they were all but sovereign, with vast estates and a toy army of their own. As I climbed the slope, looking at some mangy bears in a seedy moat and sending coins down a chute to buy them a better diet, I kept tangling with a long procession of Czech schoolchildren being taken to see their inheritance.

I took the tour, understanding one word in a hundred from the lecture the guide delivered to the children. We saw the ballroom and the chapel, and the exquisite elegance of the eighteenth-century theatre, the oldest (or was it the second-oldest?) functioning theatre in Europe. Then I broke away and wandered up the sloping garden, with its achingly beautiful views over the misty roofs of Krumlov. I felt guilty at spending time on sightseeing and asked myself whether I had learned anything about the Iron Curtain during these eighteen hours off-duty. There was nothing specific to chalk up to my credit. But my polyglot waiter had told me something about Central Europe. So had the peregrinations of the Australian musicians. So had Schiele, spending a few months here in his mother's home town just up the road from Vienna, when the whole of central Europe was one homeland under Habsburg patronage. So, for that matter, had the missing German-speakers of Krumlov, shipped out in short order half a century ago and showing no signs, as far as I could see, of coming back.

I set off from Ceske Krumlov in higher spirits than I arrived there, still intoxicated by its beauty. I intended to go east now, along the border not with Germany but with Austria. I still wanted to stay close to the frontier, but the lie of the land and the tourist attractions of southern Bohemia kept edging me away from it, northwards. The first place I came to was the Australian guitarist's Ceske bloody Budweiser – Ceske Budejovice in Czech, but it was Budweis to its German-speaking inhabitants in the old days, and the original Budweiser beer was brewed there, so he had got most things straight.

Budejovice is a big place and an open one, with a much younger feel about it than Krumlov. Like Krumlov it used to be dominated by German-speakers – merchants rather than princes here. They built expansively and well, particularly around the central square named after a medieval King Ottokar of Bohemia, that King Ottokar who fought with the Teutonic Knights far away in northern Europe and after whom they named their new capital, Königsberg.

In that square I was cornered by one of those old men who challenge you to guess how old they are. I forget the figure I offered him, but the question was only an opening gambit anyway. He was ninety-two, he said, living in a splendid old people's home: they had ladies there, as well as gentlemen. But the management were about to double the charges – 'our state is poor' – and they did not know what they would do. But old age deserved respect – 'I saw Franz Josef when he came here; he must have been the age I am now' – and no doubt someone or something would provide. Meanwhile, the Budejovice beer was good; had I tried the beer? I suspected that this was a gentlemanly way of asking for the price of a drink, but when I offered it he refused and rebuked me gently for my presumption. In the end I fled from the ancient pensioner, and when I got back to my car I found that someone had neatly winged it in its parking place.

I drove east towards Trebon, through a watery landscape of marshes and lakes and fishponds. Trebon itself has the mother-and-father of all fish ponds, as well as some glorious façades the length of its long square, some medieval, some eighteenth century, and a palace across the end of the square which mostly faces the other way, looking out of town and across the waters of yet more fishponds.

At Trebon I was close to the Austrian border, but it was too soon to cross it, so I turned north, to Jindrichuv Hradec and Pelhrimov. Throughout my journey I was looking for contrasts, usually between places east and west of the old divide, but here I found contrasts within the same country, twenty miles apart. For Jindrichuv seemed to have the fire of freedom and capitalism in its belly, while its neighbour seemed to be slothfully contented with the old, safe, Communist ways. So Jindrichuv had a splendid new hotel in the central square, with a bank next door which was glossy enough to be in West Germany, and a display of the flags of the nations from which the Union Flag was conspicuously absent. It also bore a *graffito* in English, beautifully spray-painted on a sparklingly white wall: 'Envious smokers are here'. Modernity persisted outside the town, with houses and villages protected by great glass screens from the roar of passing traffic: we might have been in Germany. But the villages themselves were dead-beat places, and Pelhrimov, beautiful though its Renaissance centre is, was hemmed in by the worst kind of Communist-era concrete and seemed infected by the old disease of exhausted sloth.

Up the road from Pelhrimov I would have reached the motorway from Prague to Brno and Bratislava. I was in danger of losing touch with the object of my journey, the Iron Curtain, so I turned back towards Austria, first to Telc and then to Slavonice. Both are glorious little places, each built round a square shaped like a slice of pie. Both seemed closed for eighteen-hour lunches, but if you went looking, in Slavonice at least, you found shops behind the Renaissance facades and people eager to sell you things. There was, I concluded, more sense of business enterprise in little Slavonice than I had found in the whole of Prague in the old days, fifteen years ago. So I bought three postcards and a roll of film which, when the time came to develop it, turned out to be reject stock.

Slavonice is right on the frontier, and from here I found a road that ran parallel to it, to Znojmo and then on to Mikulov in southern Moravia. I set myself to watch out for signs of frontier activity or traces of the Iron Curtain that once ran through these gentle hills. The first things I picked up were little blockhouses dug into the landscape, a regular kilometre apart. Clearly they were not in use, but clearly they had once served a military, frontier purpose. Were they part of Czechoslovakia's defences, built quickly when Hitler marched into Austria? If so I gave little for the Czechs' defences, for even my lay eye could see that these little blockhouses were strung out alone, too far apart to support one another, ripe for plucking by any serious attack. Or were they a generation younger, part of Communist Czechoslovakia's defences against the capitalist world? But the Iron Curtain I used to know was guarded by watchtowers, not by bunkers, and of watchtowers there was no sign.

For mile after mile there was indeed no sign of anyone minding the frontier's security. I remembered a story I had been told a couple of years earlier when I went to look at the Hungarian frontier with Romania two hundred miles away to the east. 'What was the threat?' I had asked. 'Drugs, terrorists, illegal immigrants?' Yes, they said, all those, but the real problem was cows. 'Cows?' I asked. Yes, cows. Farmers brought cows into Hungary through the recognised crossing points and back into Romania across the fields; and out of this circular traffic they made themselves rich, in a way that far exceeded my powers of Hungarian comprehension. Perhaps cows were making the same rounds

here, between the Czech Republic and Austria. There was nothing as
far as I could see to stop them.

But finally, on a crest a good kilometre away down the road in front
of me, I saw a parked police car. As I approached it I watched out for
signs of activity beside the road or in the fields that stretched away
towards Austria. There was none to be seen, and as I passed the police
car, still inquisitive, I saw why. In the back seat, comfortably at ease,
were two police officers. One was male, one female, and they had no
eyes for passing motorists, for smugglers or terrorists, or for profiteer-
ing cows.

I came at last to Mikulov, which its German-speaking inhabitants
called Nikolsberg. Under the bulk of the castle I found a cheap hotel
and as I checked in I asked the woman behind the desk about the Iron
Curtain years.

'Terrible' she said, as if she did not want to talk about them. And
when the fences came down, what did people think then? She bright-
ened. At first the peasants had been excited, had taken excursions to
Vienna. But once they discovered how expensive life '*drüben*' was, their
enthusiasm had cooled.

'Of course, it was different for us,' she added, meaning educated
people like her.

'How was it different?' I asked to keep her talking.

'We cared about freedom,' she said, 'that's why. You see,' she added,
'my father was in the SS, in Italy. My family know the value of freedom.'

I looked at her, for signs of irony or misunderstanding, but she was
impervious to my astonishment. Slowly it dawned on me that this
Czech woman of a certain age, too young for real wartime memories
but old enough to have had a father who fought in Italy, saw membership of the Waffen SS as a mark of intelligence, of cultivated tastes, even
of a sort of middle-class respectability. Perhaps she formed that conviction at her mother's knee, as Communism took away a middle-class
family's comfortable existence and reminded them of a better past.
However she got there, the woman behind the desk was talking about a
father in the Waffen SS as her sister in Godalming might have talked
about hers who had a good war in the 60th Rifles.

A few miles east of Mikulov the Czech Republic gives way to Slovakia and I thought about going that way, down the motorway that leads
to Bratislava. But Austria was an integral part of my story, and the way
things were going it was escaping me. So when I turned my back on the
Czech Republic the following morning I turned my back for the time

being on Slovakia also, and drove instead down the road to the Austrian border. I stopped, just short of the frontier, to buy Austrian Schillings. The exchange booth was in the corner of a café, bubbling with life at ten in the morning. I asked the girl who took my travellers' cheques who all the customers were.

'Austrians, from Vienna,' she said.

Were they going on to Mikulov, or Brno, or all the way to Prague, I asked.

'A few,' she said, but most of them came only this far, two hundred metres over the border.

'What for?' I asked.

'The cakes,' she said. 'We have fine cakes, as fine as Vienna, but cheaper. They come to eat cake.'

My mind went back to the hopeful notice at the beginning of this journey, encouraging people on a day out from Lübeck and Travemünde to venture across the old death strip into Mecklenburg in search of cakes and cream. A Habsburg princess become a French queen got herself a lasting bad name for a moment's frivolity when she said: 'Let them eat cake.' But down here on the Austrian border, as much as up there beside the Baltic, the freedom to cross borders to eat cake seems to have replaced the old tyranny of the watchtowers and the wire. A banal improvement, but a real one.

As I drove down the road towards Vienna the story of the cross-border traffic summoned by Mikulov's cakes lingered in my mind. To me it was a man-bites-dog story, because all my memories of Central Europe in the bad old days were of going west, not east, for a culinary treat.

Not that that was a sentiment to be uttered in polite society in Hungary. '*Jo, finom magyar étel*' was an article of faith in Budapest: it meant, 'good, fine Hungarian food', and every friend of Hungary had better believe it or else. But when I first lived in Hungary, in the 1950s, the food in Budapest's restaurants was limited and usually lamentable, and outside Budapest it was worse. Of course, there were exceptions to be searched out: fish soup here, paprika chicken there, my favourite cucumber and sour cream salad pretty well everywhere. But one rarely ate well in post-revolution Hungary.

For privileged foreigners, the trip to Vienna was therefore a prized opportunity to eat better, and above all to eat more quickly; for service in Budapest restaurants in those days was glacially slothful. Indeed, it was over a quick meal of steak, chips and red wine in the Coq d'Or in

Vienna forty years ago that I got into conversation with a British busi-
nessman who told me that he travelled widely in Eastern Europe. He
was disobliging about the help he got from British diplomats, boastful
about his business successes, and abundantly indiscreet with hints of
other activities he got up to 'over there'. I thought that to talk like that
to a stranger in a Vienna restaurant was asking for trouble; but as he
left, still boasting, he pressed his business card on me. His name was
Greville Wynne: the man who, two years later, was arrested in Budapest
and put on trial in Moscow for the help he gave Britain's spy in the
Kremlin, Oleg Penkovsky.

When we went back to Hungary, in the early 1980s, things culinary
were better, much better; but in this respect as in so many others, they
were not unrecognisably better. The range of dishes available was still
limited, the cooking still slapdash, service still slow. In a few restaurants
you could buy your way to better things and in one or two prewar standards were returning; but still a mantle of too much meat, too much fat
and too little innovation hung over everything. It was announced that a
Chinese restaurant – a first Chinese restaurant – was coming to
Budapest, and we salivated with expectation, but when it came, Hungarian ways had taken charge. Next, an 'Italian' restaurant opened its
doors, but too soon it went the way of the Chinese. '*Magyar étel*' still
ruled supreme.

The problem was, I decided, that peasant standards had come out on
top in Hungarian kitchens. Too many generations of the Hungarian
poor had gone to bed hungry. Now, with the old order swept away, you
ate well if you ate a lot. Protein was something you particularly prized,
with as much fat as possible attached; and with protein you did honour
to your guests.

Once I took my wife to visit a factory in eastern Hungary. They
asked us to stay to lunch, at a table decked in our honour with crossed
Hungarian and British flags.

They brought us a thick soup lavishly reinforced with meat, and
urged us to enjoy ourselves. We did. They brought omelettes: excellent,
we said. Chicken came next: marvellous, we said, but could we also
have water to go with the wine. We hoped to God it was over. But
chicken was followed by steak, each portion topped with a fried egg.
And after the steak came cheese; savoury pancakes; sweet pancakes;
and chestnut puree and whipped cream.

We drove away, just about animate, waving goodbye to our hosts.
That evening, back in Budapest, still well-nigh comatose, we went out

to dinner at the Swedish ambassador's; he pressed on us second help-ings of the reindeer he had flown in from the Arctic for the occasion.

Now things are changing on the other side of the Iron Curtain; but culinary change, like every other, remains hesitant and episodic. In 1999 I arrived with my busload of tourists at a grand Czech hotel. We were valuable guests, and they were eager to do us honour. So at dinner they put one course after another before us, as lavish as the food I had faced in that terrible ordeal in the Hungarian factory. We ate; we shoved our food around hopelessly on our plates; we told the solicitous waitresses that the steak was wonderful but we could not manage another scrap; we tried every trick in the book to diminish the visual impact of the mounds we left uneaten. The waitresses looked at us uncomprehending, Europe remained divided.

And yet ... Once, leaving Bratislava, I crossed the Danube to have a closer look at the wilderness of high-rise workers' flats there, the largest concentration of such homes in Europe, reputedly built to show Hun-gary that here the south bank of the river as much as the north was Slovak property. The blocks marched away to the horizon, regular and blank as soldiers on parade. I came to a bus terminus and beyond it, incongruously, a racecourse that might, with a bit of licence, have been Ascot. Beyond the grandstands and stables, the road petered our into a country lane, and a couple of miles further on into a village street. It was lunch time, and I went looking for something to eat in the down-at-heel bar-cum-café that offered the only hope of a meal in the place. I expected the worst; and there, in a village in the back of beyond sand-wiched between a bleak industrial suburb and the Hungarian border, they brought me an omelette; and to borrow Samuel Pepys's turn of phrase, ' it was the very best omelette I ever did eat in my life'.

When I got to Aš and the girl gave me my lollipop, I was not just enter-ing the Czech Republic, the ancient kingdom of Bohemia and the Hab-sburg Empire, whose traces we have seen already and which will be with us all the way to the Adriatic. I was also entering the Sudetenland, where German-speakers lived side by side with Czechs under Habsburg rule and where was played out, more than sixty years ago, one of Europe's great border crises. These were the areas which Hitler demanded as his 'last territorial claim in Europe' and which Britain and France at Munich forced the Czechs to surrender to him.

The predominantly German-speaking areas which formed the old Sudetenland extended right round the border of the Czech half of prewar Czechoslovakia. In the north they reached the Polish frontier, in the south almost as far as the border with Hungary. In Moravia the Sudeten territories dug so deep into Czechoslovakia that they came close to separating the Czech lands from Slovakia. These were places German in language and sentiment yet which had never been part of Germany. German-speakers and Czechs had lived in them together under the Habsburgs, sharing their towns and villages reasonably happily. But in the 1930s, as Hitler started to use national exclusiveness and grievance to build a dynamic new Germany, the German-speakers of Bohemia and Moravia increasingly resented their inclusion in a predominantly Slav state.

German sentiment in the Sudetenland started relatively moderate. It complained of Czech arrogance and called for recognition of the place of the German language and culture in these mixed areas. Gradually it became more strident, demanding separate political institutions and self-government. But it was the Anschluss with Austria in March 1938 which brought Sudeten emotions to boiling point. As German troops marched in, Austrians vibrant with enthusiasm for union with the Reich came out to greet them. The Sudeten Germans clamoured ever louder, first demanding recognition of their distinctiveness from their Czech neighbours and then union with the Reich.

Czech national security depended on three things: alliance with France, alliance in the Little Entente with Romania and Yugoslavia, and a strong army dug into strong fortifications in the hills along the German border. When Hitler marched into Austria he had outflanked the fortifications and, in Winston Churchill's words, driven a wedge into the heart of the Little Entente. It was clear that he would turn next against Czechoslovakia, which he for his part could represent as a wedge driven into the heart of Germany. The Czech Prime Minister said in public 'We will defend ourselves.' The Czech President, Eduard Beneš, said in private 'We shall be massacred but we shall fight.'

The Soviet Union put out feelers about cooperation against Hitler. Neville Chamberlain rebuffed them, as he had rebuffed an offer by Roosevelt in the previous year to help find peace in Europe; and historians still dispute the practical value of both proposals. The leader of the Sudeten Germans, Konrad Henlein, visited London, creating an impression of moderation, demanding only local autonomy, with international affairs remaining in the hands of Prague and Czech troops remaining in their Sudeten fortifications. Equally concerned to show its good sense, Prague gave Britain and France its proposals to conciliate the Germans in the Sudetenland. But the press wrote of mounting excitement among the Germans and the British consul in the northern Sudetenland reported that most of them were no longer even nominally loyal to the Czech state. When in June the Sudetenland went to the polls, the German parties made major gains.

Between them, Hitler and the local German leaders were orchestrating a crisis in the Sudetenland. France was committed by treaty to support Czechoslovakia. Britain, bound both by treaty to defend France and by its League of Nations commitments to defend peace in Europe, was almost as directly involved. On 26 July Chamberlain announced the despatch of a mission of investigation and conciliation to the Sudetenland. Thus a decent, elderly British politician, whose name and reputation were linked to shipping and the sea, found himself engaged in this vicious political game in Bohemia, which not since Shakespeare's time had ever been endowed with a seacoast.

Walter Runciman was the heir to a shipping fortune who started his political career by defeating Winston Churchill at Oldham in 1899, became an Asquithian Liberal, and over the next forty years held off-and-on government positions of increasingly serious weight. When Neville Chamberlain turned to him to solve the insoluble problem of the Sudeten Germans he had just ceased to be President of the Board of Trade. He went off to Czechoslovakia and told a friend when he arrived in Prague that 'if by a miracle an agreement was reached, I would be astonished'.

Runciman worked his way round the Sudetenland with a team of Foreign Office officials, who some observers said were too easily seduced by the hospitality of German landowners. They were there to find facts of demography and geography, but the political facts were obvious. Local autonomy for the Germans, which only weeks ago might have been the solution, was now nothing like enough; constantly worked upon by political agitation and envious of those fortunate Austrians, they would now content themselves only with union with Germany. The Czechs would lose their fortress line and lie at Hitler's mercy. Lord Runciman had been sent, wrote a British journalist, 'to persuade the Czechs to commit suicide'.

The local Germans held mass rallies throughout the Sudetenland. Hitler heaped oratorical fuel on their flames. The Czechs in despair extended into the Sudeten German areas martial law which was already in force in the rest of the country. In Eger, now Cheb, whose main square we admired a few pages back, two Czech policemen answered a routine call to the headquarters of the German National Party. They found them shuttered, apparently deserted. But as they scratched their heads outside, shots were fired. One policeman was killed, his partner wounded. When Czech police returned in force a siege of the building developed. Several of its occupants were killed, and the German nationalists had their martyrs.

Hitler raged; the German Army leaders, distraught at the difficulty of defeating twenty Czech divisions in fortified positions while leaving the Western Front exposed to French attack, prepared to overthrow him. Then Neville Chamberlain flew to Berchtesgaden and the officers called off their preparations. Runciman reported to the Cabinet. There was talk of the Czechs ceding to Germany only the Cheb area, which lay outside their fortress line, and pacifying the Sudeten Germans elsewhere with a cantonal arrangement of self-government under Czech sovereignty. Britain and France pressed the Czechs for more concessions to Germany. The general commanding the French Military Mission in Prague resigned his commission in disgust, took Czech nationality and offered his services to the Czech Army.

Chamberlain flew to Bad Godesberg. Hitler now rejected ideas of self-determination for the Sudetenland. The Czechs must be out within four days. Confronted with this new ultimatum, Britain and France appeared to stiffen. The Czechs mobilised and the Prime Minister was replaced by a tough old general, Jan Srovy, who at the end of the First World War had fought his way across Siberia with the Czech Legion. The world waited for war, and Winston Churchill welcomed the showdown with Germany for which he had worked: 'It seemed that the moment of clash had arrived and that the opposing forces were aligned. The Czechs had a million and a half men armed behind the strongest fortress line in Europe.' As impressed as Churchill by that army and fortress, the German generals again prepared to challenge Hitler. But again Chamberlain flew to Germany, this time to Munich. There Britain, France, Germany and Italy between them disposed of the crisis while the Czech representatives waited in the lobby, and Chamberlain flew home talking of peace in our time.

Hitler's armies marched into the Sudetenland unopposed and took control of the famous Czech defences. What was left of Czechoslovakia was rendered indefensible. The Czechs, betrayed, could look only to themselves. As the Germans marched into the Sudetenland, Henlein's few German-speaking opponents fled to Prague. The SS demanded their return to face trial. Britain refused them visas, but British do-gooders flew to Prague to beg Srovy to protect them. He refused, his face suffused with anger: 'We have been willing to fight on the side of the angels,' he said. 'Now we shall hunt with the wolves.'

Six months later, in March 1939, Hitler disposed of what was left of Czechoslovakia. His army marched through the hate-filled streets of Prague. The Czech Lands became a Protectorate, Slovakia a client state. As far as their conqueror was concerned, the Czechs were finished. But Czech pilots flew with the British in the Battle of Britain, Czech troops fought beside the British and the Russians, Slovak resistance fighters rose up as the Red Army approached in 1944. American troops were the first to enter much of the Sudetenland but they were quickly pulled back, by Allied agreement, into southern Germany. Soviet troops and the liberated Czechs moved into the Sudetenland. It was time for revenge. The Sudeten Germans were expelled with only what they could carry, to fester for years as refugees in Bavaria. The German town of Eger became the Czech town of Cheb, Marienbad became Marian-ské Lazné. When, in 1948, the Communists seized power in Prague, they created their own piece of the Iron Curtain, as absolute and lethal as any other. It ran through what had once been the Sudetenland.

Memories of the events of 1938, of 1945 and of the years between left deep and reasonable animosities between Czechs and Germans. They blended with older memories, of medieval conflict between Bavaria and Bohemia and of the oppression of Protestant Czechs by the German-speaking Catholic Habsburgs from the time of Jan Hus in the four-teenth century to the Battle of the White Mountain in 1620. For a further 300 years there were tensions between Catholic Austrians around the Habsburg court and Czech nobility who could claim that their family history went back quite as far as theirs, often with more distinction. In the nineteenth century the Czechs gradually learned a sense of identity which called out for nationhood. In the twentieth they achieved it, and until Hitler's coming they made a success of it in ways which, imperfect as they may have been, offered a solitary model of democracy in Central Europe. Like other Central and Eastern Euro-peans the Czechs learned the hard way an understandable hatred of things German. Are there traces of all this to be uncovered, I wondered, in the psyches of today's Czechs and Germans?

There is still a festering bitterness about the brutalities of 1945 among aged German expellees in northern Bavaria. You will find Czechs whose resentments of what went before those expulsions burn as brightly. Special interests will dig these emotions out of the cupboard when they can serve a useful purpose, and Presidents and Federal Chancellors have to dance a minuet around them when they want to demonstrate that the Czech Republic and Germany now understand one another pretty well. But none of this seems to matter very much to most Czechs and Germans today, who probably find it as irrelevant, and as embarrassing, as ordinary Britons find unyielding resentment of what the Japanese did to British prisoners of war more than half a century ago.

Both Germans and Czechs – and it is the Czechs who matter most here, having so much more substantial causes for historical resentment than the Germans – have other fish to fry than ancient grievance. The Czechs, for one thing, have an enduring grievance against the Russians, who installed their Communist rulers in 1948 and dealt so brutally with the Prague Spring in 1968, setting Czechoslovakia back by two decades; and a few with long memories still grieve over British and French betrayal in 1938. For most Czechs today, their grievances against the Russians far outweigh those against the Germans. They have also a need of the Germans, as friends and investors, as NATO partners and as people who can open the way for them to European Union membership. And a lot of Czechs have warm memories of the role which the Austrians played in the Cold War: naturally of the West but neutral, and with a profound historical understanding of south-central Europe and the Danube valley. I remember from my years in Hungary how smoothly Austrian diplomacy accommodated the needs of Hungarians who found themselves hemmed in by Moscow. It did the same for the Czechs, so much more clearly captives of Moscow and of its Czech Communist acolytes.

So I sense that ordinary Czechs today think reasonably well of Germans and Austrians; and that they, for their part, have every reason to think reasonably well of the Czechs. In eleven years they have put their Communist past behind them and worked their passage back into European society. German money and Czech labour work constructively together. The statesmen and the diplomats have put the fact of reconciliation firmly on the record. In Prague the Czechs have given Europe back one of its great cities. All of them, Czechs, Austrians and Germans know that they can work better together than apart. Looking back, they find their points of reference not in the terrible years from 1938 to 1945 but in a remoter history, when south-central Europe, for all its animosities and injustices, worked reasonably well together under Habsburg leadership.

But of course you can unearth grievance, injustice and cause for animosity anywhere if you try hard enough. Today's Czechs have for example a serious case to answer over their attitude towards the Roma, the gypsies, yet they would be more than human if they did not resent lectures from Germans on the subject. German businessmen and officials can be infuriatingly didactic, awakening memories of Nazi attitudes towards inferior Slavs. But from everything I hear, I believe that the balance of the record over the last decade is a positive one.

A few years ago I was in Prague, on business that had nothing to do with the Iron Curtain. It took me to a succession of offices, and finally to that of a non-governmental organisation that was trying to bring some benefit or other to the Czech Republic. There I met a well-meaning American woman, a volunteer, deeply committed to whatever it was her organisation was about. We talked about Czechs and Germans.

'Relations are appalling,' she said.

'Why?' I asked.

'Look at Skoda.'

'What about Skoda?'

'Volkswagen have bought it.'

'Isn't that good – capital, jobs, good cars, technology, industrial revival?'

'It's appalling,' she said.

'Won't they put Skoda on its feet?' I asked.

'It should have been the Czechs,' she said.

We could have been there all night, but I caught the eye of the young Czech woman who was making the rounds with me. I saw there a practical contempt for all this nonsense, this political and economic illiteracy; this Czech woman wanted to get on with building prosperity, not logic-chop her life away. The look in her eye reminded me, who love history, that you can too easily let it overburden the present.

6

The Habsburg Heartlands

Ever since we left Germany we have been among the ghosts of the Habsburgs and they will be with us all the way to the Adriatic. Now, as we drive down the road towards Vienna, we are approaching the heart of the family's glory. But beside all its glory, this was a family which in its last century of empire had more than its share of personal tragedy. Four of these tragedies were played out in places we shall pass, within thirty miles of the line of the Iron Curtain. A fifth, which reached its climax far away, began at the palace of Miramare, just outside Trieste where our journey ends.

For the first of our tragedies we go to Eckartsau, a nondescript little town on the Danube a few miles below Vienna. At its back is the Marchfeld, a flat and wearisome plain where in 1278 Rudolf of Habsburg laid the foundations of his family's fortunes when he defeated the King of Bohemia in battle. At Eckartsau the Habsburgs had a hunting lodge, which is today a dreary-looking place among a tangle of trees, serving some obscure institutional purpose. Here, in 1919, the Habsburg dynasty breathed its political last.

The last of the Habsburgs to sit on a throne was the Emperor Karl. In 1916 he succeeded his great-uncle, Franz Josef, who had ruled since 1849 and sometimes seemed to have ruled for ever. In the last years of the war everyone knew that if Austria-Hungary lost the war the Empire was doomed, and in November 1918 Austria-Hungary collapsed. Karl fled to Eckartsau with his Empress Zita, and there they hid themselves through the winter of 1918–19. Perhaps they chose the place because it was near to Vienna yet discreetly forgettable. For four months the hunting lodge sheltered Karl and Zita (the Blue Guide says that they 'subsisted' here, and the word captures the hopelessness of their position) while revolution devoured what was left of the Empire. Finally the victorious Allies, struggling to make sense of Central European chaos, despatched a British army officer to escort them into exile.

Karl was an unassuming man, but he had waited a long time to become emperor. Perhaps he found Central Europe without a Habsburg as unimaginable as did so many of his subjects. So he lent himself to two quixotic attempts to recover at least one of his thrones, with mad attempts at coups in Hungary. Neither amounted to much more than a motor-car cavalcade escorted by a bunch of officers down the road to Budapest. The Regent of Hungary, Admiral Horthy, had served Franz Josef; perhaps Karl believed that he would serve him also. But Horthy was an immoderate admirer of the English aristocracy, and from them he had learned to use the conventions of gentlemanliness to cloak an instinct for the jugular. He felt no attachment or obligation to Franz Josef's successor, and he recognised, as Karl did not, that the Allies would not tolerate a Habsburg on any European throne. So at Karl's first attempt he rebuffed him and at his second he had him arrested. A British warship was sent to take him away to exile in Madeira. There, within a matter of months, he died, the last of the imperial and royal Habsburgs to sit upon a throne; and there you can still see flowers and ribbons in Hungarian and Austrian colours laid on his tomb. But it was the departure from Eckartsau in 1919, not the death in Madeira, that marked the true end of the dynasty.

Seventy miles up the Danube in the little castle of Artstetten you can study the last act of a more famous Habsburg tragedy, one which took place five years earlier. In its chapel lie the remains of Archduke Franz Ferdinand and of the woman who was assassinated with him at Sarajevo. His love for that woman – a grace note in the character of an otherwise harsh, self-serving and loveless man – is the reason why he is buried here rather than among the other Habsburgs in Vienna.

Franz Ferdinand was Franz Josef's nephew. His wife was born Countess Sophie Chotek. Her family was one of considerable Bohemian distinction. But Sophie was not of royal blood, and she was therefore precluded from full acceptance into the House of Habsburg. Ancient rules of protocol debarred her, for example, from burial in the Habsburg crypt; and Franz Ferdinand had long since let it be known that he wished to be buried with her. So when the bodies of Franz Ferdinand and Sophie were brought back from Sarajevo, arrangements to bury them together in the chapel of the Archduke's castle at Artstetten were set in hand.

Even now, considerations of protocol got in the way, this time aided by politics. Court functionaries insisted that every last requirement of the rules of which they were custodian must be observed. They also feared that if the crowds attending the funeral procession were moved by the occasion their grief would in some way distract attention, and therefore glory, from the Emperor. So the coffins were sent off to the railway station from the Hofburg in Vienna late in the day and by the time the train reached the little Danube town of Pöchlarn it was almost dark. The bodies of Franz Ferdinand and Sophie were ferried across the river to Artstetten in the darkness, almost as if the Danube were the Styx. There was something furtive about their last homecoming. Now they lie in the castle church. The castle museum that commemorates them brings out something of the love and comfort of their bruised lives together, but it has the air of a film script about it too, as if posterity still owned and yet disdained the two of them in death, just as the House of Habsburg did in life.

To find a third scene of Habsburg tragedy you have to go up into the Vienna Woods, to Mayerling, where Archduke Rudolf died. Like Franz Ferdinand, Rudolf, the Emperor Franz Josef's only son, found himself torn between love of a mere noblewoman and the demands of his family. His baroness was Maria Vetsera, an infinitely less serious person than his cousin's wife, and his love for her was more *coup de foudre* than the enduring commitment which Franz Ferdinand, for all his faults, gave to Sophie. Rudolf was frustrated by the demands which Habsburg expectations placed upon him and by his own psychological inadequacies. He was frustrated too by all the problems which his love for Maria presented. He murdered his mistress and then killed himself. Once again Habsburg protocol played its clumsy part, trying to conceal the terrible but manifest fact that a member of the House of Habsburg was both murderer and suicide; and the mysteries which court officials made of the affair in 1888 live on to titillate investigators more than a hundred years afterwards.

At the very end of the Iron Curtain, at the castle of Miramare just outside Trieste, you can pick up the threads of yet another Habsburg tragedy. Franz Josef's brother, the Archduke Maximilian, built Miramare in 1860, on a point overlooking the sea, to be a home for himself and his new bride. She was Charlotte of Saxony, of royal birth and therefore acceptable to Habsburg protocol. In name if not in fact, Maximilian commanded the imperial fleet in the Adriatic, and he and Charlotte may have expected to live out idyllic lives together in this castle beside the sea. But politics and dynastic ambition intervened. Napoleon III was doing his restless and intriguing worst to undermine the Habsburg position in northern Italy. He was also intent on conquering Mexico. Perhaps to make amends to the Habsburgs, or perhaps out of Machiavellian purpose, he dangled the prospect of a throne before Maximilian's eyes; and the Habsburgs lacked the wisdom to say no. In

1864, Maximilian went off with his wife and a French army to become Emperor of Mexico.

But Napoleon's interest in his protégé began to wane and he began to withdraw the French troops on whom Maximilian depended. The United States, free at last of its civil war, turned its attention to this intrusion of European monarchy into the western hemisphere. The Mexicans rose up against Maximilian in a squalid civil war. Charlotte came back to Europe to try to rally support for her husband. But now Napoleon was coldly dismissive. In Vienna, dynasty and Empire were preoccupied with the consequences of Austria's defeat by the Prussians at Königgrätz. Noone could or would help Charlotte. Napoleon pulled the last French troops out of Mexico and in a scene immortalised by Edouard Manet, Maximilian ended his life before a firing squad at Querataro. In January 1868 an Austrian warship brought his body home to Trieste. From there Maximilian was taken to lie with his ancestors in the Habsburg crypt in Vienna.

The last of these family tragedies is that of the Emperor Franz Josef himself. In one sense, his life was no tragedy. He came to the throne at the height of the convulsions of 1848, and for sixty-eight years he doggedly ruled his empire. Contemporaries ruled and grew old and died; Franz Joseph ruled and grew old and lived on. An ascetic sense of duty drove him, year after year, and he brought to the task all the obsessive attention to detail that his ancestor Philip II had given to ruling Spain 300 years earlier.

He loved his wife Elizabeth with a quiet passion; she, beautiful, solipsistic and exasperatingly wayward, never succeeded in returning more than a fraction of the love he heaped upon her. She wandered restlessly throughout Europe and, like maddeningly beautiful and beautifully maddening royal women since, made herself beloved throughout the continent. The Hungarians, in particular, clutched her to their bosoms, claiming that she understood the Magyar spirit in a way no born Habsburg could. Meanwhile Franz Josef could win only the respect which his unceasing devotion to duty brought him. When a mad assassin killed her by the lakeside in Geneva he only added to Elizabeth's fame.

Her husband ruled on, to die at last in 1916, while his armies bled in Russia and Italy and Serbia. It was clear by the time Franz Josef died that the old empire of the Habsburgs was dying with him. Two years later, Karl's flight from Eckartsau proved that it was dead. A Central Europe in which different peoples, languages and traditions might hope to live more or less at peace with their neighbours died with it.

Vienna is less than an hour's drive from that cakeshop on the Czech border, down a straight road that takes you through the winelands of Lower Austria. It is even closer to the Slovak and Hungarian frontiers. Of all the cities on the western side of the old dividing line, Vienna lies furthest east, even further than Berlin. For most of the Cold War neutral Austria formed a salient of freedom between Czechoslovakia and Yugoslavia. Vienna was the place where East met West on neutral ground. Diplomacy was active here, if usually of the second-order kind. Businessmen struck deals in Vienna, assisted by Austrian bankers and go-betweens. Irregulars of every kind from the two sides rubbed up against one another here, to do their murky business or to encompass each other's clandestine destruction. Of all Europe's capitals, Vienna adapted itself most smoothly to Cold War circumstances.

It brought many advantages to the role, for Vienna is the classical Central European city, and as long as the Iron Curtain lasted it was in a sense the only one, when all the others were dragooned willy-nilly into Eastern and Western European camps, on their side of the Iron Curtain or ours. It built on experience, for its story as the prime exemplar of Central Europe goes back for centuries beyond the partition of the continent in 1945. It is by turns the story of a city on the edge of Western European civilisation and of a city whose rulers bound all of Central Europe together. In that story the years of the Cold War years of division were just the penultimate episode, and since 1989 Vienna has resumed its alternative, unifying vocation. Out of both roles the Viennese built the city we see today. It was the right size for the capital of an empire and seems absurdly too large for a country the size of today's Austria. But the heart of the place, within the Ring, is compact; and from the Belvedere Palace, where the State Treaty that gave Austria its freedom was signed in 1955, you can see right over the rooftops of the inner city to the canal on the far side. It looks a prosperous city, busy, bustling, agreeable to the visitor. Its shadow side, like that of all Austria, is something to turn to later.

Vienna lay just within the Roman Empire, whose boundary hereabouts was formed by the Danube. A Roman camp figures in its history, and so briefly does Charlemagne. When the Hungarians pushed westward in the ninth century the Germans fought a skirmish with them here. By the twelfth century Vienna had become the capital of the Ostmark, the 'Eastern March' of the Holy Roman Empire. In the thirteenth the Habsburgs took it from the kings of Bohemia, and early in the seventeenth made it the permanent residence of the Imperial court.

So Vienna became a key city, perhaps the key city, of the German-speaking world, and one of Europe's great capitals.

But already, in 1529, the city had stood its first siege against the Ottoman Turks, a brutal reminder that it lay on the very edge of the Teutonic Christendom of which it thought itself the heart. The Turkish threat persisted for the best part of 200 years, with a Turkish Pasha ruling in Buda further down the Danube, and with Turkish troops skirmishing periodically with Christian forces in western Hungary. They often penetrated into Austria and in 1683 came the last Turkish siege. The Grand Vizier Kara Mustafa brought 200,000 men through the Balkans and across the plains of Hungary to the gates of Vienna, and their siege pressed up against the walls of the old city. There were prayers throughout Christendom for Vienna's safety (although French diplomacy privately welcomed this threat to its old Habsburg enemy) and talk of getting a relieving force together. But the kingdoms of the West moved with agonising slowness while the city's garrison smuggled messengers through the Turkish lines to beg them to make haste. Eventually, Christendom rallied, and armies led by Prince Eugene of Savoy and King Jan Sobieski of Poland crossed the Danube far upstream, struck through the Vienna woods, overwhelmed the Turks and fell upon their camp. The Sultan sent the fatal bowstring to Kara Mustafa, who paid the Ottoman price for defeat. His army went streaming away, leaving a camp full of loot behind. The Turks were harried out of Hungary and back into the Balkans, where Christians were to fight Turks for a further 200 years, and where Christians seem set to go on fighting Moslems, and one another, well into the twenty-first century.

The Turkish defeat left the Habsburgs pre-eminent in south-central Europe. They already ruled Austria, Bohemia, Slovenia and much of northern Italy. They joined hands with wary Hungarian allies in clearing Hungary, and they took its crown for themselves. Hungary brought Slovakia and Croatia with it. In the Balkans the Empire established an uneasy frontier against the Turks and peopled it with soldiers turned farmers, woodsmen and border guards. In the north-east the late-eighteenth-century partitions of Poland brought the Habsburgs up against the Romanovs, as in Germany they already faced the Hohenzollerns. The Austrians suffered indignity and defeat in the Napoleonic Wars, but at the end of them they were among the victors, with peace itself made at the Congress of Vienna.

Along with Russia, Prussia, Britain and France, Austria remained one of the great powers of Europe. Throughout the nineteenth century it held south-central Europe together. In the course of it the Habsburgs were deprived of one peripheral possession after another, but in 1848 they rode out the year of revolutions and in 1867 they took the most turbulent of the nationalities, the Hungarians, into partnership with them. When war came in 1914 Austria-Hungary was still a great power, if apparently the sickliest.

Vienna was central to all this history, and its characteristics helped form those of the whole Empire. It knew how to share, for Teutons, Magyars, Czechs, Slovaks and Slovenes had always lived there. It remembered that it had been a border city, and long after the Turks had decamped from its gates Vienna's administrators knew how to guard frontiers. It was also a melting pot, welcoming all Europe to its markets and salons, and it remains a richly European city still, as the names in its telephone book demonstrate. There are more Slav names in it that German, Slav families of every provenance from Istria to Ruthenia, Italian names and ubiquitous Anglo-Saxon names as well. And until the Holocaust it contained also the names of untold thousands of Jews. Even the Turks contributed to Vienna's fame, and legend has it that they brought it both its coffee and its crescent rolls. Throughout the days of its glory it was the most cosmopolitan of the Continent's capitals.

There was every kind of contradiction in Habsburg Vienna: between Germans and Hungarians; between these dominant nations and the other nationalities; of rich against poor; between the Habsburgs, their aristocracy, the middle classes and the people; over all the confusions and cross-purposes of the constitutional arrangements of the Empire. Against all these contradictions stood the forces that bound things together: the Imperial family itself and its association with the Catholic faith practised in most of its dominions; the Army and a historical devotion to its colours; the administrative framework of the Empire, honest and efficient by the standards of the time; above all, perhaps, fear of the fragmentation that would come if the Empire fell. *The Radetzky March* by Joseph Roth will tell you how the system held together, just as that admirable film *Colonel Redl* will show you the forces that pulled it apart.

All those contradictions sapped the Empire's strength, and in retrospect there is a terrible inevitability about the decline and fall of the House of Habsburg. In 1866 Prussia drove the Habsburgs out of Germany and in 1870 established itself at the heart of a Germany which overshadowed Austria. Gradually the Italians and their French patrons picked away at the Austrian possessions in northern Italy. The Hungarians were uncertain partners in the Empire and increasing numbers of Slavs and Italians hoped to bring it to a negotiated or a violent end. To our eyes the Imperial family itself looks as fatally flawed as the Romanovs, or perhaps the Windsors. In Vienna's intellectual classes there spread a fatal ennui, anatomised, according to those who profess to have read it, in Musil's *A Man Without Qualities*. Even the Empire's brilliant intellectual and artistic recovery in its last years before 1914 reads as a last, deathbed convulsion. But punctuating the long decline were recoveries, reassertions, successes. The whole story might have looked very different had Europe not stumbled into war in 1914.

Even when it did, the Austro-Hungarian Empire went to war relatively united and resolute. Its armies sustained four years of war against Russians, Italians and Serbs, enduring longer than the Romanovs' forces and as long as the Hohenzollerns'. It was nationalism, socialism, propaganda and ideology, all of them going to work on popular discontent at the end of a lost war, together with the didacticism of Woodrow Wilson, that did for the Empire, not some fatal flaw that doomed it to extinction.

But die it did. The imperial possessions fragmented into nation states: Czechoslovakia, Yugoslavia, a grievously diminished Hungary, and Austria itself. Vienna was reduced from the worthy heart of a European empire to the capital of a diminutive republic. Four-fifths of the new Austria was mountainous, beautiful, peaceful and welcoming to holidaymakers and skiers, but economically pretty well meaningless. Vienna itself, and the Danube valley provinces of Upper and Lower Austria, were forced in upon themselves. The Austrians, deprived of their empire, could see in their little republic no role for themselves worthy of their past, and cast about for one in a larger Germany.

For twenty years successive presidents – Hans Schober (whom we have seen guarding Edward VII in Marienbad), Hainisch, Miklas, Dollfuss and Schuschnigg – tried to make sense of their doomed inheritance; but the times, and most of their people, were against them. In his efforts to save Austria, Dollfuss overthrew the constitution and made himself dictator to frustrate the Nazis, but he could not save himself from an atrocious death at their hands. For a time Italian patronage helped his successor preserve Austria's independence. But Schuschnigg was up against Nazi daemons at home as much as across the German border. In 1938 came the Anschluss with Germany. Bringing to an end his mission to a country which had ceased to exist the British ambassador reported: 'The city which served as a bulwark of civilisation against the Turks in 1683 has been converted into the eastern bulwark of a race whose cultural and philosophical outlook is the negation of the principles for which civilisation stands.' Yet as he packed his bags the people of Vienna were out on the streets, welcoming the German regiments, denouncing left-leaning neighbours and abusing defenceless Jews, celebrating that negation of the principles which at its best Vienna had represented.

Since then Austria has been denied the opportunity to show the world that it is after all prepared to suffer for those principles. In 1945 the Allies treated the Austrians as a liberated rather than an enemy people, and they were never required, as Germany was, to face up to the evil which so many of their countrymen had done. In 1955 came the State Treaty, giving Austria its nationhood, ending its occupation by the Four Powers, and binding it to a burden-free neutrality. So after a mere ten years it escaped from the occupation and division which persisted in Germany until 1989. On the wrong side of the Iron Curtain, first the Hungarians and then the Czechs tried to throw off Communism, and all the Austrians could do was to succour the refugees, as they did to their credit, with courage and generosity. Finally, when tyranny collapsed all over Central and Eastern Europe in 1989, Austria was set free to seek European Union membership.

So postwar Austria has faced few hard decisions. It has prospered peacefully, but its reputation has been repeatedly besmirched, by the fascist and racist leanings of many Austrians and by corruption scandals which have engulfed its politicians as much as its businessmen. When the world belatedly uncovered the wartime activities of their president, Kurt Waldheim, the Austrians closed ranks. Now the opprobrium is directed at Jörg Haider, a dangerously popular extreme nationalist, and it is an open question whether foreign criticism and decent Austrians will be enough to hold the line against him and his party.

But the good things remain. Vienna remains south-central Europe's strongest entrepôt of ideas, initiative and business. The lakes and mountains of Austria are glorious holiday places, the Danube above Vienna the most eternally beautiful of rivers. The country people have the simplicity of country people everywhere. The monastery at Melk, the music at Salzburg, the centre of Graz, all reach out to the sublime. The streets and squares of baroque Vienna are as beautiful as you will find anywhere in Central Europe. The Hofburg is a palace worthy of the history of the Habsburgs. And the nineteenth-century buildings along the Ringstrasse remind you that, just beyond the boundary of living memory, this was the capital of an empire as magnificent as those of the Romanovs and the Hohenzollerns, and infinitely more ancient.

If you drive eastwards along the Danube from Vienna you come to the town of Hainburg. It is a tough old town, which for centuries marked the eastern defences of the Holy Roman Empire. Cross the river from Hainburg and you are in the Marchfeld, where so many battles for Vienna were fought. Go beyond Hainburg, still on the south bank, and you reach the borders with Slovakia and Hungary, where the Iron Curtain ran. Throughout central Europe the Romans used the Danube as their northern border, all the way from Bavaria to the Black Sea. So here, just east of Hainburg, you have reached the point at which the Iron Curtain crossed the ancient world's European divide, the *limes* which separated the Roman Empire from the barbarians.

If you turn back from Hainburg towards Vienna you come to a major archaeological site, marking what is left of the Roman city and camp of Carnuntum. In AD 70, the year in which they destroyed Jerusalem, the Romans started to build a camp here to control this section of the frontier. The settlement grew into city as well as camp, and eventually the capital of a Roman province. At first the legion XV Apollinaris provided the garrison, and later XIV Germinius Martia Victrix. The settlement rapidly attracted traders from outside the Empire and became a jumping-off point for Roman expeditions into the barbarian wilderness. Later it also served a grander purpose: capital, no less, of the Roman province of Pannonia, and seat of the provincial governor.

The province of Pannonia occupied the whole of what is today western Hungary, as well as Austria east of the Alps and parts of Slovenia and Croatia. To the south was the road to the Adriatic and to Rome, to the west the Austrian mountains and the forests of south Germany. But it was Pannonia's northern and eastern border which mattered, for it was there that Rome faced military threats. Throughout its length it followed the Danube, east from Carnuntum for 100 miles to the Danube Bend, then south for 200 to Belgrade, passing the Roman city at Aquincum just outside Budapest on its way. So Pannonia formed a kind of salient protruding into barbarian territory, and quite early in the Christian era it became the Empire's single most important military concentration point.

Carnuntum, its capital, was therefore a place of importance in the Roman scheme of things. Pliny records that in Nero's time a Roman knight set off on an expedition from Carnuntum into the north. He may have been looking for warriors to fight in Nero's circus but he came back with amber from the Baltic. Hitherto barbarian traders had brought amber to market at Carnuntum, for the Romans to ship down the amber road to Aquilea at the head of the Adriatic on its way to feed the Roman appetite for luxury. Now for a time it seems to have been brought in by Roman expeditions. The market at Carnuntum saw traders from what are today Bohemia and Moravia but from further afield as well, from Poland and north Germany. At Carnuntum Roman officials negotiated with tribal leaders, threatened them, bribed them, warned them. Carnuntum's soldiers guarded the frontier and stood ready for expeditions across it. And a flotilla of the Danube fleet was stationed here.

In AD 170 the tribes of Bohemia and Moravia, the Marcomanni and the Quadi, launched a major attack across the Danube. They bypassed Carnuntum and swept right through Pannonia to the Adriatic, sacking and besieging northern Italian cities. Eventually they withdrew across the Danube, but the Empire had been humbled, its security penetrated. Marcus Aurelius went to Carnuntum to restore the situation. He first used diplomacy to divide his enemy, then launched a major attack on them. The legionaries marched out from Carnuntum across the March-feld and into the Moravian hills. Marcus Aurelius went with them and in the course of this expedition, and at Carnuntum, he wrote by candlelight his *Meditations,* those enduring commentaries on the transience of all those concerns, such as outwitting and defeating the Empire's enemies, which filled his working days.

Carnuntum endured, and it took an earthquake in AD 400 to reduce it to the state in which you see it today. There, stretching for several kilometres along the Danube and sprawling across a gentle slope that leads down towards the river, are the remains of city and camp. Parts of the site are submerged under modern buildings, but at its eastern end you can explore what is left of the legionary camp and of the town which grew up around it. Further west lies the civil city: two amphitheatres and a great triumphal arch, and the remains of the governor's palace, of wall-paintings, of water and central-heating systems, of civilisation here on the very edge of the Empire.

In its heyday Carnuntum played host to a summit conference about the future of that Empire. In AD 305 Diocletian made plans to hand over his power and retire peacefully to his palace at Salona (Split) on the Adriatic. But the voluntary transfer of power was as unprecedented in the Roman Empire as in the old Soviet Union. Things crumbled, and Diocletian's successor, Galerius, called him and his fellow-Augustus, Maximian, to a meeting in Carnuntum. Maximian begged Diocletian to come out of retirement and save the Empire. He refused. In Gibbon's words: 'His answer to Maximian is deservedly celebrated. He was solicited by that restless old man to reassume the reins of government and the Imperial purple. He rejected the temptation with a smile of pity, calmly observing that, if he could show Maximian the cabbages which he had planted with his own hands at Salona, he should no longer be urged to relinquish the enjoyment of happiness for the pursuit of power.'

A second piece of philosophy to put beside Aurelius's.

East of Hainburg, where the road overlooked the Danube and the Iron Curtain crossed the *limes*, I saw the first signs that anyone today is seriously concerned to guard the old dividing line. There, beside the road, was parked an Austrian military truck, with a red-and-white flag to emphasise that it was there on business. In the field that led down to the river was a line of little Austrian flags, with a patrol of infantry moving along it. There were more soldiers round a bend in the road, huddled round a machine-gun. Austria, it seemed, was preparing to defend its sovereignty and neutrality.

'Against what?' I asked a garrulous corporal in a bar in Kittsee, the next town down the road. It was the Roma he told me, the gypsies. They kept on slipping across the frontier. It was Austria's duty to stop them. 'Europe' demanded no less; and on a third beer my corporal began to sound like a defender of Vienna against the Turks. Slovakia did not want them. Nor did Austria, nor did Europe. They should stay at home where they belonged.

But the Roma of Slovakia were on the move that autumn just because the Slovaks were saying they did not belong in their shiny new republic. Half an hour later I crossed the border into a Slovakia which was doing no good to its reputation among liberal-minded people in the West. I came with a British passport and a respectable car, and border guards and customs officials were happy to wave me through. But for the first time on this trip I found myself politically uneasy, pondering all the bad news I had heard about Slovakia.

In ten minutes I was in Bratislava, the capital, trying to find first my way to the centre and then a place to park. It bears the marks of so many Central European cities newly emerged from behind the Iron

Curtain. There are the brash bypasses and the bleakly utilitarian blocks of flats of the Communist period. Then there are run-down offices and flats of the interwar years, wearing rather worse than the grandiloquent nineteenth-century theatre and opera house. A hill is crowned by an old fortress and in the heart of the old city, no more than 500 yards across, you find architectural repose among the baroque façades and yellow ochre house-fronts of so many towns in the Danube valley. Old Bratislava is a delightful place, with none of the pretensions of Vienna, Prague or Budapest but with quiet tranquillity compressed into a small urban space. And when, at last, you lay hands on a plan of the city, you find that, balancing the fortress at the western end, is an equally large Tesco superstore at the eastern.

So much for the tourist's first impressions of Bratislava. You can look at it from many other points of view. It is a mere thirty miles down the Danube from Vienna, one of the Habsburgs' second-order cities after Vienna, Prague and Budapest. To the Viennese it was almost a suburb of Vienna, to the Habsburgs a Danube stronghold. But Hungary is only ten miles away and for centuries Hungarians ruled the roost here, making the city their capital and holding Habsburg officials at arm's length. For eighty years until the day before yesterday Bratislava was Czechoslovakia's second city. Now for better or for worse the Slovaks are in charge, and Bratislava is the capital of a newly-minted Slovak Republic.

As such it has to answer for a country from which it is very largely detached. Slovakia straggles away 250 miles eastwards to its border with Ukraine, more Eastern than Central European. The Carpathian mountains run through the length of Slovakia, wild up-country. There is little Danube valley *gemütlichkeit* in Slovakia outside Bratislava.

Between them, that long straggle and those uplands set the rest of Slovakia apart from its capital. Bratislava today is more cosmopolitan by far than the rest of the country, but less cosmopolitan than its neighbours. Its citizens are ill at ease with both. They remember with bitterness their subordination to Czechs, Hungarians and German-speakers in turn. Yet they feel little in common with Slovak peasants. So they brandish a nervous assertiveness about Slovakia's status as a sovereign state, after so many years of second- or third-class citizenship in other people's countries.

The Hungarians came to this part of central Europe 1,100 years ago. They made the Hungarian plain their heartland, but they pushed into the hills that surrounded it. In the north they came to dominate what is today Slovakia, subduing and despising the natives of the hills in the same sort of way as the Normans subdued and despised the Welsh. As the late medieval Hungarian kingdom grew in glory and importance the Slovaks, like other border peoples, became its subjects. So things might have gone on indefinitely had the Turks not destroyed Hungary at the Battle of Mohács in 1526, captured Buda and driven what was left of the Hungarian nobility east into Transylvania, west into Austria and north into the hills of Slovakia. The Hungarians made Pozsony – today's Bratislava – their capital.

While the Slovaks succumbed to the Hungarians, the Czechs were succumbing to the Austrians; and together, the Austrians and Hungarians turned to the business of driving out the Turks. It took them the best part of 200 years, but by the end of the seventeenth century the Habsburgs on the one hand and the Hungarians on the other, in part the Emperor's subjects, in part his allies, in part his rivals, could between them call central Europe their own. Bratislava became a city of the Habsburg Empire, its affairs dominated by Habsburg administrators, Hungarian noblemen and German-speaking merchants. In Bohemia and Moravia the Czechs retained an identity and sense of worth against the worst that the Habsburgs could do to them, but the Slovaks were a simpler, almost entirely peasant people. To the Hungarians they were subjects pure and simple.

The Czechs' and Slovaks' chance came with the collapse of the Austro-Hungarian Empire and the coming of Woodrow Wilson's Fourteen Points. Czech intellectuals sold themselves to the West as the natural democrats of Central Europe. They attached the Slovaks to their coat tails. Czechoslovakia became a state, the Western democracies' blue-eyed boy among the successor states of the Habsburg Empire. It built a society whose democracy shone beside authoritarian Hungary, Poland and Romania. The country became the lynch-pin of the Little Entente, the West's counterweight to Germany in eastern Europe. In the warm glow of enthusiasm for Czechoslovakia, few outsiders noticed that people and things Czech predominated, and that the Slovaks were still second-class citizens.

So things might have remained. But we have seen the Czechs losing the Sudetenland in 1938 and impotent when Hitler marched into Prague a few months later. Bohemia and Moravia became a German protectorate, Slovakia a client state of Germany. The Roman Catholic cleric turned politician who ruled Slovakia in the Second World War got himself a bad name in the West as a rustic fascist and ally of Germany; and even the heroism of the Slovak National Rising in 1944 was insufficient to stake the country's claim to independent nationhood. In 1945 Czechoslovakia was reconstituted, and with the Prague coup in 1948, Slovakia as well as the Czech lands joined the Communist camp.

There both remained for over forty years, cowed and dutiful, their servitude punctuated only by the brief months of hope that followed the Prague Spring of 1968. It was a Slovak, Alexander Dubček, who then led the Czechs and Slovaks – the first Slovak to make a world reputation, if a short-lived one, as a hero of democracy. But when the Soviet tanks entered Prague in August 1968, Dubček was taken away a prisoner to Moscow, and when he was released it was to the obscurity of an administrative job in forestry in Slovakia.

For twenty years Czechs and Slovaks endured the enforced tedium of life in the dullest, most conformist of Moscow's client states. Their politics was no more than the story of a centralised administration seeking to extend its control into every cranny of the country's life: its economy, society, the security of the state, and the doings of individuals. Slovakia was less developed than the Czech lands; central planning called for its development, and in particular for its industrialisation. So Slovakia acquired factories, and particularly arms factories, and at first industrialisation seemed to be bringing its living standards closer to those of the Czechs.

Came 1989; and Czechoslovakia, like all of Central and Eastern Europe, made its escape from Communism. Freedom came, and the trappings of democracy soon afterwards. The country's prospects seemed golden. It lay in the very heart of Europe, with still-remembered democratic traditions, industrial assets which were advanced by Communist standards, and an educated, trained and disciplined work force. Its leaders struck out for a rapid transformation: economic freedom, untrammelled market economy, European Union membership, the works. And once again, it was in the main Czechs, preoccupied with Czech conditions, who made most of the decisions.

The Slovaks came sullenly behind. They had few of the advantages on which the Czechs wanted to capitalise, and in this new world their inheritance of heavy industry was more liability than asset. They demanded that the country be renamed Czecho-Slovakia, but the new name brought them no benefit of substance. The Slovaks went on grumbling, and talking about the advantages which Slovak independence, full nationhood, would bring them. In 1992 a populist politician came to power calling for a break with Prague. The Czechs took the Slovaks at their word and pushed through the divorce for which they had called. It took place on 1 January 1993 and left the Czechs free to go their own way, along with the Poles and Hungarians the West's favoured Central Europeans. Slovakia was left behind, at the mercy of corrupt and nationalist post-Communist leaders.

For several years Slovakia fell further behind. As Poles, Hungarians and Czechs advanced towards NATO and European Union member-ship, Slovakia was held to be lacking in democracy, transparency, accountability. The Slovaks were damned for discrimination against the country's large Hungarian minority and against the gypsies. Prime Min-ister and President quarrelled, and what remained of the old secret police got involved in insalubrious political manoeuvrings. The country seemed to be going the way of the Yugoslavs.

Then in 1999 the Slovaks seemed to pull themselves together. Out went a bad old lot at the May elections and in came shining new faces, promising honesty, transparency and accountability. There was talk of NATO membership and of joining the Czech Republic and Hungary in the favoured queue for the European Union. Today the Slovaks' prospects still look less rosy than the Czechs', Hungarians' and Slovenes', but slowly they are coming in from the cold.

From Bratislava I turned back into Austria, before setting off on my way to Hungary. I could have gone there direct from Slovakia, revisit-ing the best omelette-maker in the world, but for old time's sake I wanted to enter Hungary where I encountered it first, on a blazing hot summer's day in 1958, and where I left it, having twice lived for three years in Budapest, on a blazing hot day twenty-eight years later.

The main road from Vienna to Budapest crosses the frontier at Hegyeshalom. Today it is a motorway on both sides of the border, and the frontier control point is as busy as any you will find, one of the prin-cipal places where traffic from the east, in this case Hungary, the Balkans and Turkey, enters the European Union. It was very different when I first approached it in 1958. Then we drove out of Austria in a car that was overloaded with family, with babies' bits and pieces and with our own perturbation. We were going to a Hungary which two years earlier had been torn by revolution and war and in which, just a month ago, the revolutionary leader Imre Nagy had been executed. We were taking with us a girl of two and a boy of one, as well as our own hopes and fears about this unfamiliar business of diplomacy. There was a real feeling of tension, as much in the air at the Austrian check point as in our car. So when the Austrian frontier policeman (his pistol, we

noticed, wrapped against the elements in grease-proof paper) wished us
'*Auf Wiedersehen*' we whispered '*Bald*' in unison in reply.

The arrangements on the Hungarian side of the frontier were of a
different order of seriousness. As we drove down the empty road
towards the border itself we saw watchtowers across the fields. The
checkpoint lay at the end of an avenue of barbed wire and the guards
there had sub-machine guns slung across their chests. The system
processed us with agonising slowness, if with the propriety due to even
a brand-new diplomat. Then we drove away into Hungary down an
unkempt main road that no repairer had touched since the 1930s.

The first serious place we came to was a straggle of a big village
called Mosonmagyarovár. The name had been one to conjure with two
years earlier, when Western journalists driving to Budapest on the first
day of the revolution encountered there the broken remains of a massacre by the security police. We drove into the place expectantly, even
nervously, and found nothing but the long dusty straggle of houses you
encounter in villages and small country towns all over Hungary. (Forty
years later I found a busy, substantial town, all trace of my early memories submerged in concrete.) We needed something for the children to
drink and went looking for bottled water in the only shop we could discover, quite fruitlessly. Half an hour later, in a more substantial town
on the road to Budapest, we stopped at a traffic light. A modulated
English voice asked whether we needed help; and the Military Attaché
from the Legation, returning from a shopping trip to Vienna, shep-
herded us into the city. At a level-crossing somewhere just outside
Budapest, children came begging, till a man bristling with respectable
indignation sent them away.

So much for first impressions of Hungary. I will come back later to
describe what more mature reflection made of it, but first let us look at
the context, ancient and modern, of the dividing line we had crossed at
Hegyeshalom. It was one of Europe's more significant divides long
before the Iron Curtain.

We have seen that the Roman *limes* followed the Danube from
southern Germany to the Iron Gates in Romania and that western
Hungary fell within the Roman province of Pannonia. It was the civilian amber route from Carnuntum to Rome which ran along the present
Austro-Hungarian border, not the military *limes*. But in the ninth and
early tenth centuries the Magyar tribes came storming up to it from the
east. They raided across it, on occasions deep into southern Germany,
but for 600 years this area formed the fluctuating divide between a

growing Hungarian kingdom and the Holy Roman Empire of the German Nation. Then, in the sixteenth century, came the Ottoman Turks, surging out of the Balkans and into the Hungarian plain, pushing the Hungarians east into Transylvania and north into Slovakia. In the west the Hungarians were forced back towards the lands of the Habsburgs, and for nearly 200 years Hungarians and Turks fought a frontier war of cavalry raids and sieges and guerrilla actions up against the line of this century's Iron Curtain.

In the end, the tide of Ottoman expansion was turned at the last siege of Vienna. Defeated there, the Turks ebbed away, losing Buda in 1686, and as they went an uneasy coalition of Habsburg emperors and Hungarian magnates came to rule Hungary. Throughout the eighteenth century Hungarian agriculture flourished on land the Turks had left fallow for a century, and on the back of agriculture nineteenth-century Hungary grew rich. It was linked in a relationship with the Habsburgs composed in equal parts of circumspect love and extravagant hatred, and as long as the Habsburgs lasted, this was an internal frontier within their Empire. Yet it was a real one for all that; and east of the dividing line the Habsburgs ruled as Kings of Hungary rather than Austrian Emperors.

In 1848–49 the Hungarians fought a bitter and in the end a losing war of independence against the Habsburgs, striking twice across the border in an attempt to seize Vienna. Defeated, Hungary went under the Habsburg yoke. It stayed there until 1867 when Franz Josef, defeated by the Prussians, needed to make allies of his fractious Hungarian subjects. So he set them free and made them full partners in the Austro-Hungarian Empire. From 1867 till the fall of the Empire, the Hungarians joined the Austrians in lording it over the other nationalities, pursuing their partnership with Austria with the particular egotism which historians see as the mark stamped deep into Hungarian policy and the Hungarian psyche.

In 1918 the Empire fell, and Hungary paid the price for the enmities it had made throughout Central Europe. At the Treaty of Trianon in 1920 the Hungarians lost two thirds of the old 'Kingdom of St Stephen', great areas presented by the Allies to Hungary's lowly neighbours in Romania, Yugoslavia and Czechoslovakia. Hungary even lost a province to Austria, the Burgenland, so at most points today's Austro-Hungarian border lies significantly to the east of the old divide.

The hope of recovering all those lost territories tempted the Hungarians into a fatal, half-hearted alliance with the Germans; and indeed in the Second World War they recovered some of them from Czechoslovakia, Romania and Yugoslavia. But when they drove the last Germans and their Hungarian fascist allies across the border into Austria on 4 April 1945, the conquering Russians saw Hungary as Hitler's last ally; and all Hungary's neighbours saw it as Hitler's jackal. Like most of its neighbours it was subjected to Soviet occupation at once and to Communist rule in due course; and under them it remained, the convulsion of the 1956 Revolution apart, for forty years.

You can find places and things all over the Burgenland and western Hungary to illustrate this history of the borderlands. A consequence of the Ottoman occupation of the heart of Hungary is that most of its relatively few medieval and Renaissance relics lie on its very edges. So if you visit Hungary looking for Romanesque country churches you must go to Ják, right on the border with Austria, or Velemér, which is almost in Slovenia. Sopron is a fine old Hungarian town, but it stands surrounded by Austrian territory. When the Burgenland was ceded to Austria the people of Sopron voted to stay with Hungary. The Hungarians praise their loyalty – recorded on a tablet which calls Sopron the most loyal of cities. Others will tell you that a Hungarian soldier was billeted in every house to make sure the occupants voted for union with Hungary. And there must have been citizens who, throughout the years of the Cold War, cursed the way their grandparents chose to cast or were made to cast their votes. Now Sopron seems a happy place, its shopkeepers enriched by Austrians who come to buy their groceries here and its dentists happily serving all the tourists who come in search of crowns, fillings and extractions at half their cost within the European Union.

Köszeg is another old town right on the Austrian border, and this is one of the places that withstood a long Turkish siege, with little assistance from the Habsburgs whose lands it was defending. Sárvár, twenty miles deeper into Hungary, has a Renaissance fortress, and a museum within it tells a story even better calculated to feed the Hungarians' self-pity, for in it they are more actively betrayed by the Habsburgs to the Turks. Miklós Zrinyi, a Hungarian seventeenth-century general, fought brilliant campaigns to keep the Turks at bay here on the border of Austria, only to see his victories negated in a craven treaty with the Turks. So he, and the lord of Sárvár, rose against the Habsburgs, and in the museum you can see them standing before their judges with the executioner in waiting. It is the sort of story that appeals to the Hungarian image of themselves as the eternal victims of history.

I drove down the border to remind myself of all these places, and encountered the importance in Central Europe of the feasts of All Saints and All Souls. In every village cemetery there were groups of mourners, flowers on every grave, and candles flickering between them in the dusk. In Velemér I found a solitary old man kneeling at his wife's grave, but in the bigger villages there was something approaching a party atmosphere, with the quick sharing a drink together before happily turning to their duties to the dead. I was struck by the contrast with the protocol at Central European funerals, where every mourner is expected to show the agony of his grief and where even a quick smile of recognition of a neighbour is taken as an offence to the memory of the dead.

In the same places I found more political commemorations that would have got their authors into gaol when I lived in Hungary. For the villages have sprouted modest monuments to the 1956 revolution, each resplendent in the national colours. And these seem to have encouraged also a proliferation of monuments to the war against the Austrians in 1848–49, assertions of national pride that would, I suspect, have been frowned upon in the Communist years, not least because the Austrians owed victory in that war to a Russian intervention.

On the road that leads from Sopron deeper into Hungary lie two of Hungary's finest estates. One is the Hungarian home of the richest of all the magnates, the Esterházys. Esterháza is a yellow and white palace of a place which attracts awed Hungarian schoolchildren and Austrian visitors in equal proportions. Though the palace has been restored the job was botched and Esterháza again has an air of having seen better days. But though you can find grander Esterházy palaces in Austria, Esterháza has an importance of its own as a symbol of the wealth of the sort of Hungarian magnates who told a visiting Englishman that they had as many shepherds as he had sheep. Nagycenk is a more modest place, big manor house rather than palace, but it tells a more moving story. For this was the home of Count István Széchenyi, who in the early nineteenth century set about modernising his homeland, pretty well single-handed. Széchenyi bridged the Danube and opened it up to shipping. He preached modern agriculture and the value of railways and the importance of using credit constructively. Concern at the war with Austria in 1848–49 brought his mind to breaking point and in 1860 he shot himself, like Zrinyi and the lord of Sárvár a Hungarian who found himself trapped between his homeland and the Habsburgs.

When we were leaving Hungary an artist we had befriended wanted to give us a present. He offered us a choice of two bronze bas-reliefs.

One depicted a pastoral scene, of man with horse and moon, the other, more moving by far, showed Jews being driven through a western Hungarian town in the winter of 1944, on their way to extinction. We swallowed hard and chose the less demanding gift. Now, when I went back rediscovering Hungary, I went looking for the prison at Sopron Köhida where some of these Jews, and some of Hungary's few anti-Nazi resistance fighters, died in the last desperate months of the war. It is a functioning prison still, with high blank walls and razor wire and guards with guns. There are plaques on the walls, to the victims of fascism who died here in 1944–45 and to the 'several thousand' Hungarians who were imprisoned here by Soviet occupiers between 1945 and 1948. But there are advertisements on the walls too, in good free-market style. When I was there they were promoting life insurance and condoms to repel Aids.

On that same journey I discovered some new aspects of western Hungary. Just inside the country from Austria is a gleaming new factory labelled 'Opel of Hungary'. Further up the road I passed what was left of an agricultural estate. There at the end of an avenue of trees was the old manor house, dilapidated and ruinous now, and there were the farm labourers' barracks, which in the bad old days of the estates offered human beings less comfort than carriage horses found in the stables. Now I could see curtains at the windows and three satellite dishes along the eaves. At last the people were living better than the horses.

I went looking for a mechanic to fix the damage done to my car in Budejovice. By the roadside I found a workshop which, on the face of it, had all the glitz of Western business. They went to work on my car and I wandered off in search of a toilet. Behind the scenes I found myself in living quarters more squalid than anything I have seen in the Third World, an abomination of bachelor desolation.

A few miles further on I stopped for petrol and saw that they were selling toys for doting fathers to take home to Laci. The biggest attraction on the shelves was an American army truck in IFOR Bosnia lettering, with the name of the NATO base in Hungary, Kaposvár, blazoned on its side. When I left in 1986, I reminded myself, Hungary was a member of the Warsaw Pact in good standing, a country that even smelt of Eastern Europe, with that mixture of dust and diesel exhaust and doubtful drains. Now it is a pillar of NATO and as capitalist as they come, selling replicas of NATO trucks for little Hungarians to play with. The Iron Curtain is gone, and with it so many of the presumptions that made Hungary Eastern European. But as I paid for my petrol

and bought a bar of chocolate and went back to the car, I caught
another whiff of that smell I remembered so clearly.

We stayed in Budapest for three years on our first diplomatic posting,
years at the turn of the 1950s and 1960s which showed just how harsh
life behind the Iron Curtain could be. There were Russian garrisons all
over the country. The Communist regime pumped out a stream of propaganda about popular contentment that nobody believed; for the
place then was dirt-poor, the people shit-scared. Rumours ran around
Budapest: so-and-so had been arrested for his part in the Revolution,
tried, imprisoned or executed. It was rumoured then and has been
established as fact now that the regime was executing young men on
their eighteenth birthday, when they reached the age of legal responsibility. A campaign began to drive the peasants back into co-operative
farms which they had abandoned as soon as they got the chance two
years earlier. Every so often we drove to Vienna to stock up with supplies and breathe free air, and each time we crossed the border we saw
more of the complexity with which the Hungarian side was defended.
We came to take the watchtowers, the wire and the border controls for
granted; but to encounter, twenty kilometres inside Hungary, a pair of
frontier guards manning a machine gun in the ditch beside the road was
a reminder of just how lethal this border could be for those who, unlike
us, had no right to be there. And even we were not allowed to travel
freely near the border if we were not on our way to Austria. The contrast between the tension and terror in Hungary and the casual ways of
neutral Austria in those years was a stark instruction on the differences
which the Iron Curtain had driven through the heart of Europe.

For us there were lighter moments along that border, even in the late
1950s. Once we went out of Hungary not on the road to Vienna but at
the other end of its border with Austria, at a place called Rábafüzes.
The frontier station there was even simpler than at Hegyeshalom, but
the same sense of siege brooded over it: watchtower, barbed wire,
ploughed strip, bored young men with guns. While we waited for our
passports we saw that the guards had penned a young faun in a hand-
kerchief of a field behind the frontier post. It was shut in by barbed wire
but it was looking for greener grass in pastures new, poking its head
under the barbed wire. Just beyond the wire was one of the little pen-
nants in the national red and white with which the Austrians staked out
their sovereignty. It would have made a splendid propaganda photograph if we had had the nerve to take it. Instead we contented ourselves

with composing a sentence in broken Hungarian: 'That animal is as free as the Hungarian people'; but we had the sense not to use it when the guard wordlessly gave us back our passports. (I rediscovered that crossing point recently. It was as unrecognisable as Hegyeshalom, with a smart new customs post manned only by a young girl idly glancing at passports. She had an enormous pistol strapped to her broad backside, but as I handed her my passport I saw that she had a child's jigsaw puzzle of Donald Duck on the shelf in front of her. Two or three pieces seemed to have defeated her, and I stretched over and slipped one into place. *'Köszönöm szépen'* she said, without looking up: 'thank you very much', with all the commitment of a child trained to say thank you before she gets down to play.)

Whenever we crossed the frontier, we did so as privileged foreigners. Things were different for Hungarians. An old Hungarian said to me recently: 'To talk about taking a trip to the moon today is more realistic – I mean it, literally more realistic – than the thought of our taking a trip to Vienna in the early 1950s.' Once I went shopping for something or other in the Bond Street of Budapest. I turned down the only thing the shopkeeper had to offer me, saying 'I'll get it in Vienna next time I go.' To this day I remember with shame the expression my carelessness painted on his face.

We saw the difference between diplomats and Hungarians one day when we drove a Hungarian friend to Vienna and into emigration. Mária worked as a translator in the British Legation. For a variety of reasons – wrong class background, sons who had fled in 1956, refusal to report on the Legation's doings – she got across the secret policeman to whom she had to report for a regular interrogation. He could have clapped her in gaol. But she was sick and getting sicker, and working as she did in a Western legation she had at least a modicum of protection. The interrogator and his masters decided they would be better off without her. They told her she could leave the country, and they would drive her into an asylum if she stayed; so, innumerable documents and rubber-stamps later, she drove away with us down the road to Vienna. At the frontier the passport people and the customs people turned out her pockets and her handbag and all that was left of her possessions in a crumbling suitcase. They asked her what she, a Hungarian citizen, was doing in the car of her country's capitalist enemies. They warned her that she could never come back. Finally they let her go and we drove her to Vienna to meet her sons. (Forty years later, well into her nineties, she went back every year to Hungary, to take a cure for her rheumatism, make a retreat in a convent, and drink coffee and play bridge with the handful of her friends who still lived in Budapest.)

Mária too was privileged in her own way. Those who tried to get out of Hungary illegally were not. For most of the Cold War it was a potentially fatal business to try to flee the country. The Hungarian frontier guards did not keep their guns wrapped in grease-proof paper. Even in the early 1980s, when I was back in Hungary as ambassador, by which time Hungary was supposed to have become an easygoing place, the BBC reported that an Austrian couple out boating on the Neusiedlersee, the lake that straddles the border, had drifted into Hungarian waters and been shot dead by the frontier guards. I asked our cook about it, for in an earlier incarnation he had done his national service with the frontier troops. Oh, yes, he told me, there were regular shootings on the border. But he had escaped patrolling when he volunteered for the cook house. There he learned the finer points of *gulyás* and *pörkölt* and now he found himself in our kitchen, cooking them for Princess Margaret and Margaret Thatcher.

There were, nevertheless, two great illegal migrations across the border into Austria: in the late 1940s, as the Communists tightened their grip in Hungary, and in the autumn of 1956, when the revolution went down to defeat and 200,000 people took the chance to get away to freedom. Pál Nagy went with the first wave, Tom and Kati Zombory with the second.

Nagy started his journey from Budapest in style, on the Arlberg express. His cover story was that he had family business to settle in western Hungary. So far, so good. He changed trains safely, then went into hiding with friends. That night he boarded a third train that would take him close to the border. He found himself in the suspicious company of frontier guards going back to duty, and matters were made worse when two friends joined him, dressed in their best shooting clothes and all too obviously prepared for a yuppy yomp to freedom. But Nagy had paid a guide, who was keeping an eye on him from the next compartment. They made a dash for it, jumped from the slow-moving train and escaped into the darkness. Four hours hard walking followed; fear at the frontier; a dash past heaps of barbed wire not yet put in place; and safety in Austria.

The Zomborys fled in 1956, after the defeat of the Hungarian revolution, when half the young people of Budapest were on their way to the West. They also took a train, intending to cross the frontier near a place called Levél, which in Hungarian means 'letter'. A cousin had gone before them and she sent them a message on Radio Free Europe from Vienna: *Levél megy* – which to the world meant 'letter on its way' but to them meant the Levél route to freedom was still open. But the railways were erratic in those tumultuous days, and their train dumped them miles away further south, ten miles from the border. In the station yard men were waiting: 'Can I help you?' They could have been villains, or agents of the secret police, or honest men who for a price could show them the way to freedom. Tom and Kati gambled, successfully. Their guide took them on a six-hour route march across frozen plough and sent them on their way across a canal that forms the border with Austria. In the darkness a flapping flag told them they were safe and they struggled on for five more miles towards a single light in the darkness. Behind them they saw flares and heard shots. In a sleeping village they found a sign in Hungarian: 'Refugees this way'. It led them to an empty schoolroom strewn with hay. There they slept. The following morning a clerk registered their arrival and a local farmer gave them the fare to Vienna.

From then on, the Zomborys' story reads like a fairy tale. Vienna was packed with refugees. Austrians gave them money, took them in, gave them clothes. The Zomborys went to the British Embassy, where the British Council representative gave them tea, sausage rolls, cake and sympathy. Within a week of their arrival they married – the first refugee couple to do so, with the man from the British Council giving Kati away. Within two weeks they were in Britain. When, as they told me their story, I carelessly remarked that nowadays they would be rejected as economic emigrants they were understandably offended; but the fact remains that we do not manage today to give refugees the welcome which poor post-war Britain extended so unquestioningly forty-four years ago.

These are two stories among 200,000. Nagy ended his days in South Africa, a gentleman farmer doing much what he had wanted to do in Hungary. The Zomborys made good lives in England. Yet both stories could so easily have ended differently. Nagy might have found the barbed wire fence completed, the guards in wait, a bullet in his back. The Zomborys' guide could have betrayed them to years in gaol. Or they might have turned back, as the hero does in the film *Daniel Takes a Train*. Daniel and his friends, like the Zomborys, take a train out of Budapest in November 1956. When the moment of decision comes some go on, to danger and freedom. Daniel hesitates, turns back. The film, made in Communist Hungary in the early 1980s, was the subtlest kind of propaganda, suggesting that for the refugees of 1956 there were choices, and the choice to go back was as valid and attractive as the choice to go on. It did not seem like that to the Zomborys in 1956, and they had not changed their minds when, in 1999, they told me their story.

Nearly fifty years after Pál Nagy, more than forty after the Zomborys, I went looking for traces of the two exoduses. I looked in western Hungary and, more particularly, in the quiet corner of Austria in which most of the refugees arrived. It is the Seewinkel, the flat stretch of fields and marshes that juts into Hungary on the eastern side of the Neusiedlersee, infinitely remote from Vienna only forty miles away. I went to Andau, where hundreds of refugees inched across a broken bridge across the canal that follows the border. It is a nondescript little town which has forgotten that once upon a time people wrote books about what happened there. But a back road which leads the six miles to the bridge has been christened 'Freedom's Way'. Artists from all over Europe have punctuated it at regular intervals with bits of modern sculpture made from trees and boulders and *choses trouvées,* which are worthy if unconvincing tributes to freedom and human rights for all. At the end of it, I found the bridge – or rather a reconstruction of the bridge, in brand-new timber. Beside it was a viewing tower, for those who wanted to peer into Hungary. In front of it was a little notice marking the border five yards short of the bridge, and threatening criminal prosecution for those who crossed it.

That autumn Western Europe was full of the dangers of East European gypsies fleeing into the European Union from persecution at home. On the previous day I had seen those Austrian troops watching the Danube near the Slovak frontier, and everywhere I had been along the frontier there had been patrols – men on foot, in jeeps, in frail bivouac tents – out to stem the flow. Two men in uniform were moving away along the canal as I arrived at the bridge at Andau. I studied their backs; the minatory notice; and the satisfaction to be had from setting foot on the famous bridge. It was getting dark, they were lost already in the darkness, it would be absolutely safe to go over into Hungary. Timidity held me back, a timidity which even in safe little England blushes when it sees a policeman. And as timidity defeated temptation I saw, ten yards away in a ditch, two other Austrian gendarmes, who must have been watching me in the November dusk. It was nothing more respectable than craven fear that saved me from exposure as the ex-ambassador who was arrested for illegally crossing from Austria into Hungary over the bridge at Andau.

We have looked at western Hungary and at some episodes from Hungarian history. Let us now consider the Hungarians themselves.

Objective Hungarians – and they do not grow on trees – will tell you that they are a brilliant, bumptious and unique people. Outsiders, who in their turn find it difficult to be objective about the Hungarians, tend to agree with them. They love them or loathe them, and those of us who know them well sometimes entertain both sentiments at the same time. Hungary and the Hungarian Diaspora have produced far more than their share of brilliant individuals. Go to a party in Budapest and you will find that Hungarians, particularly male Hungarians, more often than not are bumptiously aware of their own merits. 'With a Hungarian for a friend you don't need an enemy' caricatures but encapsulates an aggressive lack of love of fellow-Hungarians and the nation's neighbours. And listen to spoken Hungarian or glance at a Hungarian newspaper to be convinced that these are a unique people with a unique language, their only remote European relatives the distant Estonians and Finns.

You could as easily make a different list of Hungarian characteristics. Hungarians strike me as extraordinarily personable, flexible and quick off the mark. There is charm about them, and striking physical and moral beauty. Their loneliness in Europe makes them exceptionally self-aware, which makes them yet more personable; but self-awareness makes them selfish. Hungary's policy in the late nineteenth century provoked a usually mild-mannered observer, Edward Crankshaw, to write '... it is hard to discover in the history of modern Europe any nation which has exhibited such sustained and unmitigated egocentricity as the Hungarian nation, any nation which at no time in a century of rapid change ever showed the faintest, the most embryonic, flicker of interest in anything at all but its own immediately selfish interests.'

The dying East German regime in 1989 would have said amen to that, as it watched the Hungarian government open its frontier to Austria and release that flood of East Germans to the West which brought down Communism in Europe. Yet the comparison brings us to the inescapable point that the Hungarians did the right thing in 1989, for Europe and their own interests. If, yet again, the Hungarians were last into the revolving door and first out of it, they opened the way for others to follow them.

Criticism such as Crankshaw's easily provokes the Hungarians to self-pity. They think they are unusually badly done by. Geography exposed them to the ravages of Mongols, Tartars, Turks, Habsburgs

and Russians. When the Turks were gone they were left as junior partners of the Habsburgs, who could never persuade Vienna to take their
preoccupations as seriously as they took them themselves. Geography
surrounded them with people, whom on the whole they despise, with
historical grudges against them. And these despised Romanians, Slovaks and South Slavs came out on top in 1920, when the Treaty of Trianon gave them so much of historic Hungary, leaving Hungarian
minorities languishing under alien rule and a truncated Hungary
bewailing its misfortune. Resentment of Trianon led the Hungarians
into Hitler's arms, which was followed by Soviet occupation and then
by failed revolution.

But after the tragedy of 1956, the Hungarians' famed agility once
again stood them in good stead. They found their way relatively quickly
out of the worst excesses of Communism. They escaped from it altogether in 1989, back into the Western company in which they believe
they naturally belong but from which malign fate has too often separated them. Now they are members of NATO and on their way to
membership of the European Union. No lasting grounds for self-pity
here (though the day they joined NATO it went to war with the Serbs in
their very back yard).

The Hungarian revolution of 1956 calls for reflection. For thirty
years after it, no one told the exact truth about it, at least in public. The
Communist regime wanted the Hungarian people to forget about their
moment of glory when they tackled Soviet tanks; for them, as for
Moscow, Budapest 1956 was a neuralgic memory. But Hungarians in
the West had an interest in painting a highly-coloured picture of what
had happened in their homeland that autumn. Memoirs were slanted
while the archives remained closed.

Yet the revolution itself needs no embroidery and deserves to be
remembered. It was the greatest event in Hungary's twentieth-century
history, and the country rightly takes 23 October, the date on which it
began, as its national day. In 1956 the Hungarians abandoned their
usual caution and went for broke. For once, they used to say, they
behaved like the gallant and impractical Poles. In this Hungarian version, the Poles that year behaved like Czechs and the Czechs, as usual,
behaved like pigs.

For a fortnight, Hungarian freedom fighters fought gallantly against
Soviet tanks. The Hungarian people succoured them, fed them and
nursed them. A few Communist apparatchiks and secret policemen
apart, no Hungarians went over to the enemy. Between the Second

World War and the wars in Yugoslavia, this was the only European war between sovereign states in half a century.

Once the revolution was defeated, all concerned breathed 'Never again'. The Hungarian people wanted no more bloodshed; the regime no challenge to its authority; Moscow no more damaging images of its tanks in action in city streets. The Hungarians had had their moment of glory; now they reverted to their more traditional caution. That caution played its part in bringing them by careful degrees to where they stand today, eighty per cent reintegrated into the European body politic, a Central European country latching itself onto the West, distancing itself as best it can from Balkan neighbours. Still Hungarians see themselves as unique in Europe, as the victims of history and as the worthy objects of their own self-pity. And to the rest of the world they remain the agile, intelligent, personable and often impossible people their history has made them.

My next-door neighbour in England is back from four happy years in Hungary. I told her that I was trying to describe my time there for a book about the Iron Curtain. 'I never knew the Iron Curtain,' she said, and for a moment she took my breath away; for me life in Hungary and life behind the Iron Curtain had always been synonymous. But even nostalgic old men must keep up with the times. In today's Hungary the Iron Curtain is history.

As we talked, I realised that there were many other ways, too, in which Nina and I saw Hungary differently. Mine was the macro view, based on history, politics, society and diplomacy, leading me to broad and questionably-founded generalisation. Her preoccupations had been very different: children in Hungarian schools, giving tea to Hungarian school friends, taking children to Hungarian music-teachers – a micro view. I asked her to put down her impressions, give me a view of Hungary from the school gates. This is the essence of what she wrote.

The school population – teachers, children, parents – was a far cry from the Westernised Hungarians whom most foreign diplomats and businessmen naturally meet. Few of them spoke English; few of them wanted to learn it; all rejected Russian; for them Hungarian was good enough and always would be. They took pride in their language, as an academic discipline, a gloriously ingenious linguistic jigsaw puzzle and an essential part of national identity. At school meetings the teachers begged the parents to insist on its correct and punctilious use and on resisting foreign influences. This kind of concern, together with the formality of the Hungarian language (which was resisting democratic

slovenliness as effectively as it had resisted Communist levelling),
meant that Hungary, Nina thought, was making a better fist than its
Western neighbours at holding unwelcome outside cultural and social
influences at bay.

Most of the time, Nina found that she was the only parent in the
gathering at the school gates waiting for Laci and his little sister Eva.
Hungarians in their thirties and forties were too busy holding down
multiple jobs to make ends meet. Grandparents came instead, when
they could; and when they couldn't, eight-year-old Laci took five-year-
old Eva home himself, right across Budapest with three changes of bus
if necessary. Mum's Volvo-run was not an option in middle- and working-class Hungary.

All this meant that children were self-reliant to a degree no longer
imaginable in the West. By and large they were serious, too, about their
work. By Christmas the first grade were reading fluently and writing in
a neat cursive hand, by the end of the year they knew their tables up to
10. By Western standards the curriculum was narrow but rigorous, and
teachers put their back into their work, for pitifully small financial
reward. As a result, by the end of elementary school everyone had mas-
tered basic literacy and numeracy.

Nina found all this impressive – as one might have found English
education two generations ago. She was impressed too by the efforts
the school made to help a rare gypsy child. She was gifted, but her
father was a caricature of everything that underpins eastern European
prejudice against the Roma. He seemed determined to frustrate the
school's attempts to help Ilona keep up, as if education would threaten
her gypsy identity. Finally Ilona went elsewhere, and her teachers
grieved for her.

But musical education was something else. Music gives Hungary's
gypsies a rare opportunity to break out of the mean framework of their
lives, and gypsy families put everything into supporting musically gifted
children. Nina found her own violinist children competing with gypsy
children for approval and applause, and the gypsy parents treated her
and her children almost as if they were competitors for their family
business.

All this is a far cry from the broader themes of other parts of this
book. It is everyday stuff, the stuff of ordinary lives. There is nothing
heroic here to put beside Armageddon and death on the wire, or beside
the Habsburgs' tragedies and the future of Trieste. But it tells us something about the values of ordinary life today on the other side of what

was once the Iron Curtain, and it demonstrates that now Europe is undivided there is quite as much that its Western half can learn from the East as East from West.

Nina's memories reminded me of a different group of Hungarians who took their language seriously. In both the periods in which we lived in Hungary, the poets, writers and translators occupied positions in society more central by far than their confrères in the West. In Central Europe, the literati mattered.

In some ways, they always have. The nations of Central Europe have faced hard struggles to survive or to emerge from under alien rule. Their languages have played an essential role in that struggle. The writers and poets who used them had a political as well as a cultural importance. Mickiewicz in Poland, Petöfi in Hungary, Czeslaw Milosz in Lithuania are all figures of literary and political, and hence of heroic, stature. Their words gave expression to nationality, and so helped build nations.

Each of them wrote in languages with little resonance outside their own countries. They needed translators to convey their message to the world. At the same time, the intellectuals of Central and Eastern Europe wanted to bathe in Western culture as well. They cried out for translations of the works of Shakespeare, Dante, Voltaire and the rest. So Hungarians, and no doubt Poles and Romanians as well, will tell you that Shakespeare reads even better in their language than in English.

Translators in Central Europe share in some of the veneration accorded to poets and prose writers. Many writers use translations to supplement what they earn from their own writing. In the hard years of the 1950s and 1960s others, such as Hungary's first democratic president after 1989, Árpád Göncz, turned to translation when their political sins brought a ban on the publication of their original work. Then and now they form an integral part of the literary world.

When we first lived in Hungary, it was this literary world which stood out most distinctly for Hungarian values, in mute protest at the socialist internationalism which the country's rulers wished upon their people. Some of its members lived dangerous lives, and they made the danger worse by their appetite for things Western. So even in the worst of times they took risks to keep in touch with Western diplomats, accept invitations, lay their hands on Western books.

Faced with the literary giants among them, the authorities shared something of the nation's awe and admiration. So poets like Gyula

Illyés and novelists like Géza Ottlik created limited freedoms for themselves, and used those freedoms to pick away, almost imperceptibly, at the bonds that had been fastened on Hungary. Boldly daring, they used to come to our house, and talk about Hungarian literature and art; and wrapped up in the parcel with the poems, heroic novels and short stories were fragments of Hungarian politics too. And when the British Council invited them, they sought, and sometimes won, permission to go to Britain and see its cultural world.

By the time we went back to Hungary in the 1980s, everything there was easier. The cultural figures went back and forth more or less at their pleasure, doing a term at an American university here, attending a literary conference in Italy there. By now, politics was beginning to express itself without the old literary camouflage; dissenters, like the man in the speeding Trabi, were speaking almost openly of their political aspirations.

Some of the political zing had vanished from literary and cultural gatherings. What had once been whispered among friends now appeared, suitably modulated, in the literary magazines. Still the writers wrote, the poets sang their song, the translators filled the bookshops with the work of Western writers. Still the state subsidised this cultural world, accepting that in some ways it reflected the aspirations of ordinary Hungarians who did not open books from one year's end to the next. We saw the way things worked through the lives of many of our friends: materially cramped, living in two-roomed flats on the scrapings of a literary income, but free of the whole world's ideas, and confident that they spoke for the true Hungary.

1989 brought them real freedom to replace the limited, cloistered freedom their reputations had won them under the Communists. It also brought them sudden bruising acquaintance with the costs of capitalist freedoms. Now ordinary readers were free to back their preferences, and more often than not they chose the easily accessible, the meretricious. The people we had known winced at the changes that came over the Budapest bookshops. At the same time their state subsidies vanished and they were thrown back on what they could earn. The value of their state pensions diminished with inflation. Beside the new rich their status, once unchallenged, dwindled. They worked harder to scrape a living.

They continued to read widely, and their judgement and taste, as much for foreign as for Hungarian work, remained sound. To talk to Hungarian writers was to be reminded of how much valuable new work in English was passing one by, and of how much time one was giving to things that were less than first-rate. I gave one of Patrick O'Brian's novels to one of them, suggesting he consider translating it, telling myself that the language of topgallant staysails in a force nine gale would take some rendering into Hungarian. A week later he returned it, saying thanks but no thanks; and he explained himself not with the problem of interesting Hungarian readers in Nelson's navy but with a wonderfully shrewd analysis of O'Brian's deficiencies in such particulars as plotting, literary pace and character development.

As long as Hungarians worship their language, Hungary's writers will be people of national importance. I see no sign of them ceasing to be men and women of taste, judgement and literary ability, bravura performers in their own right as well as mainstays of their country. But in a free Hungary their role is going to be less central, less political, in the end less zestful than it was under Communism. By and large, the writers of Central Europe enjoyed the curse of living in interesting times. Now they have to come to terms with the curse of living in easier ones.

7

From the Alps to the Adriatic

Szentgotthárd is the last place we visit in Hungary. It is the country's westernmost town, hemmed in between Austria to the north and west, Slovenia to the south. It is a pleasantly undistinguished kind of place, but historians remember it for a great Habsburg victory over the Turks in 1664, which you can see depicted in gruesome detail in frescoes in the church in Peace Square. The man who drove the Turks to their deaths in the River Rába was the Habsburg general Montecuccoli, and just over the border, in Heiligenkreuz, the army of Austria, that modestly neutral republic, has a barracks improbably named after that victorious imperial general. You can fill an interesting half hour with all this, but our immediate problem in Szentgotthárd is to decide where the Iron Curtain went from here.

For Winston Churchill it started not in Lübeck but in Stettin. But when he spoke at Fulton in 1946 he was clear that it ended at Trieste, dividing Austria and Italy from Tito's Yugoslavia. Following him, we are going to go westward from Szentgotthárd, along Austria's southern border westwards all the way to Italy, before we turn south through the mountains that lead to the Adriatic.

But Churchill was speaking immediately after the war. In 1949 Tito broke with Moscow. Yugoslavia became officially 'non-aligned', one of the leaders of the association of Third World states that cursed East and West with splendid impartiality. Yugoslavia remained an authoritarian society, a police state. But the West smiled on its separation from the Soviet camp; its economy blossomed; its lakes, mountains and Adriatic coast welcomed Western holidaymakers. The old tensions along its borders with Italy and Austria were relaxed. Belgrade came in from the cold, and Westerners began to feel that the Iron Curtain ran not where Churchill had placed it but along Yugoslavia's frontiers with a Hungary prostrate after the 1956 revolution, with Ceausescu's Romania and a still-Stalinist Bulgaria, and with Maoist Albania.

On that reading we should today be making our way along Hungary's frontier with Slovenia, Croatia and Serbia in turn. In the Habsburg era, Slovenia's links were with Vienna, but Croatia was constitutionally tied to Hungary, giving it an access to the sea; and in the 1990s arms smuggled from Hungary helped establish Croatia as a state capable of defying and then defeating the Serbs. Further east Hungary faces the northernmost province of Serbia, the Vojvodina. It contains a Hungarian minority 300,000 strong, the only substantial minority within Serbia so far left in peace by Slobodan Milosovic.

We are in the heart of the Danube basin here. We left it on the Austrian-Slovak border and we find it again at Mohács, where in 1526 the Turks destroyed the Hungarian monarchy in battle. Here the Danube leaves Hungary on its way to Belgrade, and we could count bombed bridges if we came this way today. Further east still, beyond Szeged, Romania takes up the running from Hungary, and Serbia's border runs across the flat expanse of the Banat. Beyond it, this alternative pursuit of the Iron Curtain would take us into the Balkan mountains. Among them we would reach the Bulgarian border with Serbia, scene of bitter Balkan wars in the years before 1914, then the border between Greece and Macedonia, and finally that between Bulgaria and Turkey.

So this alternative route would be more adventurous by far than the one which takes us between Austria and Slovenia and then between Slovenia and Italy, but historically it makes less sense for us than Churchill's line to the Adriatic. For non-aligned Yugoslavia remained a one-party Communist state, whose federal constitution was held on a tight rein by Belgrade. Before 1989 the Yugoslav leaders never paid more than lip-service to Western ideas of pluralism and accountability. For years they maintained vicious little concentration camps on barren rocks among the Adriatic archipelago. Throughout the 1960s and 1970s Yugoslavia was more one of 'them' than of 'us'; and as long as an Iron Curtain divided Europe, however tenuous it became down here, Yugoslavia lay on its further side, 'over there'.

At Hungary's westernmost tip, therefore, we turn west, not east. But the fact that we faced a choice reminds us that Europe is full of dividing lines and that even the most ancient retains a resonance today. There is an illustration of the point on Szentgotthárd's doorstep. Just south and east of the town stretches the Örség, an area of unspoiled country and primitively beautiful villages, inhabited by the descendants of men planted here in the Middle Ages to watch the Habsburgs' south-eastern borders. For thirty years under Communism it was out of bounds to visitors and development, lying as it did right up against Hungary's frontier with Yugoslavia, and naturalists say that its wild life flourished in the peace and quiet which this political juxtaposition brought it.

Europe had bigger and grander divisions than the border which the Örség represented. On the Elbe we saw the old divide between Slav and Teuton, and on the Danube the Roman *limes*. Between Thuringia and Bavaria we followed the line of the Iron Curtain between Lutheran and Catholic Germany. Away to the south east from Szentgotthárd the troubled border between Croatia and Serbia marks the divide between Orthodoxy and Roman Catholicism. If we were to go into Italy from Austria we should be leaving the Teuton world for the Mediterranean and when instead we enter it from Slovenia we shall be leaving the Slav world for the Latin. When I went hitch-hiking as a schoolboy in 1948 I saw on the Rhine a border between France and Germany almost as ferociously defended as the Hungarian-Austrian border when I discovered it ten years later; and now one is going the same way to oblivion as the other. But if you go to the Finnish-Russian border on the road between St Petersburg and Helsinki you will find it still as closely watched by the Finns as it was ever watched by the Russians. And in Budapest I have talked to nationalists who thought that the existence of a few Croat-populated villages along the western border of Hungary, each of them going back centuries, represented some kind of Slav threat to encircle the Hungarians and cut them off from their natural place in Western European society.

In our own time too there were divides quite as absolute as those we are exploring along the continental Iron Curtain. In the far north there was the short land frontier between the Soviet Union and Norway's northernmost province. Here NATO faced Warsaw Pact direct, and in an area of particular sensitivity, for behind the Norwegians were the North Cape and the North Atlantic, and behind the Russians Archangel, Murmansk and their naval bases in the Kola peninsula. I went there in 1997, bumping in a bus from Kirkenes through a snow-bound wilderness. On the way there was nothing to be seen except a single Norwegian soldier walking purposefully into nowhere, and a stream whose far bank was Russia. At the frontier you could get post-cards stamped with a very particular postmark, buy Russian dolls and a clumsy carving of a reindeer, or acquire at exorbitant cost a map which showed you that here you were as far east as Istanbul. There was a barrier across the road and an empty sentry-box. Down the road, veiled in snow flurries, was a more substantial-looking checkpoint, and beyond it endless and eternal Russia.

The long line of the Russo-Finnish border south from Kirkenes to the Gulf of Finland also formed part of the Iron Curtain, and a part which had once been fought over in earnest. Here the Finns fought two wars against the Russians. In Western eyes the first, fought through the winter of 1939–40, was a glorious defensive war of David against Goliath. At first the Finns, swathed in white camouflage against the snow, swift and silent on their skis, cut the clumsy Soviet columns to ribbons. Then gradually the Russians built up overwhelming strength, forced back the Finns and finally drove them to negotiate a peace which gave Moscow most of what it had gone to war to secure. In April the West, which had talked in the winter of sending military support to the Finns and hence of taking on the Communist world as well as the Nazis, found itself trying unsuccessfully to halt the German seizure of Norway; and a month later the British and French armies were fighting for their lives on their ways to Dunkirk and to capitulation.

A year later, when Hitler invaded Russia, the Finns tried to recover some of what they had lost, fighting a second war against the Soviet Union. This time the West thought it less than glorious; and at the end of it the Finns were again the losers and Karelia, which some Finns think contains the essence of their national identity, became definitively Russian. The outcome of two defeats was that Finland throughout the Cold War was a cautious neutral, wary of saying or doing anything that could annoy Moscow. But still the Finns guarded their own 600-mile Iron Curtain against the Soviet Union with watchful tenacity.

Greece and Turkey had their own Iron Curtains, stretching across southern Europe from the Black Sea to the Adriatic. The Turks watched the Bulgars, the more angrily because of Bulgaria's persecution of its Turkish minority. The Greeks held a much longer border, first with Bulgaria and then with Yugoslavia and Albania. They had memories of battles fought along this line, first against Italian and German invaders and then against Greek Communist armies supplied and supported from Yugoslavia. Now, more than half a century later, this is the bit of the old Iron Curtain most vulnerable to new war if the Kosovo settlement comes apart and we see a wider Balkan conflict.

For their part the Turks had yet another Cold War frontier to watch. Their eastern border faced two of the Soviet Union's southern republics, Georgia on the Black Sea and Armenia in the high mountains of eastern Anatolia. Here Turkish troops confronted Soviet units at heights up to 15,000 ft. They were under the command of Allied Land Forces Southeast Europe, whose commanding general in the late 1970s was the same Bill Knowlton whom we have seen as a lieutenant, many pages back, bluffing his way across north Germany in the last days of the Second World War, looking for Russian hands to shake rather than Russian aggressors to deter by force of arms.

Now there is another divide in Europe, almost as manifest as the Iron Curtain used to be. It separates Estonia and Latvia from Russia. It comes between Poland and Lithuania on the one hand and Belarus and Ukraine on the other. Kaliningrad is cut off from Mother Russia on the western side of this divide. For a time it seemed likely to leave Slovakia, Romania and Bulgaria 'over there', but the demands of political and material reconstruction after the Kosovo war have shifted that demarcation line. For the moment, Serbia is 'over there', Croatia and Bosnia 'over here'. In ten years' time, expansion of the European Union will have drawn new lines between insiders and outsiders. Already, Poland, Hungary and the Czech Republic rejoice in NATO membership; others will come to join them.

Among all those who deal with central and eastern Europe, there is a determined effort to fudge and blur these distinctions. The Organisation for Security and Co-operation in Europe is an inclusive, soft-edged organisation. So is the Partnership for Peace. The search is on for ways to accommodate Russia and Belarus and Ukraine, and even Yugoslavia once Milosovic has gone. An enlarged NATO and an enlarging European Union threaten noone. But for all the soft words and soft soap the fact remains that in eastern Europe today there are first-class passengers and second-class passengers on the train that takes them to join the West. The divide that used to run through the middle of Europe now runs through eastern Europe, still leaving places and people 'over there'.

So I left Szentgotthárd on the road to the west. At once I was in Austria, in the southern tip of the Burgenland. The road ahead would take me into Styria and eventually to Graz. I had started late, and before very long I turned aside for a meal. I was sitting in a bar, contemplating what was left of my beer, when an astonishing figure walked in. He was immensely tall, catastrophically emaciated, gangly beyond all description, contrasting hugely with the squat regulars at the bar and in the best corner.

The proprietor greeted him with that gentleness of the nicest kind of Austrian, and he probably asked what the newcomer wanted to drink, but the reply was addressed to the room in general rather than anyone in particular. 'I am a philosopher' he announced. He said it as if it were a challenge, speaking in a pure, high-pitched high German which added to the impression he made on me but which seemed to alienate the rest of the company. But one of the regulars drew back a net curtain and peered out into the street. '*Sieh die Machine*' he said. The others looked where he pointed and moved in a phalanx towards the door. I followed them.

Drawn up on the curb was a tricycle. It was a tricycle such as none of us had ever seen before. From the juxtaposition of seat and handlebars it looked as if the rider sat tipped backwards, almost reclining between the wheels. It was decorated with the paraphernalia of a multiplicity of gears. The rear wheels were draped with panniers. A control panel worthy of a light aircraft was attached to what passed for a crossbar. A whippy aerial sprouted from the rear axle, a good fifteen feet long. The whole affair gleamed with modernity.

'Why,' asked one of the regulars, 'what sort of a machine is this?' And then, seeing the philosopher gangle out of the pub door, again 'Why?'

'Transport,' he told them, 'this is my means of transport.'

'Where to?'

'The Mediterranean.'

'Where from?'

'From Munich.'

'But you are no Münchner.'

'I am a Berliner. But I am a human being' – this with a touch of exclusivity; and then, almost defiantly – 'I travel where I will.'

Question and answer continued. Philosopher turned materialist, he explained the mysteries of the machine. With the umpteen gears he could climb any hill, it weighed I forget how many kilos. In the pannier bags he could transport '*meine Sachen*' – his things. He had books with him, 'Philosophy, poetry. … And necessary clothes.' With his machine he was a free spirit, 'a world citizen'. Radio kept him abreast of conditions, of world events. A satellite navigation device – a sort of bubble on the handlebars – told him where he was.

I asked him about his philosophy. He turned coy, one might almost have said wary. 'Through it I find myself,' he said.

'But what school of philosophy?' I asked him, piqued by his disdain for non-philosophers.

'I write poetry also,' he said, brushing the unworthy question aside. 'In it I express myself.'

How much a day was he spending, one of the regulars asked him. The philosopher dismissed the question with the same disdain as mine about his philosophy.

'Today I cross the pass. Tonight I pitch my tent in Slovenia.'

We looked suitably awed.

'It is forty kilometres yet,' a member of his audience told him.

An uninteresting fact, the philosopher's expression suggested.

'Drink up,' said one of the regulars, moving back into the bar.

Another offered the philosopher a drink, which he accepted with a silent inclination of the head.

I paid my bill; and as I left I heard him suggesting – still with an air of infinite condescension – that they buy him a meal to go with the drink.

Leaving my philosopher friend tucking in to the meal ordinary mortals were paying for, I went on my into Styria. Here one is on the very edge of German-speaking Europe; and here, as in the next Austrian province to the west, Carinthia, you can still hear Slovene spoken. For once again we are in an historic borderland, disputed over the centuries between Slavs and Teutons, and a region which might, if things had gone otherwise in 1945, be a part now not of Austria but of Slovenia.

Styria and Carinthia are delectable places, idyllic compositions of vineyards, high hills, dark woods, deep lakes and fast-flowing rivers, with mountains rising up on every horizon. They extend for more than 100 miles from east to west, the Austrian Alps to the north, the mountains of the Slovenian border to the south, further west the Julian Alps of the Slovenian-Italian border and then, further west still, the Dolomites. The towns – Villach, Klagenfurt, Spittal – are old places with charming, almost rustic, centres; and Graz, capital of Styria and Austria's second city, is one of those urban masterpieces which too many travellers so mysteriously neglect.

The region has its troubles: friction with the Slovenes, economic problems, concern about immigrants, and now the nasty kind of near-fascist politics which so often disfigure such idyllic places. They have come to a head with the emergence of the Freedom Party in the governing coalition in Vienna, for the Freedom Party is particularly strongly supported here in southern Austria and its star performer, Jörg Haider, is the Governor of Carinthia. The problem posed by the rise of the Freedom Party, by European distaste for doing business with it and by Austrian defensiveness raises all sorts of issues for us Europeans. It is worth turning aside from the beauties of Styria and Carinthia to think about it.

Jörg Haider caught the world's full attention just as it was celebrating the new millennium. He was a skeleton at the feast, reminding us all of what another Austrian fascist had done to the twentieth century. For once, members of the European Union acted decisively, saying that they did not want to do business with an Austrian government which included fascists. Right-minded, left-of-centre Austrians came into the streets in protest against the Freedom Party, but Austria as a whole, not unnaturally, turned stubborn against outside pressure, as it had done before, over world criticism of the less than salubrious past of Kurt Waldheim.

Austria's critics, it seems to me, were right and wrong, in roughly equal proportions. We have learned the hard way the need to nip racist sentiment in the bud. But none of us is without sin; and we do business with many governments as sinister, or potentially dangerous, as the Freedom Party. The argument by analogy with Hitler is a seductive one – 'if only we had acted decisively ... threatened war when he marched into the Ruhr ... stopped the Anschluss ... defended Czechoslovakia' – but it seems fanciful to see a new Hitler in the Governor of Carinthia or to imagine little Austria stamping across Europe like the Third Reich. And there are the small matters of democracy (the votes freely cast for the Freedom Party) and of sovereignty (what right have outsiders to tell Austrians whom to vote for?) Finally, and again it is a factor that weighs on both sides of the argument, there is the character of the European Union itself. Is it arrogantly imposing itself on one of its smallest members? Or are its members worthily trying to formulate standards of what is acceptable and what is not in our 'ever closer union of the peoples of Europe'?

So much for Haider, a story to be explored at greater length in a second edition. Now we turn back to another southern Austrian drama, which developed in 1945 when Styria and Carinthia played host to tragedy.

In the first week of May 1945, troops of the British Fifth Corps advancing from Italy entered Carinthia. Ahead of them lay an anticipated meeting with Soviet troops coming through the Burgenland and Styria from Hungary, and the fear of collision with Yugoslav partisans coming up fast from the south-east. As we shall see, the Yugoslav Communists had made a bid to seize Trieste, an attempt only narrowly frustrated by the advance of the New Zealanders of the Eighth Army. The fear was that they would try the same in Carinthia.

Ahead of the British there were German units, both Wehrmacht and SS, all that were left of the defenders of the Italian and the Eastern Fronts, some desperate to surrender, some still resisting. With the Germans were divisions of auxiliary troops, and in particular the Croats, as well as Georgians and, above all, Cossacks. These auxiliaries had with them wives, children, horse-drawn caravans containing all their worldly goods, camp followers in their thousands. And milling around Carinthia, as around all Europe that spring, there were also men and women on their own or in small groups, displaced persons of every kind, stragglers, released prisoners of war, refugees and outright bandits.

The British units' orders were daunting. They were to take control of Carinthia, receive the surrender of their enemies, subdue any of them foolish enough to continue fighting, keep the Yugoslavs out of the province, establish contact with the Russians and link up with American troops who had entered Austria from the west on the other side of the Alps. They were at the end of a long war that had brought them up the length of Italy and, some of them, across North Africa before that. They were leaving behind them the simplicities of war for the confusions of peace, dealing with people of whose stories they knew next to nothing. They longed for rest after their exertions. But as they entered the natural paradise of Carinthia they were plunged into a political and human maelstrom. Their story has been told by Nicholas Bethell in *The Last Secret,* and by Nikolai Tolstoy in a book which provoked a celebrated libel action and which, when he lost the case, was withdrawn by the publishers. On any interpretation it is a terrible story, one of the most horrific to unwind anywhere along the line of what was soon to become the Iron Curtain.

At first things went smoothly. A Cossack force camped at Tolmezzo in northern Italy withdrew over the border into Austria, surrendered itself to British troops and, as instructed, set up camp in the valley of the upper Drau between the Austrian Alps and the Dolomites. The Cossacks gave up the bulk of their weapons but were allowed to keep their sidearms. Other Cossack forces further east similarly gave themselves up to the British. But a small British unit still further east, at Bleiburg on the Yugoslav border, encountered difficulties that foreshadowed those which were about to engulf all the units of Fifth British Corps in the area.

Out of Yugoslavia came a host of Croats, 200,000 strong. They had fought in loose coalition with the Germans against the Communist partisans and rightly feared vengeance. Their leaders told the British officer who stood in their way that there were more behind them, and as many camp followers again. This was 'an emigration of the whole Croat nation', who refused to live under Communism; they wished to settle overseas. A strong force of partisans was in the area, and their leaders demanded that the Croats, who they asserted were fascists to a man, be returned to face 'allied justice'. Had the Croats continued their march into Austria they could have overwhelmed the few British troops who barred the way, and the Communists would have pursued them into what was to be the British zone of occupation. Totally unprepared, the man on the spot found himself face to face with the lethal complexities of Balkan politics. Finally, he cajoled and threatened the Croats into surrendering to the partisans.

Back went the Croats, to be led away as prisoners on a forced march through Slovenia, Croatia and Serbia. It was clear that the British were despatching them to face rough justice. But only later did it emerge that what had started as a forced march had turned into a death march, in the course of which thousands were massacred. It was the first example of the fate which might await all Hitler's allies and auxiliaries.

The case of the Cossacks was more complex. At Yalta it had been secretly agreed that all Soviet citizens who fell into Western hands, whether as German prisoners of war or as allies of the Nazis in German uniforms, would be returned to the Soviet Union. Already many who had surrendered to the British during the fighting in France had been so returned, and the few British officials involved had grim suspicions about their fate. But the men of Fifth Corps knew nothing of this, or of the secret agreements of Yalta. Most British soldiers had been conditioned to think of the Red Army as their trustworthy allies; some few knew that the Cossacks had won themselves an unsavoury reputation as ruthless enemies; their return to the country from which they came seemed the obvious course; and if the bad hats among them faced punishment on their return, that was the price which war criminals could expect to pay when they lost a war.

To the Cossacks none of this reasoning would have seemed comprehensible. They were, understandably, obsessed by the horrors which the Soviet regime had visited upon their people. They thought it self-evident that they should fight against the Communists when they got the opportunity. To any British officer who would listen they explained that they had no quarrel with the British or Americans; indeed, they expected to become their auxiliaries as soon as fighting was resumed, as they assumed it soon would be, this time pitting the Soviet Union against the Western allies. And they were in no doubt about the fate that awaited them if they were handed over to the Russians.

All was ready, therefore, for misunderstanding and worse, as soon as General Keightley, commanding Fifth Corps, ordered his men to act upon the Yalta Agreement and hand over to the Russians those of their prisoners of war who were Soviet citizens. This he did, in an order issued on 24 May, two weeks after the end of the war. It made clear the importance of handing over the Cossacks, and particularly their leaders, to the Red Army, and it did so in terms which ignored the important distinctions – between, for example, Soviet citizens, who were to be returned, and prewar Russian émigrés, who were not – which had been drawn in the Yalta Agreement.

What followed was the most terrible story to unwind in that sort of idyllic mountain landscape for half a century, to be exceeded in horror only in the 1990s, with the prison camp tortures and massacres of Bosnia and the massacres and clearances of Kosovo. At first the British, wittingly and unwittingly, had lulled their captives by the very decency and friendliness with which they had treated them. Now they set about carrying out their orders to hand them to the Russians. The Cossack officers were invited to a mythical 'conference', so separating them from their men, and the next day they were handed over to the Russians. At Judenburg in Styria you can see the point at which the handover took place and the bridge from which many of the Cossacks flung themselves rather than fall into the Russians' hands. When, thereafter, the Cossack rank and file and camp followers resisted despatch to the Russians, British troops used clubs and bayonets to break their resolution and threatened them with a Bren gun and a flamethrower.

The story seen from the Cossack side is an even more poignant one. They thought of the British as their friends, and could not understand the hostility – quite often justified – with which their record was viewed. They could not imagine that the Western democracies were truly committed allies of the Communists who had destroyed their own communities. They never understood that the British did not believe that they faced death or fatal imprisonment. They ignored hints about what was to come. When the truth broke in they resisted with an animal sense of hopeless solidarity.

Hardened infantrymen wept as they consigned the Cossacks to their fate, but discipline held, and consign them they did. By 7 June Keightley was able to report to London that the handover of the Cossacks was substantially complete. Over in the Soviet zone the returning Cossacks were handed over to the security police, their leaders to face the hangman, the rank and file to long terms of imprisonment in the Gulags. The very title of Bethell's book, *The Last Secret*, comes from Solzhenitsyn who met them there.

Both Bethell and Tolstoy bring out the horror of all this. Tolstoy added what he claimed was evidence of deliberate misinterpretation of the Yalta Agreement, so as to rid the British Army of its troublesome prisoners, and it was these claims that took him as a defendant into one of the costliest libel actions in recent legal history. He examined signal traffic between London and the commander-in-chief in Italy, Field Marshal Alexander, and between Alexander and the commander of Fifth Corps, General Keightley, and he laid the blame for what he saw as evil conspiracy at the door of one of Alexander's senior staff officers. To read his book long after the libel action is to read an obsessive, righteously engaged in the search for that most slippery of objects, absolute truth in a political and practical world of relative values. Bethell tells a more convincing, because a more modulated, tale of a corps commander who cast aside the complexities of the Yalta Agreement and so despatched to their fate many Cossacks whom the Yalta terms exempted, and of British officers who knew nothing of the political background, nor of the peoples – Cossacks, Croats, Georgians – with whom they found themselves dealing. They could not see their prisoners, rogues and patriots both, as anything other than fellow fighting men. But nor could they conceive that the Soviet ally would visit on the Cossacks the punishments which the Cossacks took for certain if they were returned to the Communists. They were tired, at the end of a long war; they wanted simplicities; they had their orders. So they played their part, unhappily but dutifully, in the horror which unwound in Carinthia in May 1945.

In Klagenfurt I turned my back on these ancient horrors and drove south over the Loibl Pass. The crossing into Slovenia was notably easy and informal, a model of a modern European frontier, and I had to remind myself that the we owed the tunnel to the Nazi slave labourers who died digging.

Straight ahead lay the road south to Ljubljana, and beyond it the seductions of a motorway to Trieste. But I still had 100 miles of the old Iron Curtain to trace and to do so I had to turn west, towards the Julian Alps, through Kranjska Gora. It is a neat little, prim little place, a ski centre which has caught the scent of globalisation, learned the art of prosperous blandness and comes across like anywhere of its kind in Switzerland or Austria. It is a good introduction to Slovenia, the lucky country.

For over forty years, Slovenia was a Yugoslav republic, the most prosperous if one of the smallest of the six. That it has not succumbed like the others to war and ethnic hatreds is mostly due to pure good fortune. To it must be added its geographical position and Western European sympathy, an ethnic composition simpler by far than those of its former partners, national unity in deciding for independence in 1990, and political ruthlessness when Belgrade challenged that decision in 1991. The consequence was that Slovenia escaped from the Yugoslav federation almost without loss of life, and with a cleaner reputation than the chicanery of its leaders deserved. Today it is a peaceable Alpine republic, its back turned resolutely against the troubles of its old Yugoslav partners, a candidate for membership of the European Union and NATO, and a society more than twice as prosperous as its Croat and Hungarian neighbours. It looks now like a simple and unsophisticated Austria. Its story is less straightforward.

The Slovenes are a Slavonic people whose ancestors came here as the Roman Empire dissolved. In the eighth century they fell under the dominion of the Carolingian emperors. From them, and more improbably from Irish missionaries too, they acquired the beginnings of Christianity. But soon they were overrun by Magyar raiders, and when the invaders were driven out half a century later it was by Germans, who dominated the Slovenes in their turn. For nearly 1,000 years thereafter the area was ruled by Teutons under one guise or another, a rule which gradually developed into incorporation into the Habsburg Empire. Slovenia became a distinct but integrated appendage of Austria, known as Carniola, just as Croatia was of Hungary. Between them they gave the Austro-Hungarian Empire a window to the Adriatic.

There was an interruption at the beginning of the nineteenth century, when Napoleon, having defeated the Austrians, carved his Illyrian provinces out of parts of Slovenia and Croatia. That lasted for only four years, but the modernising ideas which the French brought with them awoke a sense of Slovene identity and the beginnings of a sense of nationhood which subsequent events never quite extinguished. They also brought an astonishing series of French governors to Slovenia. Marshal Marmont, whom Napoleon put in charge of the Illyrian provinces, flung himself with passion into their development and awakening. But Marmont the zealot was succeeded by Bertrand the cynic, and Bertrand by Junot, the Duke of Abrantès, who made his capital in Ljubljana, 'gave a state ball, and came down the great marble staircase, under the blazing chandeliers, stark naked and raving mad'. Junot's successor was Napoleon's sinister policeman, Fouché, who abandoned France's Illyrian empire to the returning Habsburgs. They were to hold it, and the rest of Slovenia and Croatia, until 1918.

Most of the history of Slovenia in the last 500 years is therefore the story of a sub-Alpine people under Habsburg rule. The inheritance is manifested in the order of the countryside and the architecture of cities like Ljubljana, the capital, and Maribor in the north-east. Yet the Slovenes were and are a predominantly Slavonic people, if Slavs who see themselves as different from their more turbulent cousins in the true Balkans. Above all, the Slovenes are pretty well undiluted by minorities, for 88 per cent of the people are Slovene.

The hand of the Habsburgs was relatively light. Vienna exercised ultimate political power. Slovenia's landowners were mostly nobles and gentry of German blood, just as its key administrators were mostly Austrian. There was friction, and the occasional peasant rising, in particular where Slovenes and Germans lived cheek by jowl. But the people's relationship with Vienna was not all that different from the relationship of the peasants in Tyrol or Upper Austria, or for that matter in southern Bohemia. And the underlying ethnic differences were overlaid by the far greater differences embraced within the multi-ethnic empire of the Habsburgs.

To the Habsburgs themselves, Slovenia was one of their innumerable family possessions. We have seen Archduke Maximilian residing at Miramare outside Trieste before going off to wear an imperial crown and face a firing squad in Mexico, and other members of the family before and after him made homes for themselves in Slovenia. And as in the course of the nineteenth century the Empire was by degrees stripped of its territories in Italy, the importance of Slovenia grew. In 1849 the railway from Vienna to Ljubljana was completed, just in time to help bind together an Empire shaken by the revolutions of the previous year. When the line was later extended to Trieste it made an economic reality of Austria-Hungary's access to the sea. Trieste was developed into a major commercial seaport, as Pola in Croatia became a base for the warships of the *Kaiserlich-und-Königlich Kriegsmarine*. Ships of the Lloyd-Trieste Line carried hundreds of thousands of emigrants from the Balkans to new lives in North America. In the war of 1866, warships from Pola were launched in an ironclad cavalry charge against a larger force of Italian vessels in the Adriatic. They brought a new style of naval warfare to the world and new pretensions to the Habsburg administrators in Vienna. Between them Trieste and Pola made of

Austro-Hungary something more, if tenuously more, than a central and eastern European power. The Empire owed them to its possession of Slovenia and Croatia

Italy came into the First World War in 1915 to ensure that it should have a seat at the Peace Conference table and a share in the booty of victory. Her generals drove their men into terrible offensives against the Austro-Hungarians in the mountains. The return on that terrible investment of men's lives was their seat at the Peace Conference. The Conference gave them their booty, specifically Trieste and western areas of what is today Slovenia; and that poetic freebooter and charlatan d'Annunzio snatched for them the Istrian peninsula south of Trieste in a lawless *coup de main*.

The rest of Slovenia joined Serbs, Croats and Montenegrins in the Kingdom of Yugoslavia. Yugoslavia became a steadily more oppressive state, but throughout the interwar years it was the issue of Slovenes under foreign rule, far more than their sufferings at home, which haunted Slovene politics. The Italians, inflamed as much by the exaltation of d'Annunzio as by common-or-garden fascism, committed themselves to nationalist absurdities: 'Have bugs a nationality when they infect a dwelling?' the *Popolo d'Italia* once inquired. 'That is the historical and moral position of the Slovenes living within our borders.' Rebecca West, who gave that sentiment hardback immortality, may have had it in for the Italians. She believed that the 600,000 Slovenes were the worst-treated minority in Europe except for the German-speaking peoples of the south Tyrol, who were also subordinated to Italian rule.

In April 1941 Hitler attacked Yugoslavia. Italian troops occupied most of Slovenia, German and Hungarian forces the rest. But in the four years that followed partisans, here as elsewhere in Yugoslavia, created a powerful resistance movement, which in Slovenia became even more active when Italy left the war. Until the very end of the war it failed to clear the Germans from Slovenia but when, in May 1945, British troops entered Trieste and southern Austria they ran up against aggressive and potentially hostile partisan forces, all of them committed to the Communist cause. We have seen how the encounter played out in Carinthia and we shall come to the Trieste crisis – a crisis that briefly seemed to threaten all-out East-West war – at the end of our journey.

The victorious partisan leaders in Slovenia, as elsewhere in Yugoslavia, were convinced Communists. They had their national loyalties, but they believed in the union of the south Slavs. They took the province, less Trieste, into a Yugoslav federation. Within the federation, all power was concentrated in Communist hands; and the Communist parties of each of the republics were committed to holding the federation together. For them, Communism mattered and nationality within the federation did not; as Milovan Djilas quotes Tito as saying during the war, 'For us, these demarcation lines will be no more than administrative frontiers.' The break with Moscow in 1948 reinforced their need to hang together if they were not to hang separately, and for thirty-five years Tito (himself part Croat, part Slovene) and the men around him suppressed any over-vigorous expression of national sentiment in the republics.

Yugoslavia was run as a centralised federation. Over the decades that followed a little more initiative was surrendered to the individual republics. Nevertheless, Yugoslavia remained a tightly-controlled, authoritarian country, of a kind familiar throughout Eastern Europe, right up to the collapse of the Iron Curtain in 1989. But that marvellous year changed the face of every familiar thing in the whole region. In Yugoslavia it called in question the authority of the men on whose cooperation the cohesion and survival of the federation depended. In their republics they faced national pressures, and the temptation to play the national card to keep themselves in power.

The whole world knows the malignity with which Milosevic and Tudjman exploited Serbian and Croatian national sentiment. The political leaders in Slovenia's modestly elegant little capital, Ljubljana, played the same game, but with greater delicacy. In April 1990 Slovenia held free elections. The incoming government proposed that a looser Yugoslav confederation should replace the old federation. Staunch federalists, and particular the traditionalists in the high command of the Yugoslav Army, saw such a change as the death-knell of Yugoslavia. A majority of the Council which ran the federation rejected the Slovene proposal. The Slovenes declared themselves sovereign in their own land. Two days before Christmas 1990, they voted for independence, to take effect within six months; and on 25 June 1991 Slovenia withdrew from the Yugoslav federation.

Yugoslav troops moved into Slovenia. It was a tentative move, designed to secure the external borders of the federation, and the soldiers, most of them raw conscripts, had little idea what they were about. The Slovene leaders, however, represented the move as an all-out assault on their new country's nationhood and democracy. There was fighting and a few casualties, most of them among the federal army's infantry and peaceable lorry drivers caught in the crossfire.

In any of the other republics, all this could have led to one of Yugoslavia's bloodbaths. But the Slovenes had no serious non-Slovene minority to contend with. They had engaged sympathetic outsiders in their cause. They showed themselves determined, and had made themselves well-armed. The army withdrew. Slovenia had started a process which destroyed Yugoslavia as a state and opened the way for the wars of Serbian aggrandisement. It had also achieved its independence and separated itself from the fate that lay in store for the rest of Yugoslavia. Nine years later it is numbered among the first five candidates for European Union membership. And the rebuilding of the Balkans in the wake of the war in Kosovo can only benefit the Slovenes. Once again they will come up smelling of roses. This is indeed Yugoslavia's lucky country.

I called Kranjska Gora a good introduction to Slovenia. It was also the starting point of the hairiest part of my journey. It stands at the foot of the highest mountain in the eastern Alps, Mount Triglav. To explore Slovenia's border with Italy, the last stretch of what was once the Iron Curtain, I would have to go into the mountains to the west of Triglav, the Julian Alps. To get there I would have to climb to the summit of the Vrsic Pass, 5,000 feet above sea level. It would be a nightmare journey in high summer, and this was early November. You follow a twisting, precipitous, only-just metalled road that worms its way up into the clouds, and when you get there the pass is as bleak as anything you can imagine in Europe. On the way up you pass a Russian Orthodox chapel, erected in memory of 400 Russian prisoners of war who were swept to their deaths by an avalanche when they were building this road for their Austrian captors in 1916.

By now I had a companion on board, a man I have known for half a century. I had put him in charge of the map-reading and he had no difficulty in finding the way out of Krjanska Gora (population 2,800). He then remarked that the map suggested that the road ahead might be a little tortuous but there was no danger of my getting lost. At that he fell asleep, taking his ease as I coaxed our little car round the innumerable hairpins to the snow-covered top of the pass. There he awoke, got out, stamped his feet, looked at the view, said he'd seen better when he went to Switzerland in 1953, and announced that he was chilly. Back in the car its warmth soon put him back to sleep, while I took us gingerly down the other side of the pass. It wriggled its way down into the valley of the Soca, which the Italians call the Isonzo, through hairpins which made the ascent feel like a motorway. At the foot of the pass my map reader awoke and remarked that he could do with a cup of coffee. We drove on down the valley, through Soca and Bovec and Zaga. Finally we got him his precious coffee in a place called Kobarid.

At the other end of the Iron Curtain, we looked at preparations for the great battle in the north German plain which was never fought and which, if it ever had been, might have put an end to our world. In the Marchfeld beside the Danube we passed the site of one of Napoleon's few defeats, at Aspern, and of one of his bloodiest victories, at Wagram. But here in Slovenia we are looking for a battle fought right on the line of the divide that in due course became the Iron Curtain. Different parties call it by different names. To the Austrians it was fought at Karfreit, to the Slovenes at Kobarid. To the Italians and their Allies in the First World War it was the Battle of Caporetto.

To a generation that thinks it can fight wars without casualties, any First War battle is close to unimaginable. Perhaps we can vaguely encompass what happened at Verdun or on the Somme, and even more vaguely imagine the Battle of Tannenberg in East Prussia. But Caporetto and the Isonzo offensives that preceded it are beyond conception: land battles fought in three dimensions, attacks up death-trap valleys, outposts on snow-covered mountainsides, supplies brought up, casualties evacuated in swaying cable cars, that and more was the war between Austria and Italy in 1915–17. Ernest Hemingway is honoured for his account in *A Farewell to Arms,* but it tells us only a sentimental story of an ambulance volunteer who falls in love, is wounded, wearies of defeat, and makes off with his love to neutral Switzerland.

I first tried to visit Caporetto forty years ago. We had been on holiday in Venice and were on our way back to Budapest. Outside Udine I saw a signpost to Caporetto, and persuaded a deeply sceptical wife that we could go back to Hungary that way as easily as on the main road to Villach. We set off up a fast-deteriorating road that twisted up into the mountains, and suddenly we came to the Yugoslav frontier. Caporetto was no longer an Italian town for the Yugoslavs had swallowed it up in 1945. Without a visa there was no way forward. We turned back to Udine, my wife muttering about some people, impractical foolishness and feckless irresponsibility. When I finally got to Kobarid in 1998, still shaken by the nightmare twists, turns and precipices of the Vrsic Pass, I thanked my stars that the guards had turned us back at the frontier in 1960.

The Italians entered the war in 1915 eager to show their mettle as a nation and win themselves a profitable place among the victors. They massed their armies in the plains north-east of Venice, with an Austro-Hungarian army facing them in the north and another Habsburg army to their east, all the way down through the Julian Alps to the head of the Adriatic. In whichever direction the Italians attacked they faced mountain barriers; and even an attack along the coast, to seize Trieste, would first have to clear the mountain escarpment that overlooked the coast road. So everywhere the Italians would be fighting up-hill, advancing into ever more forbidding mountain country.

Nevertheless, between the summer of 1915 and the autumn of 1917, the Italian commanders threw their men into a series of offensives. At first they were successful, advancing out of the plains, up the Isonzo valley into the mountains, and occupying Caporetto. But impassable mountains lay ahead: the only way forward lay up the Vrsic Pass. The Italians were attacking into a cul-de-sac. Yet for the best part of two years they kept up their attacks, ten Isonzo offensives in all, first around Caporetto and then further south around Gorizia and on the escarpment that dominated the approach to Trieste. In the museum at Kobarid you can see bits and pieces of the story: mock-ups of command-posts carved out of cliff faces, photographs of mountain ropeways, incomprehensible models of the disposition of the two sides across the mountain sides, horrifying picture of faces carved into obscenity by flying splinters of mountain rock. If anything exceeded the horrors of the battles on the Western Front it must have been these pointless battles in the Julian Alps.

And yet, God knows how, the Italians got close to breakthrough. Vienna turned to Berlin for help and Ludendorff produced his assessment: 'In the middle of September 1917 it became necessary to decide for the attack on Italy in order to prevent the collapse of Austria-Hungary.' The Russian armies were dissolving, going home to revolution; the Germans and Austrians could safely transfer troops here from the Eastern Front. They brought division after division over those dreadful mountain roads, gradually building up numbers more or less comparable with those the Italians were still flinging into the attack.

By now, in the late summer of 1917, the Italians were concentrating their attacks at the southern end of the front and were within sight of Trieste. Everywhere they were still positioned for the offensive, not defence, but the men were weary of pointless war. Then in October the Germans and Austrians (for by now the Germans predominated on this Austrian front) attacked in the northern Isonzo valley.

In the words of a Slovenian guide book, Caporetto was 'the greatest mountain battle in the history of mankind; it was the first successful blitzkrieg operation in the history of warfare; it was the most successful breakthrough operation in World War I; it was the greatest battle on the Slovenian territory.' It was all of these things, as well as a vast human tragedy, and it came close to knocking Italy out of the war. It was also the only major battle to be fought right on the line that was to become the Iron Curtain.

Erwin Rommel, who came to fame in the North African desert in the Second World War, was at the head of the attack. He was a junior officer of the Württemberg mountain troops. He had already made a name for ferociously aggressive spirit in the Vosges and the Carpathians. Now they put him in charge of the 'Rommel Detachment' of three mountain companies and one machine-gun company and told him to clear the Italians off a mountain overlooking the road from Caporetto to Tolmin. He set off in a storming march along the mountainside and along the Italian front line. In fifty-two hours of non-stop movement the Rommel Detachment, less than a battalion strong, took 9,000 prisoners, losing six dead and thirty wounded in the process. It was the kind of headlong advance which, with tanks, dive-bombers and infinitely larger numbers, he launched into Poland and France in 1939 and 1940.

Everywhere the Italians streamed away from the battle, back into Italy. They fled across the Tagliamento and were only just halted on the Piave. The King feared for his throne and the Venetians for Venice. Somehow the Italians held; but they needed massive British and French reinforcement before they were able, a year later, to take their part in the Allies' last victorious advances, ending the war at Vittorio Veneto. We have seen that in the peace settlement they got their reward, taking Trieste and Istria and western Slovenia, but you need to be a passionate Italian expansionist to believe that those gains, two out of three of them reversed twenty-five years later, were worth the lives of the Italian conscripts driven against mountain defences in those ten terrible offensives and finally flung back into the plain from Caporetto.

Kobarid today is a quiet little town, and at first sight little identifies it with all these horrors. It is, indeed, one of those towns among mountains which, in Austria and Switzerland, lead placid and blameless lives and which, in Bosnia and Kosovo, witness such appalling atrocities. Kobarid, like all Slovenia, has gone the Swiss and Austrian way, thank God, a place where people come to walk in the mountains, raft on the Soca and fish in the mountain lakes. A British television researcher was there when we discovered it, talking distractedly about a programme on the Battle of Caporetto. They showed her the same models that had puzzled us and took her off to look at the remains of an Italian defensive line further up the valley, but I should be surprised if she got a programme out of it. Now the museum reminds you of the battle, and so do the mountains looming above the town if you can identify where it was that Rommel pursued his mountain Blitzkrieg. But the most vivid commemoration of what happened here is a vast white ossuary crowning a hill above the valley floor. The Italians built it in the 1920s and filled it with the bones of 7,000 soldiers who died on these mountains in those incomprehensible battles over eighty years ago.

From Kobarid we drove on down the Soca valley and now, safely back on level ground, my map-reader was sprightly, refreshed, engaging me in cheerful conversation. The road stayed close to the river, through Tolmin and Kanal to Nova Gorica; and away to the west, in the last mountains before the northern Italian plain, the line of the frontier followed every twist and turn of the valley. We passed cemeteries from the First War and partisan memorials from the Second; dams and hydro-electric stations; rapids where you might go rafting and pools where in summer you could swim in clear aquamarine water; and throughout the journey the mountains of western Slovenia towered over our road.

At Nova Gorica, however, the mountains begin to give way to the Italian plain. The Soca, turning west, becomes the Italian Isonzo. And across the border from Nova Gorica stands the more venerable Italian city of Gorizia. For Nova Gorica is, to tell the truth, little more than a modern shadow of Gorizia, flats in boxes of stained concrete, created by Tito's Yugoslavia to assert that it is here, not further back up the valley and in the mountains, that Yugoslavia meets Italy, and on equal terms.

Gorizia itself is a pleasant place, in spirit an Italian provincial town; it is the sort of place where you can walk under shady arcades, finger the fruit and vegetables in the market, and spend two hours over lunch. Yet for 400 years of its history it was Habsburg property, and it was Austrian when the Italians declared war in 1915. They captured it in 1916 and held it for a year, the period in which it figures at the start of *A Farewell to Arms*. They lost it after Caporetto and got it back again a year later. With most of western Slovenia it became Italian *de jure* in the post-First War settlement.

There was never a chance that a defeated Italy could hold on to all those gains after the Second World War, but when it lost most of them it kept Gorizia, if by a whisker, with the Yugoslav border running just to

the east of the old town centre. For years tensions ran high, while Nova
Gorica was built and the two towns glared at one another. There were
times when Trieste and Gorizia were the most volatile places along the
Iron Curtain, and the border which curled around them both was a line
on which cold war might suddenly have turned hot. But in the end deals
were done, accommodations found. Gorizia and Nova Gorica still look
each other in the eye, but peacefully now, separated by nothing more
than a jumpable fence, and united in what looks like mutual amiability.

If you follow the Isonzo from Gorizia on its journey to the sea you
come to Aquilea, whose ruins remind you that for the Romans this was
an important place, where the road from the Danube reached the Adriatic. It served them for centuries as a provincial capital; when the barbarians came, refugees from it fled to the islets of the Adriatic lagoons
and eventually created Venice. Grado, just beyond Aquilea, stands at
the point where Italy's old border with the Habsburg Empire reached
the sea. Here Italian patriots, pining under the rule of Vienna, would
come secretly to breathe free Italian air, so much finer than the Habsburg air back along the coast.

But we were concerned with more recent divides, with the Iron Curtain itself. We set aside the temptation to go exploring Aquilea and to
take ourselves off to Venice. We drove south from Gorizia along the
Slovene border, and then south-east towards Trieste. On Italian territory, at sea level and refreshed with pasta and Soave, my old friend
rediscovered his sense of responsibility, finding us short cuts, bypasses
and a British war cemetery in which lies buried a soldier who won the
Victoria Cross in battle here in 1918. But as we approached Trieste, as
rain and dusk descended, matters were taken out of his hands. We were
trapped in an unbroken stream of traffic, crawling bumper-to-bumper
along the coast road towards the border city and Adriatic port which
marks the end of our journey. Once again he fell back into deep repose.

The streets of Trieste were daunting on a wet Friday night in the rush
hour, so we went beyond it, to spend the night in a flashy hotel-cum-
casino on Slovenia's abbreviated Riviera, looking back across the bay at
the lights of Italy, and we came back to explore the city in the quiet of
the weekend. It is a serious kind of place, 250,000 inhabitants strong,
its business connections going back a long way and its more recent role
as the capital of an Italian province giving it governmental gravitas as
well. So there are a fine theatre and a stock exchange and banks, an
echoing railway station and insurance companies and churches. But

Trieste is squeezed between its waterfront and the mountains which crowd in upon it, rearing up to the Slovenian frontier. So a few hundred yards back from the water's edge the streets turn precipitous, and as you climb them you get increasingly dramatic views over the rooftops and out to sea. Out in the roads there are ships at anchor or creeping towards a mooring, for with Venice, this is the biggest port on the Adriatic.

I had expected great things of Trieste. As we shall see, it has a complicated and interesting history, and a reputation among the cities of Italy. I had read Jan Morris's panegyrics about the place. All the way from the Baltic I had looked forward to a grand arrival here: journey's end, Latin civilisation, Mediterranean food, 'the sea, the sea'. So we set out with high hopes to see the sights that brisk Saturday morning in November.

Trieste has a splendid square beside the harbour, flanked on three sides by nineteenth-century buildings of a magnificence as splendid as those on Vienna's Ring. Marking the fourth side are two soaring flag poles, at whose feet *Bersaglieri* parade at dusk amid musical pomp and circumstance while they bring their enormous Italian tricolours down to earth for the night. On the very water's edge, monuments commemorate the supreme moment in Trieste's twentieth-century history: the arrival of the destroyer *Audace* in November 1918, bringing Italian troops to take possession of this Italian city at last recovered from the Austrians.

Further inland, the castle on the hill offers the most sweeping of all Trieste's views, extending all the way to Miramare, Maximilian's white palace beside the sea. Just below it there are the remains of a Roman forum, half-converted to the purposes of war memorial and jingoistic regimental declarations; and a strange, rather lovely, Siamese twin of a church, formed when two ancient churches, built side by side, were knocked into one to form the cathedral of San Giusto, with their adjacent aisles forming a new nave.

But aside from these attractions, Trieste seemed to me to have little to offer a visitor in search of art, beauty and the material of historical reminiscence. Jan Morris, who served with the British army in the city immediately after the war and has conducted a strange love affair with it ever since, disagrees. She will tell you about its glorious cafés, where you can capture its Italian nature, its Habsburg inheritance, the quiddities of the customers, the cultural and literary vitality of the city. Perhaps I went looking in the wrong cafés, but as something to look at, to explore, I found Trieste a vaguely dispiriting end to my European journey.

All the same, the place is packed with history to console you for the sparseness of its historical and cultural monuments. It goes back to before the Romans, and legend claims that the Argonauts came here, dragging their boat overland from the Danube to the sea. It was mentioned by Strabo, Livy, Virgil and Julius Caesar, colonised by Italian settlers in 138 BC, and made a Roman city 100 years later. Attila the Hun came this way, and it may have been he who laid Trieste waste in 453. Then the Byzantines and the Lombards fought over it. By the fourteenth century the names of Habsburg princes begin to crop up in the story, locked as often as not in competitions for influence with the Venetians. By the sixteenth century, however, Trieste was securely Habsburg, and Habsburg it remained (with the short exception of Napoleon's kingdom of Illyria which we noticed a few pages back) until the *Audace* arrived in 1918.

The nineteenth-century story is worth telling in a little more detail, for in the course of it Trieste developed into a major city of the Austro-Hungarian Empire and the main link between south central Europe and the wider world. For centuries the Habsburg Empire had been one of the major European powers, but it was a land-locked state, cut off from oceanic expansion. Croatia and Slovenia had always given it but tenuous access to the Adriatic; but when the railways came, and the steamship lines, Trieste became the Empire's seaport, its window on the world. It had always attracted people of every nation, class and kind: German-speakers, Slovenes, Italians, Jews, riffraff minorities from all over Europe. Now it attracted industry, world trade, modern commerce too.

The place also attracted artists and intellectuals, who helped make Trieste society as richly various as any in Europe. James Joyce and Richard Burton lived here around the turn of the nineteenth century, the one teaching English for Berlitz while he wrote *Finnegan's Wake*, the other safely ensconced in a sinecure as British Consul in the city while he quarrelled with his wife. Stendhal came here from France, Rilke from Germany; and Italo Svevo, as celebrated as he is unread, whom Joyce introduced to the joys of literature when he was not teaching him Berlitz English, is Trieste's own. Egon Schiele came here briefly, as a teenager and again in his early manhood, and Bandmaster Franz Lehár brought a touch of personal distinction to the music with which a regiment of Habsburg infantry entertained the city's promenaders of a Sunday afternoon.

Different people have always seen Trieste differently. To the Italians it is an Italian city, and its possession put a final feather in their country's cap of self-assertion as a European power. To the Habsburgs, Trieste was a city of central Europe, their window on the world, as Austrian as the Ring in Vienna itself. But the Slovenes were there first, or can argue that they were. Other observers claim not that Trieste belongs to them but that, by accommodating everyone, it makes itself nothing – that it is nowhere. They note a sense of displacement, of otherness, the sense that the city is on the edge of things. So in a letter to his wife Chateaubriand, who turned back before he got to Trieste, explained its unexamined shortcomings: 'It is situated ... at the foot of a chain of sterile mountains; it possesses no monuments. The last breath of civilisation expires on this coast where barbarianism starts.' 'One has the sense of being nowhere at all' wrote a German visitor in 1909. Jan Morris sees matters differently. For her, the sense of being nowhere makes Trieste unique, mistress of herself: 'If Trieste ever felt impelled to advertise itself on road signs, like towns in France ("*Sa Cathédrale, Ses Grottes, Ses Langoustines*"), it would have no problems. This is a city unique and altogether original, and it could simply announce, on one very large placard, "*Sua Triestinità*": its Triesteness.'

So for most of the nineteenth century Trieste's history was a story of peoples of very different backgrounds from very different worlds, living, doing business and making music together. But it also embraced two conflicting political forces. One was Habsburg power, a dead weight in occupation. The other was the swelling passion of Italian nationalism, whose influence in the city grew as the rest of northern Italy gradually threw off Habsburg rule. But the more the Habsburgs lost in Italy proper, the more valuable to them was this half-Italian city on the edge of their dominions and of the sea. The city's nineteenth-century story was marked by an occasional riot, an assassination attempt, a rare execution of a patriotic Italian freedom fighter. And so the way was prepared for Italy's entry into the Great War in 1915, precisely to make good at last Italian claims to Trieste.

The outcome was Italian victory, at a terrible cost, and the annexation of Trieste to Italy. Western Slovenia and Istria, the peninsula at Trieste's back door, were annexed to Italy also and for over twenty years played their part in Mussolini's tragi-comic pantomime. We have seen how harshly Italian rule bore down on the Slovenes. For the Italians of the region it was a story of nationalist hopes at first fulfilled and then proved hollow, of disillusion and, with the Second World War, disaster.

Yugoslav partisans fought the Italian Army all over the mountains in Trieste's hinterland. Then, when Italy pulled out of the war, came the Germans, proclaiming a short-lived German province of the Adriatic. The mountain war continued, and in Trieste itself Jews and Communists and resistance fighters were dragged away, first to Trieste's own concentration camp and then to their final destruction.

The last days of the Second World War found British and New Zealand troops of the Eighth Army advancing across the Piave and the Tagliamento towards Trieste, while Tito's partisans closed in on it from the hills. Churchill urged his men forward across the Isonzo as well, to seize the city before the Yugoslavs, just as he ordered the armies in northern Germany to force a crossing of the Elbe and occupy Lübeck before the Russians. Finally, on 1 May 1945, British reconnaissance units encountered Yugoslav units on the Isonzo, fifteen miles short of Trieste, and a day later men of the New Zealand division, rubbing shoulders uneasily with Yugoslav fighters while they tossed oranges to the children, occupied the city. Here on the Adriatic, just as much as on the Baltic, the line that was to become the Iron Curtain was established as the fighting stopped and the rejoicing began.

In and around Trieste, trouble came quickly. When the armies first met, good-fellowship between allies only thinly disguised mutual suspicion and animosity. Here as in Carinthia, word spread on the one hand of Yugoslav brutality and on the other of British imperialist ambition. Practical arrangements were knocked together, with the immediate vicinity of Trieste divided into two. Zone A under the British and Americans occupied most of the city itself and the Yugoslav Zone B most of its hinterland. But there was friction along the divide, and before the summer of victory was over, governments and capitals were engaged, with London complaining that Yugoslavs in Trieste and western Slovenia were doing their best to frustrate the British military authorities.

Five thousand Yugoslav activists were rumoured to have remained in the area under Western control as 'stay behind' agitators, getting their orders from partisan headquarters in Ljubljana. Meanwhile the Yugoslav press trumpeted charges that the British were installing Italian 'fascists' in the areas under their control. The British ambassador in Belgrade took up with Tito himself anti-British attitudes among the Yugoslav General Staff. Meanwhile my friend Gordon Campbell of Croy, whom we saw at the crossing of the Elbe at the beginning of this story, was at work with his colleagues in the Foreign Office in London, casting around for ways to divide the incompatible with the minimum of friction. They quaintly called the whole area 'the Julian March' and saw 'the ethnical principle' as paramount among mutually incompatible *desiderata*.

1947 brought the Paris Peace Conference and the need, if Italy were to get its peace treaty, to fix its border with Yugoslavia. The Conference remained loyal to Zones A and B, and decided that they should jointly constitute the Free Territory of Trieste. But relations between East and West were fast deteriorating, and in 1948 the Berlin blockade brought them close to breaking point. With Yugoslavia and the Western Powers locked in disagreement, the Free Territory was as unworkable as any other arrangement which called for a modicum of trust between the two sides. In Italy, a general election was imminent, the campaign bitterly contested between Christian Democrats and Communists. If Italy went Communist so, London and Washington believed, would Western Europe. Britain and the United States, as concerned to swing votes in the elections as with the situation on the ground, pressed the case for Trieste to be united with Italy. The Yugoslavs were bitterly resentful but impotent; for six years the situation remained deadlocked. Finally, in 1953, Britain and the United States proposed that Zone A should go to Italy, Zone B to Yugoslavia. A year later an agreement was signed: Trieste became part of Italy, linked to it by a coastal corridor all the way back to the Isonzo, and the hills which overlooked the city as well as the Istrian peninsula to the south passed to Yugoslavia.

There the frontier remains, nearly fifty years later, though now it separates Italy from Slovenia, and until the summer of 1989 it formed its own, very particular part of the Iron Curtain. To understand how particular requires a grasp of the topography of both city and hinterland.

Trieste is squeezed between the Adriatic and the limestone uplands which rear up so abruptly five or six miles back from the coast. If you go up through the city streets you are soon among the suburbs which straggle up the hillside, bent and narrow streets gradually giving way to steep lanes between vineyards. When at last you burst into the open at the top, human lungs or combustion engine bursting with the effort of the climb, you are close to the frontier; and with a bit of licence you could imagine Yugoslav border guards in the bad old days not looking out into the capitalist West, but spitting down its chimney pots. So the Iron Curtain did more than curl round Trieste; it also loomed over it from above. And to complete the city's sense of isolation, of constriction, the border ran parallel with the road to the west along the coast all the way back to the mouth of the Isonzo. In the bad old days of the cold war, Trieste lay at the very extremity of the Western world.

Those hills do more than confine and dominate Trieste. They form the end of the line of uplands which runs down the Slovene-Italian frontier all the way from Austria. These are the hills of the Karst, a strange limestone world in which rivers and streams dive underground, to emerge far away on the other side of hills, and in one case at least on the other side of the Italian border, thirty miles away. The soil which covers the limestone is poor, supporting only woods and scratchy fields. The hill villages are primitive, and some of them still bear the scars and scorch-marks of partisan stroke and Italian or German counter-stroke, with hostages shot, houses destroyed, whole villages burnt out. There is a sense of emptiness, of decompression, ten miles, 1,000 feet of altitude and a whole world removed from Trieste.

There are attractions to be found up here. The most remarkable are the caves at Postojna and Skocjan, echoing chambers ornamented with stalactites and stalagmites, carved out by the rivers which plunge so erratically through the limestone into the underworld. The most famous is the ranch at Lipice, where the Lippizaner horses are prepared for the Spanish Riding School in Vienna. There has been a horse farm here for 400 years, first royal, now state-owned. Here horses from Spain were crossed with the local breed, and they flourished on the limestone. Wars and rumours of wars have washed round Lipice, with horses shipped elsewhere, to Bohemia and Hungary, and with other places disputing the claim to be the true home of the Lippizaner. At Lipice the state farm is turning itself by degrees into a holiday resort, with casino and golf course, and with a restaurant that a bit of Italian cooking could do a lot to improve; but the horses themselves remain the real attraction of the place.

So the line of the old Iron Curtain reaches the sea at last. Italy and Slovenia share Trieste Bay between them, Slovenia with a twenty-five-mile coastline squeezed between the Italian and Croatian frontiers. Back from the sea they are separated by the great height of land which sets Slovenia towering above the city. But the hills depend on the city and the city upon the hills. So Italians and Slovenes are simultaneously linked and separated, as the different inhabitants of this area always have been: linked by trade, by marriage, by everyday conversation, separated by rivalry and language and too often by war.

Europe has not been made self-evidently whole here, at the very end of our journey, any more than anywhere else along the way. But Slovenia and Italy, Slovenia and Trieste have the freedom to choose how much they will see of one another, how much they will commit their futures to trust in one another, how far they want to make themselves friends and define themselves as fellow-Europeans. After decades as an outpost of the West, Trieste is back in its historic business as a Central European city and as Central Europe's window on the sea.

8
Whole and Free?

In a few short months in 1989 the Iron Curtain was suddenly swept aside. For forty years it had been an immutable fact of European politics, a feature on the map of the Continent which seemed perdurable. When I left Hungary in 1986, at the end of my second tour of duty there, something was stirring under the country's surface appearance of happy conformity with Moscow's views. I even thought I might just live to see Hungary recover its freedom of action and Hungarians some degree of personal liberty. But as we drove out of Hungary it never occurred to me that, the next time I came that way, there would be no watchtowers, no barbed wire, no need for visas on the road from Vienna to Budapest.

When it came, change affected all of central and eastern Europe; but the process started in Moscow and spread first to Warsaw and Budapest. In my book, Gorbachev is the hero of the story, a man who, whatever his personal shortcomings, had the realism to accept that the Soviet Union was morally and materially bankrupt and the courage to insist that things must change. His recognition that the Soviet Empire in eastern Europe was one of the things that must change signalled the end of the road for Communist rulers throughout the area. Some – particularly the Poles and the Hungarians – accepted that fact, others fought against it.

The origins of this particular Polish and Hungarian flexibility went back a long way: thirty-three years, to be precise, to 1956. When in that year reforming Communists took power in Warsaw, Khrushchev descended on them to bully them into submission. They resisted; and when he talked of Soviet troops they talked of the Polish army. Khrushchev blinked first, and the Poles won a limited degree of independence which they never quite lost thereafter. Within days the Hungarians tried to move down the same road as the Poles. Their Communist leaders had less skill than the Poles, Hungary less luck than Poland; and the Red Army could not swallow humiliation twice in one year. The result was the Hungarian Revolution in October and the brief Soviet-Hungarian war in November which put it down.

We have seen that for a month or so that autumn the Hungarian Iron Curtain vanished. The refugees streamed westwards over the open border into Austria, leaving behind a cowed and broken nation. Hungary lost its independence as Poland did not. But ever afterwards Moscow, the Hungarian Communists and the Hungarian people themselves all had reason to walk warily and to make sure that, come what may, nothing like the 1956 tragedy ever happened again. Hence the relative moderation of Communist rule in Hungary; the economic reform of 1968; the increasing respect for individual liberties; the timid attempts at reconciling people and Communism which I observed in the mid 1980s while I lived in Budapest.

The consequence was that when Gorbachev started to set the countries of the Soviet Empire free, Poland and Hungary knew how to respond. In June 1989 the Poles held free elections. The Communist candidates were routed and Poland became a multi-party democracy. Here the Poles, far from the Iron Curtain, bow out of our story. The Hungarians remain central to it for it was they who, after Gorbachev himself, did most to sweep away the Iron Curtain and so bring Communism in eastern Europe to its ignominious end.

While the Poles were conducting their free elections, the Hungarians, on 16 June 1989, reburied the mortal remains of Imre Nagy, the mild, reform-minded Communist who had led them in 1956 and been executed two years later. The event took the best part of a summer's day; it attracted hundreds of thousands of ordinary Hungarians, who heard hitherto little-known dissidents speak out freely about Communism's crimes; it was the most moving ceremony I have ever attended; and by the end of that long day there was no future for Communist rule in Hungary.

The Communists themselves knew it. The day after Nagy's reburial I talked to one of their old leaders, a man who had grown grey and weary in the Politburo. I asked him if power was slipping out of his Party's hands. 'Not slipping,' was his reply, 'it has slipped.' Younger Communist leaders knew that if they were to make their peace with the West and with the Hungarian people, the Iron Curtain had to go; and when the American President, George Bush, came to Budapest in July, his hosts presented him with a symbolic strand of barbed wire from the dismantled frontier obstructions.

Hungary's frontier with Austria was no longer fortified, but it was still controlled. But members of the emerging Hungarian opposition, encouraged by that ubiquitous European politician and descendant of

Emperors, Otto Habsburg, were planning a happening on that very frontier. They announced that they were going to hold a Pan-European Picnic. The idea was that right-minded people from all over Hungary and both sides of what was left of the Iron Curtain should meet on the very line of Hungary's border with Austria just outside Sopron. They gathered there in their thousands on 19 August 1989. It was at one and the same time a people's party and a political demonstration. What was left of Communist authority was persuaded, cajoled and bullied into opening the gates on a back road that led across the frontier into Austria. Customs officials stamped passports on demand, or more often than not were gently ignored. The picnickers strolled back and forth between East and West; and some of the Easterners did not stroll back. The Iron Curtain was abolished for the day; but the principle still remained that this international border, like any other, was subject to all the mechanisms of immigration, customs and frontier control.

For years East Germans had been coming on holiday in their thousands to Hungary. They came for the warm waters of Lake Balaton, for Hungarian food, wine and prices, and for a taste of the easygoing nature of Hungary's Communist rule, so different from the rigidities of their own. Many of them came also for the chance to holiday with friends and relatives who had got into the habit of coming to meet them from West Germany. This summer, 1989, they came as usual, and gradually it dawned on them that on the border with Austria only bureaucracy stood between them and freedom in the West. The East Germans piled up in the Balaton resorts; they besieged the West German embassy in Budapest; they asked for asylum and places in Hungarian refugee camps while they waited for the frontier to open.

Diplomacy was hard at work. East Berlin demanded that the Hungarian authorities should keep the Austrian frontier closed and send the East Germans back. Bonn urged that the frontier should be opened. The Austrians feared trouble along their borders. The Hungarian government and what was left of the Communist party wrestled with a dilemma which, every twenty-four hours, grew more intense. Prime Minister and Foreign Minister travelled to Bonn to talk to the West Germans. Finally, on 10 September they declared that the frontier would be opened at midnight on the following day. The East Germans were free to leave. Out they went in their thousands, through Austria and on into West Germany, taking the pollution of their unloved Trabants and Wartburgs with them or abandoning them by the roadside.

The East German government barred any further tourist traffic to Hungary. The Hungarians' crisis was over. But East Germans turned to Czechoslovakia instead, hoping that the Czech government could be driven to do what the Hungarians had done and set their visitors free. They found a country as aroused as Poland and Hungary, but one that confronted an unyielding government. So in Prague too they besieged the West German embassy, and again the Bonn government demanded that they should be set free to travel to the West. Now the Czech government yielded. Special trains loaded with East German refugees, first with 6,000, then with 7,600 of them, rumbled on their way to West Germany.

Their route took them through East Germany, and the crowds came to Leipzig station to cheer them. Now it was the East German government that found itself facing an aroused and angry people. As the authorities anxiously tried to orchestrate celebrations to mark the fortieth anniversary of the founding of the German Democratic Republic, they found themselves confronted with very different, hostile demonstrations. The crisis dragged on, through October and into November, with daily demonstrations in all East Germany's major cities. Suddenly, out of the blue, on 9 November, came the opening of the Berlin Wall. If Moscow's signals had been different or if argument within the East German leadership had tipped the other way, there would instead have been a massacre on the Wall. Some of the East German leaders had imagined that they were opening the Wall not for good but for the day. But once the East Germans had tasted freedom there was no going back, and by 3 December the Communist leadership followed those of Poland and Hungary into the wilderness.

The events that marked the collapse of Communism in the rest of Central and Eastern Europe dragged on. The Czech Communists fell, then the Bulgarians. In Romania the regime fought on into December. But finally, on the 25th itself, Nicolai and Elena Ceausescu were tried at drumhead court martial, condemned, dragged out protesting and shot to make a Romanian Christmas holiday. In the Soviet Union itself change was to come more slowly; but by the end of 1989, Communism, the Warsaw Pact and the influence of Moscow in Central Europe were dead. Suddenly Curtain and Wall, so long brutal facts of European politics, became curiosities, embarrassments, anachronisms. For a short euphoric period, Europeans, Easterners and Westerners alike, convinced themselves that at a stroke Europe had been made whole.

After the euphoria came the hard labour. The work of tearing down

Curtain and Wall themselves was a joyful business, scarcely labour at all, and while it was going on neighbouring towns and villages separated for forty years started to discover one another. Egon Schwintowsky gave me heartwarming accounts of what happened when the people of Horst came over the old border to discover the delights of Lauenburg, discoveries that were replicated throughout the length of the old Inner German divide from the Baltic to the Czech border. Elsewhere, the cross-frontier outings began. Hungarians went to the Burgenland as freely as Austrians had long come to Körmend and Sopron for cheap shopping and bargain dentistry. Czechs and Slovaks set out to explore Vienna. But behind all these easy assertions of common humanity lay the hard work of reordering political and economic systems.

Germany – still, as the process began in early 1990, two Germanies – faced the most complex reshaping. The two states were each leading partners in their respective alliances; there were thousands of Soviet troops in East Germany and thousands of American, British and French troops in the Federal Republic. The Soviet Union and the three Western allies still claimed the rights and responsibilities of conquerors throughout the two Germanies. The Germans were set on unification: one nation, one people, one currency. They were encouraged by the Americans, watched with pursed lips or worse by their British and French allies. This whole cat's cradle of interdependent issues demanded protracted, complex diplomatic negotiations.

While they proceeded, the nature of East German society was changing. One-party politics, the command economy, collectivised society were all dying. But systems to replace them had to be contrived, constructed, established; and as the changes came winners went out to exploit them, losers to lament them and try to hinder them. All these complexities – the stuff of fat volumes of analysis and still unwinding now, eleven years afterwards – flow from that moment of euphoria when Wall, Curtain and continental divide vanished down the memory hole.

We have seen that Yugoslavia faced problems quite as difficult as Germany's, and many times as lethal; and that Slovenia's escape from them in the summer of 1991 was as fortunate and uncovenanted as anything that happened in 1989. Sovereign and independent, Slovenia faced the same problems of reconstruction and reordering of politics, society and economy as East Germany. Its old partners in the Yugoslav Federation were impotent to interfere, its Western neighbours on the whole benevolent, except when issues like compensation for Italians driven from Istria half a century earlier raised their troublesome heads. Unlike East Germany, Slovenia had no problem of occupying powers and foreign armies, but no rich big brother like the Federal Republic to smooth its way.

For Hungary, the way ahead looked relatively straightforward. Like Czechoslovakia and Slovenia it wanted sovereignty and democracy, plus NATO and European Union membership as soon as it could achieve them. But the problems of Hungarian minorities outside its frontiers, in Slovakia, Yugoslavia and above all Romania, raised issues that had been carefully concealed in the years of Communist-bloc conformity. So Hungary's leaders went to work on two fronts: reordering the nation's politics, economics and society, and building relations of confidence with its neighbours.

Lastly, the Czechs and Slovaks. They first set out to build a free Czechoslovakia and then, when strains between Prague and Bratislava became too acute, to negotiate a peaceable divorce. In the first years of their new democracy and free markets the Czechs seemed to lead the way for other central Europeans, while the Slovaks were stuck with the authoritarianism and corruption of the old ways. But gradually, with economic setbacks and accusations of corruption in high places, the gloss wore off the Czech Republic. Meanwhile, in its 1999 elections Slovakia began to pull itself together.

Seen from Berlin, from Prague and Bratislava, Budapest and Ljubljana, has Europe been made whole? The answer is not yet; but in their different ways the people of each of these cities see past progress and future promise. For Berliners, Germany is politically united and Berlin its capital again. Some 'Ossis' still dislike and distrust 'Wessis', and all of them see continuing differences in the social and economic levels of the new Germany. Political and popular attitudes alike will continue to reflect those differences, but in its decentralised, federal way Germany today is almost as whole a country as any of its neighbours. Through this new wholeness it contributes to making Europe whole.

For the other cities of Central Europe, the signs of wholeness are the Western visitors on their streets, the Western companies setting up business in them, the émigrés returning to rebuild or exploit the lands of their birth. Bar the obstacles of language, the centres of Prague and Budapest today feel like those of Western European cities, the poverty of their working-class suburbs comparable with those of southern Europe. Bratislava has further to go, and so has Ljubljana, even though the country which it leads is so much more prosperous than Slovakia. For all four countries, the political catchwords are NATO and European Union, with Hungary and the Czech Republic already members of NATO and all four looking forward to joining the Union within the decade. So though today's answer of all four to the question 'Has Europe been made whole?' is 'Not yet', all four look forward with confidence to a secure and integrated place on the European map.

From the other side of the old continental divide the picture again is reasonably positive. Germany has achieved its political aim, unification. Now it has to make a social and human reality of it. The Italians see a friendly Slovenia rather than an unpredictable Yugoslavia on their north-eastern frontier and the world trade of all south-central Europe beating a path to Trieste's door, with no Slovene in the foreseeable future likely to question Italy's rights to the city.

Austria, the country which alone through the Cold War kept alive something of the qualities of the old Central Europe, perhaps stands to gain most from the Iron Curtain's end. For there, at the heart of Central Europe and of what was once the Habsburg Empire, Austria faces all ways: south over the mountains to the Mediterranean, east into the old Communist world, west towards the German cousins. Vienna could be – in some ways is – the quintessential European city, open to all its neighbours, open to all the European winds that blow. But for the moment, other winds blow around the Hofburg, along the Ringstrasse and across Schwarzenbergplatz. At present many Austrians, perhaps most Austrians, think not of openness and of Europe but of national distinctiveness and exclusion. Their compatriots are out on the streets to object, and the countries of Europe are shouting their dissatisfaction; but Jörg Haider and the Freedom Party are defiant, and many ordinary Austrians rally to them in national solidarity. So Austria may, as this book goes to press, be building a new divide, a petty one this time, in the heart of Europe; or it may rediscover its inheritance from the Habsburgs and opt for universal inclusiveness instead.

And now, to make an end, how does it all look to outsiders, interested in this European saga but uncertain what they should make of it? Focus groups are to hand, for although throughout this book I have been describing a solitary journey, supplemented only in the last chapter by the company of an amiable somniac, late in 1999 I twice travelled from Lübeck to Trieste with a coachload of fellow-travellers. They had signed up with a cultural and artistic tour organiser to explore the Iron

Curtain with me. On them I tried many of the ideas in this book, and I have used their reactions to refine them before committing them to print.

They were interesting and various groups of fellow-travellers. Some had personal reasons for the journey: a father born in the Sudetenland, a mother dead in Auschwitz, memories of a German childhood. Others, like me, had professional connections, and one of these was a Slovenian journalist who, I suspected, wanted to see the whole story, and particularly her country's story, through an outsider's eyes. Some were looking for an introduction to the history of Central Europe. Others again came only because they had lived through the Cold War as distant observers, and wanted to see some of the places along the Iron Curtain at which it was played out.

Few of my customers were in the first flush of youth, and for people of our age the tour was heavy going. In a fortnight we travelled getting on for 2,000 miles, slept in eight different hotels. They were a captive audience, and I talked at them all the way; by God I talked – in the coach, in formal sessions in the hotels before dinner, as we walked beside the Elbe at Lauenburg, among the ghosts at Buchenwald, through the tired splendours of Marianské Lazné and on the virgins' bridge in Ljubljana. They were patient, interested listeners, and good talkers. Early on I warned them that on our last evening, in Trieste, I was going to ask them to turn the tables on me and make me listen, while they told us, each one of them, what they had made of the journey. I suggested a question we might ask ourselves, at the end of our journey along the old divide: what evidence had we seen that Europe had at last, in George Bush's words, been made whole and become a continent united in freedom?

I knew what I thought; indeed, I had been preaching it, if indirectly, for a fortnight. We had seen seven countries: four 'Eastern', two 'Western', and a united Germany created out of a fusion of East and West. Each of these countries had its full sovereignty, trammelled only by membership, or the desire for membership, of an alphabetic soup of organisations. Within these seven countries, all their citizens had their democratic rights, and most of their inhabitants – gypsies, minorities, immigrants sometimes excepted – their full entitlement of human rights as well. By world standards, all seven countries were prosperous as well as free; and even the poorest of them, Slovakia, was prosperous by comparison with European countries further east. Four of the seven were members of NATO; Slovakia and Slovenia looked forward to joining; and Austria's neutrality was guaranteed by international treaty. Germany and Italy were founder-members of the European Union, Austria a latecomer whose position in the organisation was handicapped only by its own leanings towards far-right politics. All four 'Easterners' – Czechs, Hungarians, Slovaks and Slovenes – were eager candidates for membership and all four were likely to be admitted before the first decade of the twenty-first century was out.

On the other hand, we had seen very different standards of well-being. The change when we crossed the border from Germany into the Czech Republic had been striking. So were conditions in Slovakia outside the very centre of the capital. Hungary was a vastly poorer place than Austria or, for that matter, than Slovenia. And one could sense that politics and society in the old East were less self-consciously democratic, government less transparent, human rights less firmly established than in the West.

And yet, and yet ... Italy's recent political history was as chequered as such things can be, its governmental record as corrupt. Already the story of Helmut Kohl's depredations in Germany was beginning to unfold. As for Austria, when we talked in Trieste Jörg Haider was only a potential threat, not the challenge to 'European' values which he had become before the year was out; but already Austria was looking a less than impeccable member of the democratic world. In terms of economic and political righteousness and well-being there was, in short, no absolute distinction to be drawn between 'East' and 'West'.

There was also the rebirth of Central Europe to celebrate. Before the Iron Curtain divided the Continent, the people of most of the places we had visited would have thought of themselves not as Eastern or Western but as Central Europeans. The division of the Continent into two camps had forced people to be 'Easterners' or 'Westerners'; and as long as it lasted perhaps only neutral Vienna among all the cities we had seen had been able to enjoy the luxury of thinking of itself as Central European. Yet even in the worst of times Czechs, Hungarians, Slovaks and Slovenes privately cherished the idea that they were Central Europeans, temporarily corralled into the Eastern bloc. Occasionally even the Communist façade cracked, as a story I told my fellow-travellers illustrated.

Back in the mid 1980s, I was complaining about something or other in the impeccably Communist Hungarian Foreign Ministry. 'You know,' I said, 'we British sometimes still find it difficult to get business done in Eastern Europe.' 'Ah yes, Mr Ambassador,' the Deputy Foreign

Minister across the table responded, with all the unction of a Habsburg counsellor of state, 'How much easier you must find it here in *Central Europe*.' And within a decade, by which time I had moved to diplomatic pastures new and the Deputy Foreign Minister had been kicked out of public service into more lucrative employment in the private sector, Hungary was avowedly Central European again, as Hungarians had only dreamed of being for the last half century.

So if Central Europe was itself again, and if Central Europe was open equally to East and West, it seemed to me that you could begin to talk about a Europe made whole. Of course, the countries we had visited, like those further west, were still distinguished from one another by a multitude of particulars. Language distinguished them, rivers and mountain ranges divided them. So did their very different histories and their places on the map. They had historical reasons for disliking one another. Their interests varied with their economics, their political systems, their size and their ambitions. But we lived today not in a Europe artificially divided by the Iron Curtain but as members of a European orchestra. Day-to-day differences within the orchestra produced discordant passages, even at times cacophonies of sound; but we were trying to play in harmony, in concert; and more often than not we were succeeding.

I conceded that further east the picture was different and that a new divide was being driven through Europe. What had been Yugoslavia was bitterly fragmented, with only Slovenia safely a member of the European orchestra. When we talked in Trieste the war with Yugoslavia was not long over, the refugees were still making their way home in Kosovo, the Serbs still fulminating against the fate that they had brought upon themselves. All south-eastern Europe was still affected, still divided by unsettled business with Milosevic. Further east again, where the former Soviet Union met the former Soviet Empire, there were more and deeper divisions.

The gradual absorption of the countries of Central Europe into NATO and the European Union would codify those differences, make them more absolute; and there was little that I could see that we could do to ease the pain. The West could look after the Baltic States, give them European Union membership. But I could not see it doing the same for Ukraine or Belarus. And only the Russians themselves could find an answer to their existential dilemma, their age-old doubts about their country's relationship to Europe: part of or distinct from, friendly or constitutionally hostile, a European nation or a uniquely Russian identity, European or Russian values? Over there in the east, I had to admit, Europe had not been made whole or free. But in Central Europe, along the line which we had travelled, I believed that wholeness and freedom were in the making, indeed already apparent, if not yet fully accomplished.

My fellow-travellers were having none of this. There was no consensus, but the weight of opinion was far more sceptical than mine. Perhaps I had provoked them by looking too hopefully to the European Union as the instrument which would complete the process of making Europe whole. Faced with that belief, some were sceptical, some downright hostile; and they came back time after time not to what we had seen in Central Europe but to Brussels and the sins of the Commission, to Paris and the age-old differences between Frenchmen and Englishmen, to Bonn and Berlin and the suspect ambitions of the Germans.

To almost all my friends at those two meetings in Trieste, what still mattered most was national character, identity and interest. They had seen the differences between the countries we had visited. The familiar stories I had told them about frictions between Germans and Czechs, Hungarians and Austrians showed how hostile these peoples had been to one another in history. What reason was there now to imagine that their attitudes to one another had changed?

My friends were doubtful even about the desirability of wholeness. They had seen the peasant-girls-turned-tarts along the roadsides in western Bohemia, waiting for German sex-tourists to bring them Deutschmarks; if that was what being made whole meant they saw nothing to commend it. I had talked about the hundreds who had died along the Wall and the Iron Curtain, but what about the 'Ossi' children killed at a traffic black spot just east of Lübeck by speeding 'Wessis'? They saw not a European orchestra but evidence of national selfishness acted out day-in-day-out in Brussels, with every example of cross-purposes there reported in their morning newspapers. The things I had shown them and the stories I had told them illustrated those differences, not the wholeness that George Bush had talked about and that I claimed to detect.

I had promised my friends that in Trieste I would listen while they talked; but I found myself answering back. 'What about multiple identities, layered identities?' I asked. I thought of myself as an Englishman, a Yorkshireman, someone who could talk more easily with Americans and Canadians than with Germans, yet a European also, all at the same time. Throughout their history, Germans and Frenchmen, Italians and

Hungarians had thought of themselves also as Europeans; and I quoted Voltaire to illustrate the point: 'I have always considered the Christian powers of Europe as one great republic, whose parts all correspond with each other, even when they endeavour at their mutual destruction.' If Voltaire could write of the war of 1741 in such terms could not we, after the twentieth century's two vicious European civil wars, recognise the reality of Voltaire's great republic, of my European orchestra?

They were unpersuaded, and when I went to bed I found myself thinking about mankind's two legs. Each of us has his own views about the balance between his private world and the public one. We decide for ourselves where we place most of our weight, on the private leg or the public. It is the same when we think about domestic politics: more freedom or more equality, high taxes or low, more public welfare or more money in your private pocket? Views of international affairs divide in the same way. Are you interventionist or isolationist, a do-gooder or a national interest man, a believer in international groupings or a nationalist? None of us is solely one thing or the other; when we judge individual issues as much as in our general approach, all of us choose how we will place our weight: 60/40, 70/30, 50/50?

Almost to a man and woman, my friends seemed to place most of their weight on the national leg, far less on the European. And these, I had to remind myself, were natural Europhiles, people who had invested time, money and energy in our voyage of exploration, our journey through the heart of Europe. If internationalists such as these still viewed developments in Europe with such wary suspicion, what about the little Englanders, the Germany-firsters, the French national-ists and the hard, suspicious men of the once-Communist world? Per-haps my enthusiasms had got out of hand and cried out for a cold shower of scepticism about the old continent.

Perhaps they have, but I still think I am nearer the truth about all this than my friends in the conference room of our Trieste hotel. I concede that the countries of the region have far to go before we can talk of a Central Europe made whole. I accept that further east Europe is split by a new division. Events in Austria show us that old Adams are not dead but merely slumbering. But at the end of my travels, solitary, with my somniac friend and with all my tour-companions, I am still more hopeful than not. Europe today is manifestly freer than it was, and to my eye it is on its way to being made whole.

At the end of it all, when my travels along the Iron Curtain were over, I told a psychologist friend of mine what I had been about. Inevitably, he asked me why. I said it had started with a desire to look again at some of the places I had known when I lived in Germany and Hungary and see how the new world had changed them. I had talked airily then of 'taking a swing through Central Europe', to rediscover old haunts and explore new ones. But the journey needed a discipline. The idea of tracing the line of the Iron Curtain had provided that. Then there had come the thought of a book, and after that my new career as lecturer, tour leader and general wiseacre about the affairs of Central Europe.

'And now what?' he asked.

Write the book, was my reply.

'Why?' he asked.

To bring what I had seen together, I said. He looked doubtful about that, so to turn the tables I asked him what he thought the psychological significance of the Iron Curtain had been.

He polished his glasses and began.

The Iron Curtain, he acknowledged, was about real differences. But even if it had not been, the mere fact of its existence would have given Western society a heaven-sent opportunity to project its own shadow upon the East. The reverse was equally true. Even democratic societies presented themselves by reference to their differences from others: think about European opinions on America or American views of Europe. Authoritarian ones felt more strongly and expressed themselves more freely: hence 'running dogs' and 'great Satans'. But between societies not instinctively given to Chinese or Iranian levels of exaggeration, the absolute nature of the Iron Curtain provided an excuse for projecting a darker shadow than would have been the case without it: think about a President of the United States calling the rival superpower the 'evil empire' and the Kremlin returning the compliment in dialectical spades.

But, shadow projection apart, there were differences of real psychological significance between the societies on either side of the Iron Curtain. The West started out with a belief in the individual. Its churches preached the worth of every single human being. Its laws held all men equal. We believed in human rights for the individual. Our democracy asserted the importance of the individual's opinions. All the many things in the West which diminished that individuality were aberrations, departures from the central ethic of society.

The Communist East started out with the collective and with the aim of making the individual a worthier member of it. In society's terms it was a glorious vision, in some ways finer than the West's; it sought perfection and it could produce heroic individuals. But in psychological terms it could only rarely work, for a search for psychological development and understanding must of necessity start within the individual. It is after all the individual man or woman who is seeking to understand himself, develop himself, achieve the completion of self and of self-awareness which Jung called individuation.

This did not mean that the West had a monopoly of psychological wholeness. Western society could demonstrate a huge capacity to damage, to cripple the individual. It too could show itself materialist, authoritarian, violent. Sometimes Communist policies – on employment, for example, or on education – showed more respect for man than ours did. But from a psychological point of view, the West was carving with the grain of humanity while the East had tried to cut across it. And as Communism found it impossible to recruit ordinary people to believe in the splendour of its vision, it had had to turn to force, to an authoritarianism which further alienated the individual.

And East and West had aggravated one another, projecting decade after decade hostile stereotypes onto one another. Hence Ronald Reagan's caricatures of his opponents. Hence too the Communist world's caricature of a capitalism sated with the blood of the workers. When in 1947 George Marshall launched his famous plan, America saw it as a disinterested proposal to save Europe from ruin. Moscow saw it as a plot to destroy the socialist world. NATO was based on the premise that the Warsaw Pact was the aggressor; the West stood resolutely on the defensive. To the East the truth was the diametric opposite, and NATO exercises might turn without warning into aggressive war. Both sides built their perceptions on truths, developing them into massive structures of half-truth or untruth. The West's vision was, to repeat, nearer to the truth than the East's, and the relative openness of its societies served to check too wild a proliferation of falsehood. But both deceived themselves about the other and fed obsessions with 'us' and 'them'.

The Iron Curtain itself played a dual role in all this. Physically it kept the two sides rigidly apart. Psychologically it dramatised their differences and made it easy to exaggerate them. It left no room for those who wanted to hedge their bets between their societies and ours, compelling even neutral Austria and non-aligned Yugoslavia to see themselves as 'Western' and 'Eastern'.

But it had kept the peace, I suggested. It had had much the same effect as partition in an ethnically mixed society, doing damage and

providing security at the same time. Yes, said my friend, and he began
to talk about the psychological significance of borders, boundaries,
limits. The collective unconscious thrives on distinctions. So did the history of nations. Individuals felt safer in familiar surroundings, shut in
by the distinctions which separated them from the unfamiliar. Hence
the Roman *limes;* and hence, much earlier, the distinction which the
Greek settlers on the northern Black Sea littoral made between themselves, the people of civilisation, and the wild men of the steppes who
came to trade with them.

Hence, for that matter, the satisfaction which propagandists took in
Robert Frost's twice-repeated phrase in his poem *Mending Wall:* 'Good
fences make good neighbours'. It is a sentiment that has gone into the
anthologies, a poet's justification of practical policies that keep people
apart for their own good. But it is not Frost's sentiment but that of a
curmudgeonly neighbour. And in the same poem Frost twice uses a
phrase that argues for human togetherness, 'Something there is that
doesn't love a wall'. So there, in a single poem written in 1914, you
have two views you could have applied to the Iron Curtain, practical
necessity to one eye, brutal obscenity to another.

Now the Curtain was gone, my psychologist went on, it was easier
for societies on either side of it to learn from each other. But there were
still psychological obstacles in the way. The West was arrogant, the East
resentfully dependent, yet perversely proud that through the bad years
it had preserved qualities which the West thought it had outgrown.
Now neither Western wealth nor Eastern poverty liked the look of the
other. Each of us had half a century's conditioning to overcome. It
would be a generation before we could look at each other reasonably
calmly. Each side had lost its enemy; and here he quoted Cavafy:

'And now, what will become of us without the barbarians?
Those people were a kind of solution.'
'All the same,' I asked, 'Is Europe whole? Psychologically whole?'
'Not yet,' he said.
'But it's getting there?'
'Perhaps,' he said.
'But it's healthier than it was before the Wall came down?'
'What do you think?' he said.
'I think so,' I said.

Bibliographical Note

This is a book which starts more hares than it catches. I have acknowledged in the Preface the few books that I have mentioned directly, and to suggest further reading on so discursive a subject without listing a library's worth is difficult. But a good starting point, for all its faults as the book of the television series, is *Cold War* by Jeremy Isaacs and Taylor Downing (London: Bantam Press, 1998). It sets in global context the creation of the Iron Curtain, its long and infamous life-span, and the events which swept it aside.

More specifically, I know of four books in English which, like this one, trace some or all of the line of the Iron Curtain, three of them written when it still seemed a permanent feature of the European landscape. The first is David Shears's *The Ugly Frontier* (London: Chatto and Windus, 1970). A decade later came Anthony Bailey, another journalist, with *Along the Edge of the Forest* (London: Faber & Faber, 1983). In 1985, Adam Nicolson produced *Frontiers* (London: Weidenfeld & Nicolson), a more episodic and erratic yet in some ways more ambitious book than the first two. Finally, there appeared last year Oliver August's *Along the Wall and Watchtowers* (London: Harper Collins, 1999), a young man's book which has the merit of describing the situation now that the Iron Curtain has been swept into oblivion, but which is incomplete in that it deals only with the German part of the Iron Curtain story.

To go more deeply into the story of the Cold War, turn to John Lewis Gaddis's *We Now Know: Rethinking Cold War History* (Oxford: Oxford University Press, 1997), to Mary Fulbrook's *The Two Germanies 1945–1990* (London: Macmillan, 1992), to Charles Gati's *The Bloc that Failed: Soviet-East European Relations in Transition* (Indianapolis: Indiana University Press, 1984) and to Timothy Garton Ash's *In Europe's Name: Germany and the Divided Continent* (London: Vintage, 1994). For its ending, read Michael Beschloss and Strobe Talbot in *At the Highest Levels: the Inside Story of the End of the Cold War* (London: Little Brown, 1993) and Konrad H. Jarausch's *The Rush to German Unity* (Oxford: Oxford University Press, 1994).

There are hundreds of books about Germany and the Germans. Three good ones are Gordon A. Craig's *Germany 1866–1945* (Oxford: Oxford University Press, 1981), the same author's *The Germans* (London: Penguin, 1982), and Mary Fulbrook's *A Concise History of Germany* (Cambridge: Cambridge University Press, 1990). Barbara Jelavich is good on Austria in *Modern Austria: Empire and Republic 1800–1986* (Cambridge: Cambridge University Press, 1987). For the Czechs read Derek Sayer's *The Coasts of Bohemia: a Czech History* (Princeton: Princeton University Press, 1998). There is no obvious modern book about Hungary, but C. A. Macartney's *Hungary, a Short History* (Edinburgh: Edinburgh University Press, 1962) is still valuable. For the Hungarian Revolution see my own biography of Imre Nagy, who played the central role in it: *Voice in the Wilderness* (London: Macdonald, 1991). On the Cold War story of Berlin see James S. Sutterlin's and David Klein's *Berlin: From Symbol of Confrontation to Keystone of Stability* (New York: Praeger, 1989) and, in lighter vein, *The Berlin Blockade* and *The Last Division* by Ann Tusa (London: Hodder & Stoughton, 1996).

There are many travellers' tales that touch on or cross the line of the Iron Curtain, with a number of great books among them. In *A Time of Gifts* (London: John Murray, 1979) Patrick Leigh Fermor takes us on foot through Austria and Hungary in the early 1930s on his way from London to Constantinople. In his heroic mountain march from Santiago de Compostela to Constantinople, Nicholas Crane passed through Austria and Slovakia. He describes the journey in *Clear Waters Rising* (London: Penguin, 1997). Claudio Magris brilliantly illuminates Central Europe in his *Danube* (London: Collins Harvill, 1989) and Jan Morris's *Fifty Years of Europe: An Album* (London: Viking, 1997) sparkles on Trieste and other cities along the old divide.

For travel details, use Rough Guides in Germany, the Czech Republic and Slovakia; Blue Guides in Austria, Hungary and Italy; and the Lonely Planet Guide in Slovenia.

Index